WITHDRAWN

Shady Characters

The Secret Life of Punctuation, Symbols
& Other Typographical Marks

Keith Houston

W. W. NORTON & COMPANY
New York · London

For information about permission to reproduce selections from this book,
write to Permissions, W. W. Norton & Company, Inc.,
500 Fifth Avenue, New York, NY 10110

For information about special discounts for bulk purchases, please contact
W. W. Norton Special Sales at specialsales@wwnorton.com or 800-233-4830

Manufacturing by Courier Westford
Book design by Judith Stagnitto Abbate/Abbate Design
Production manager: Anna Oler

Typeset in 10 point Hoefler Text, with Courier, Didot, Gotham,
Myriad, Requiem, Semilla, and Symbola (among others).

Library of Congress Cataloging-in-Publication Data

Houston, Keith, 1977–
 Shady characters : the secret life of punctuation, symbols, & other
typographical marks / Keith Houston. — First edition.
    pages cm
Includes bibliographical references and index.
ISBN 978-0-393-06442-1
1. Punctuation—History. 2. Signs and symbols—History.
3. Type and type-founding—History. 4. Writing—History. I. Title.
P301.5.P86H68 2013
411—dc23

                                                    2013017324

W. W. Norton & Company, Inc.
500 Fifth Avenue, New York, N.Y. 10110
www.wwnorton.com

W. W. Norton & Company Ltd.
Castle House, 75/76 Wells Street, London W1T 3QT

1 2 3 4 5 6 7 8 9 0

For Leigh ❧

Contents

Preface

¶ Some years ago a friend recommended a book to me. The book was *An Essay on Typography*, written in 1931 by Eric Gill, one of England's most famous modern typographers.[1] Although it was both diminutive in size and short on actual instruction (Gill preferred polemic to practical advice), *Essay* was a joy to read, full of philosophical asides and painstakingly hand-cut illustrations. Most of all, though, my interest was piqued by a character resembling a reversed capital *P* that peppered the text at inscrutable intervals. What was this ¶ for? Why did it appear at the start of each paragraph, and between some sentences but not others?

I hunted down the symbol in my copy of the *Typographic Desk Reference*, though its perfunctory definition was less than satisfying. As it explained, this character was called the pilcrow and once upon a time it had been used to separate paragraphs:

> *pilcrow*
>
> An old mark, rarely in use today, representing the beginning of a paragraph or section. Today it is used as an invisible character in word processing applications to represent a paragraph break. Also called *blind P*, *reverse P* or *paragraph mark*.[2]

This curt description invited more questions than it answered. I started to notice the same mark in other places: websites, glossaries of other typographic reference works, and even computer applications such as Microsoft Word.

How did the pilcrow's curious reverse-P form come about? Was it related to the letter *P*, as the *TDR* seemed to suggest, or was it something more subtle? What were the roots of its pithy, half-familiar name? What had caused this "old mark" to fall out of use, and having done just that, why did Eric Gill see fit to place it seemingly at random in his only published work on typography?

What, in other words, was the pilcrow all about?

A web search yielded a list of books to read and sites to browse. Once I'd finished with those, I had a heaping pile of notes and a list of yet more sources to be investigated. The story of this one character took in the birth of punctuation, the ancient Greeks, the coming of Christianity, Charlemagne, medieval writing, and England's greatest twentieth-century typographer. I started to research other marks—not only those, like the pilcrow, that hovered on the margins, but also everyday characters such as the dash (—), the ampersand (&), and the asterisk (*). An ever more diverse set of episodes, actors, and artifacts emerged: the creation of the Internet; ancient Roman graffiti; the Renaissance; Cold War double agents, and Madison Avenue at the peak of its powers. Their stories described a fascinating trail across the parallel histories of language and typography.

In February 2009, my meandering note-taking and browsing snapped sharply into focus. While investigating a symbol called the interrobang (‽), a hybrid question mark/exclamation point created in the 1960s, I came across a website dedicated to the symbol at www. interrobang-mks.com. At first sight it seemed unremarkable—a single page bearing a picture of the interrobang and a few paragraphs relating its story—but at the bottom was an e-mail address for one "PennSpec." Without much thought, I dashed off a message asking whether PennSpec happened to know anything more about the character, and promptly moved on to other things.

The penny dropped the next day. The "mks" in "interrobang-mks. com" must surely refer to Martin K. Speckter, the interrobang's creator; PennSpec, who habitually sent her e-mails without a signature, had to be Martin's widow, Penny. I was astonished: I was corresponding with the wife of the man who had invented one of the first new marks of punctuation for decades, if not centuries. The story of the interrobang was suddenly a living, breathing piece of history.

Emboldened, I sought out other people involved in the world of unconventional punctuation, and more conversations followed. I talked on the telephone to Josh Greenman, a New York journalist who had invented a sarcasm mark, and to Paul Saenger, an expert on spaces between words—invisible punctuation, if you will. I corresponded with Bas Jacobs, the Dutch designer of an irony mark for the type foundry Underware; with Doug Kerr, the AT&T engineer responsible for the appearance of the hash mark (#) on telephone keypads; and with William H. Sherman, the world's foremost authority on the "manicule," or pointing hand (☞), who helped me out of an etymological dead end.

These typographic conundrums, these shady characters hiding in plain sight, were too good to be passed over like so many periods and commas. This book is here to bring them into the light of day, and I can only hope to do justice to Penny Speckter and all the others who have helped me on the way here.

How to Read This Book

There's no wrong way to read this book, but be aware that later chapters occasionally use terms explained earlier in the book. Where possible, cross-references have been added to help guide readers who jump straight in to a particular chapter.

Shady Characters

Chapter 1 ✌ The Pilcrow

This is a pilcrow: ¶. They crop up with surprising frequency, dotted about websites with a typographic bent, for instance, or teaming up with the section symbol in legal documents to form picturesque arrangements such as §3, ¶7. The pilcrow also appears in Microsoft Word, where it adorns a button that reveals hidden characters such as spaces and carriage returns.

For all this quiet ubiquity, the pilcrow gets short shrift in books on typography and punctuation. Take the trouble to look it up and in most cases the humble pilcrow warrants only a few lines, dismissed briskly as a "paragraph mark" that is "only appropriate when brevity is important."[1] More generous definitions might run to mentioning that it has fallen out of common use and that it is sometimes used to indicate a footnote.[2] No mention of where its reverse-P shape comes from, or its name; for the pilcrow, this is as good as it gets.

This is a crying shame. The pilcrow is not a mere typographic curiosity, useful only for livening up a coffee-table book on graphic design or pointing the way to a paragraph in a mortgage deed, but a living character with its roots in the earliest days of punctuation. Born in ancient Rome, refined in medieval scriptoria, appropriated by England's most controversial modern typographer, and finally rehabilitated by the personal computer, the pilcrow is intertwined with the evolution of modern writing. It is the quintessential shady character.

* * *

The orthographic world of ancient Greece was a sparse old place. When reading a contemporary manuscript, a literate Greek of Homer's time would be faced with an UNBROKENSTREAMOF LETTERS, all uppercase (because at that time there *was* no other case), with lines running alternately left-to-right and then right-to-left across the page in the boustrophedon, or "ox-turning," style, after a farmer driving his oxen across a field.³ Perhaps most cruelly, the visual signposts of punctuation that today we take for granted were completely absent. It was the reader's unenviable lot to tease out words, clauses, and even sentences from this densely packed zigzag of characters.

Despite some recent scholarly murmurs to the contrary, it is generally held that the painstaking task of interpreting a document like this would have been accomplished by reading it aloud.⁴ At the time,

☞ *Figure 1.1*   Boustrophedon writing at Gortyn, Crete, circa sixth/fifth century BC.

the written word was very much an adjunct to spoken language, and silent reading was the exception rather than the rule. Physically pronouncing the syllables helped a practiced reader to decode and retain their meaning, and to discover the rhythms and cadences lurking in the unbroken text.[5]

Aristophanes of Byzantium, librarian of the great institution at Alexandria in the third century BC, was the first to give readers some room to breathe when he created a system of marks for augmenting texts written according to the rules of classical rhetoric.[6] Statements were broken into clauses of varying length and meaning, and a skilled orator would pause or draw breath to emphasize each such unit. Aristophanes defined a system of dots, or *distinctiones*, to indicate the points at which these pauses should take place—a boon for non-native readers, such as the Romans, who were attempting to decipher Greek literature.[7] A century later, the grammarian Dionysius Thrax described the system in his essay *The Art of Grammar*:

> There are three punctuation marks—the full [or high dot], the intermediate [or middle dot], and the subordinate [or underdot]. The full marks the completion of the sense, the intermediate is used to show where the reader can take a breath, and the subordinate is used if the sense is not yet complete but still lacks something. What is the difference between the full and the subordinate? It is one of duration; in the case of the full, the time interval is long, whereas it is without exception short for the subordinate.[8]

The so-called intermediate (·), subordinate (.), and full (˙) dots, signaling short, medium, and long pauses respectively, were placed after corresponding rhetorical units called the *komma*, *kolon*, and *periodos*. Though it took centuries for these marks of punctuation to crystallize into the familiar visual forms we know today, their modern names are not so far removed: "comma," "colon," and "period."*

Unlike modern punctuation, which authors use chiefly to make clear the semantics, or meaning, of their words, Aristophanes's dots were intended solely as aids for reading aloud; *distinctiones* were to be added retroactively by a reader preparing a text to be performed in front of an audience.[9] An intermediate dot, for instance, did not turn the preceding words into a formal rhetorical komma, but rather marked the pause for breath that a reader would take after speaking such a clause aloud, while texts were not terminated with a *periodos*, or high dot, since after the final letter there was nothing more to punctuate (or read!).[10] Even now, many marks of punctuation still act wholly or largely as vocal stage direction: parentheses denote the typographical equivalent of a spoken aside; the exclamation mark implies a surprised, rising tone of voice; and the question mark is as much about inflection as it is about interrogation.

Aristophanes's system found use only fitfully, and later, as Rome usurped Greece with characteristically brutal efficiency, his *distinctiones* had to contend with the Roman disdain for punctuation in general.[11] Cicero, for instance, an orator, philosopher, and politician from the first century BC who crops up with indecent frequency in any discussion of punctuation or grammar, looked down his aquiline nose at it. He considered that the end of a sentence "ought to be determined not by the speaker's pausing for breath, or by a stroke interposed by a copyist, but by the constraint of the rhythm."[12] And although the zigzag boustrophedon style of writing had long since been replaced with lines running uniformly left to right, a brief, unrelated Roman

---

* See Figure 10.1 in chapter 10, "Quotation Marks (" ")," for an early example of Aristophanes's points at work.

experiment* of SEPARATING·WORDS·WITH·DOTS had by the end of the second century been abandoned in favor of the Greeks' monotonous, unspaced *scriptio continua*.[14] For the most part, the Romans had no truck with punctuation.

With all this emphasis on reading aloud, it might come as a surprise that the paragraph—a purely semantic construct, with no counterpart in spoken language—had been marked up in texts even before the advent of Aristophanes's multifarious dots, and continued in common use throughout punctuation's dark days at the hands of the Romans.

The *paragraphos*, from the Greek *para-*, "beside," and *graphein*, "write," first appeared around the fourth century BC and took the form of a horizontal line or angle in the margin to the left of the main text.[15] The exact meaning of the *paragraphos* varied with the context in which it was used and the proclivities of the author, but most often it marked a change of topic or structure: in drama it might denote a change of speaker, in poetry a new stanza, and in an everyday document it could demarcate anything from a new section to the end of a *periodos*.[16] In some uses, the symbol itself marked the start of the new section; in others, it served only to draw attention to a break elsewhere on the specified line.[17]

The concept of the paragraph weathered changing tastes in punctuation better than word, clause, and sentence breaks, and by the second century AD, paragraphs were marked in a number of ways even as Aristophanes's dots found themselves out on their ear. The *paragraphos*

---

* The origins of the Romans' flirtation with dots between words, which were used mainly in monumental inscriptions, are not certain. Scholarly speculation fingers Greek influences, though the obvious candidate—Aristophanes's system of dots from the third century BC—may not be to blame. Instead, it is suggested that Roman stonemasons revived and modified an even older Greek practice, employed sporadically during the fifth century BC, of separating words with vertical rows of three dots (⋮).[13]

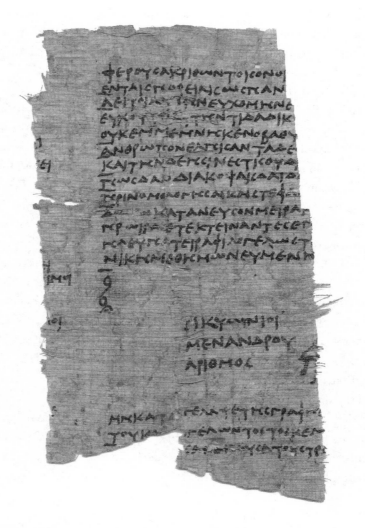

Figure 1.2 Each horizontal mark, or *paragraphos*, in this copy of
Menander's *Sicyonians* from the third century BC, indicates a change in
speaker somewhere on the corresponding line. The final *paragraphos* of the
main text is accompanied by a *coronis*, a decorative symbol marking the end
of a section or work.[18]

soldiered on in a growing variety of forms such as Γ and γ, while some readers dispensed with a mark altogether and instead outdented or enlarged the first few letters of each paragraph to yield *litterae notabiliores*—literally, "notable letters."[19] Still others inserted the letter *K* for *kaput*, or "head," to mark the "head" of a new argument or thesis, and it was this particular convention that would eventually give rise to the pilcrow.[20]

This motley collection of paragraph marks was typical of the state of punctuation at the dawn of the first millennium: written by one person and marked up by another (who most probably shared Cicero's distaste for the form), texts were punctuated inconsistently or not at all. Writing was, however, about to be well and truly shaken up by the biggest upheaval since Rome's fall from Republic to Empire. The emergence of Christianity a scant few decades after Jesus's death would change the face of written language on a grand scale, and almost as an afterthought, it would kick-start the pilcrow's journey from *K* for *kaput* to a fully formed mark in its own right.

☞ *Figure 1.3   Third line at left: K* for *kaput,* set off by a dot on either side, signaling the "head" of an argument, in a copy of Cicero's *In Verrem* from the first century BC/AD.

* * *

C ompared to Rome's traditional pagan religion, Christianity was a different beast altogether. Whereas paganism relied on oral tradition and its practices varied according to local custom, Christianity emphasized conformity and universal, written scriptures.[21] If Judaism had been the prototypical religion of the Book, cleaving to the written Word of God, Christians embodied this ideal with unprecedented vigor, driving the evolution of punctuation as they built and consolidated a concrete, written dogma. After all, the Word of God had to be transmitted with as little ambiguity as possible.[22]

The torrid period of lion-baiting, crucifixions, and humiliation that had beset early Roman Christians finally came to an end in the fourth century. In 312, on the eve of a battle that would decide the ruler of a united Roman Empire, the presumptive Emperor Constantine was reported to have witnessed a vision of a cross in the sky.* If Constantine had been in any doubt as to the import of this symbol, it was accompanied by a helpful inscription, HOC SIGNO VICTOR ERIS (BY THIS SIGN YOU WILL CONQUER—one might forgive the Almighty for His melodramatic use of capitals when one recalls that His subjects had not yet developed lowercase letters). Constantine's vision was followed that night by a dream in which God instructed him to march into battle under the sign of the cross.[23] The next morning, Constantine did as he was told. The battle was won and Constantine's devotion to the new religion was ensured.[24]

As the first Christian emperor, Constantine rolled back the institutionalized persecution that Christians had suffered for 250 years. Christian worship was decriminalized, Church lands were granted

---

* The sign that Constantine saw in the sky was not a crucifix but an early Christian cross called a "Chi Rho" (☧), formed by the superposition of the Greek letters *chi* (X) and *rho* (P) and which represented the name of Christ.

exemptions from tax, and the state provided labor and materials for the construction of new churches.[25] Having set Christianity on the road to legitimacy, though, after Constantine's death his legacy came under threat from one of his own descendants: his nephew Julian was intent on giving the old religion a second chance.

When Julian became Caesar in 355, he brought along a mystical strand of paganism and a desire to return polytheism to the center of Roman religion.[26] Under the guise of various edicts enforcing religious tolerance, he subtly aimed to reduce Christianity's influence throughout the empire. The proponents of this pagan revival understood the value of the written word as well as their Christian counterparts: as a reaction against the encroachments of Constantine's religion, several of Rome's aristocratic families sought to preserve, edit, and elucidate old pagan texts.[27] Julian's reforms were reversed upon his death, and the turning point finally arrived in 380, when Rome adopted Christianity as its official state religion. The pagan revival had failed, though writing practices were nevertheless strengthened by it.[28]

As the new, wordy religion swept through Europe, it drove the development of much of what we take for granted in modern-day writing. Aristophanes's venerable system of dots, for example, was revived by the fourth-century grammarian Donatus and popularized in the seventh century by Saint Isidore of Seville.[29] In his meandering reference work *Etymologies*, which would remain one of the most important books in the West for more than eight hundred years, Isidore described a reorganized system in which the *comma*, *colon*, and *periodos* now lived at the bottom, middle, and top of the line respectively—though the words they punctuated were still welded together without spaces.[30] The reorganized *distinctiones* were joined by new marks of punctuation, while some old symbols assumed new meanings: the ancient *positura*, a 7-shaped mark, now signaled the end of a section of text (in contrast to the *paragraphos*, which marked the start); questions were terminated with a *punctus interrogativus* (?), and the *diple* (>)

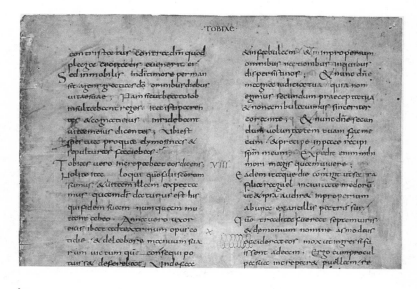

Figure 1.4   This leaf from a Bible, circa 800 AD, shows the use of Carolingian minuscule lettering, word spacing, *litterae notabiliores* to mark paragraphs, and various marks of punctuation, including ampersands.

called attention to quotations from sacred scripture, leading in turn to quotation marks (" ") and guillemets,* the speech marks used in many non-English languages (« »).[31] The technology of writing changed too: far from the reed beds of the Nile delta, religious scholars of northern Europe forsook rough Egyptian papyrus for smooth animal-skin parchment, freeing their scribes to create a variety of flowing "uncial," or "inch-high" scripts.[32]

In the eighth century the first chinks of light appeared in the claustrophobic *scriptio continua* that had dominated writing for a millennium. English and Irish priests, in an attempt to help readers decipher

---

* See chapter 10, "Quotation Marks (" ")," for more details.

texts written in unfamiliar Latin, began to add spaces between words.[33] Also in the eighth century, the crusading Frankish king Charlemagne commissioned the first standard lowercase letters to create a unified script that all his literate subjects could read. No longer bound to the solemn, square "majuscules" that suited the stonemason's chisel, the monk Alcuin of York used the scribe's dexterous quill to massage the Holy Roman Empire's divergent regional scripts into a single lowercase alphabet known as Carolingian minuscule. Sporting distinctive ascenders, descenders, and flourishes, Alcuin's script is the direct progenitor of today's lowercase roman letterforms.[34]

Amid all this innovation and consolidation, the paragraph mark finally, truly, arrived: the pilcrow came about in the fertile, scholastic world of the monastic scriptorium.

* * *

Just as the Latin word *kaput* stood for a section or paragraph, so later the diminutive *capitulum*, or "little head," came to be used in the same fashion. Even though the Roman letter *C* had all but seen off the older Etruscan *K* by 300 BC, the orphaned *K* for *kaput* persisted in written documents for centuries more.[35] By the twelfth century, though, *C* for *capitulum* had taken *K*'s job, and many of the religious documents that formed the bulk of Western civilization's written works were studded with *C*'s dividing them neatly into *capitula,* or "chapters."[36]

The interdependence of Christianity and the written word is nowhere better illustrated: *C* for *capitulum* was enthusiastically adopted by the monks who painstakingly copied the Church's books, and their use of *capitulum* to denote a section of a written work ultimately gave us the name and concept of the "chapter." *Capitulum* and "chapter" were so closely identified with ecclesiastical documents that they soon permeated Church terminology in a bewildering number of ways: monks went *ad capitulum*, "to the chapter (meeting)," to hear a chapter from the book of their religious orders, or "chapter-book," read out in the "chapter room."[37]

Monastic scriptoria worked on the same principle as factory production lines, with each stage of book production delegated to a specialist. Depending on the relative wealth of a given monastery, this process sometimes began even before a scribe put pen to paper, with the preparation of animal-hide parchment using the skins of livestock reared on the monastery's land.[38] With parchment in hand, whether produced by the monastery itself or bought from a professional "parchmenter," a scribe would then painstakingly copy out the body of the text, often by lamplight (candles were forbidden because of the risk of fire).[39] He would take care to leave spaces so that a "rubricator" could later embellish the work with elaborate initial letters (or "versals"), headings, and other section marks. Named for the Latin *rubrico*, "to color red," rubricators often worked in contrasting red ink, which not only added a decorative flourish but also guided the eye to important divisions in the text.[40] In the hands of the rubricators, *C* for *capitulum* was soon accessorized by a vertical bar, as were other *litterae notabiliores* in the fashion of the time; later, the resultant bowl was filled in and so ¢ for *capitulum* became the familiar reversed-P of the pilcrow.[41]

As the symbol's appearance changed, so too did its usage. At first it only marked chapters, but soon after it started to pepper texts as a paragraph or even sentence marker, breaking a block of running text into meaningful sections as the writer saw fit. ¶ This style of usage yielded very compact text, harking back, perhaps, to the not-so-distant practice of *scriptio continua*.[42] Ultimately, though, the utility of the paragraph overrode the need for efficiency and became so important as to warrant a new line—prefixed with a pilcrow, of course.[43]

¶ The pilcrow's name—pithy, familiar, and archaic at the same time—moved with the character during its transformation from *C* for

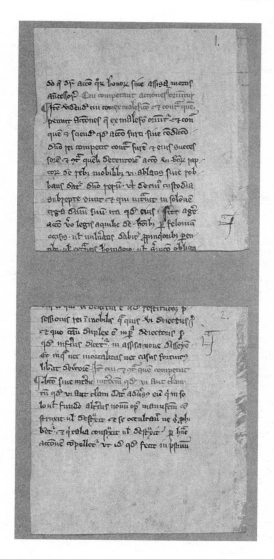

Figure 1.5 Taken from Henry Bracton's *De legibus et consuetudinibus Anglie* [The laws and customs of England], dated to the second half of the thirteenth century, these fragments show familiar, *c*-like *capitula* placed at the start of lines to mark paragraphs.

capitulum to independent symbol in its own right. From the Greek *paragraphos*, or paragraph mark, came the prosaic Old French *paragraphe*, which subsequently morphed first into *pelagraphe* and then *pelagreffe*. By 1440 the word had entered Middle English, rendered as *pylcrafte*—its second syllable perhaps influenced by the English *crafte*, or "skill"—and from there it was a short hop to its modern form.[44] The pilcrow had been given form, function, and name.

¶ Having attained such a singular importance, the pilcrow then did something remarkable. It committed typographical suicide.

¶ Taking pride of place at the head of every new paragraph, the pilcrow had carved out a niche for itself at the heart of late medieval writing. Boldly inked by the rubricator, the marks grew ever more elaborate and time-consuming to add. Unfortunately, the deadline is not a modern invention. On occasion, time would run out before the rubricator could complete his work, leaving undecorated the white spaces carefully reserved for pilcrows, versals, and other rubricated marks. With the advent of the printing press in the mid-fifteenth century, the problem was compounded. The first printed books aped handwritten works as closely as possible, leaving gaps in the printed text for the rubricator to later fill by hand, and as the volume of printed documents grew exponentially, it became increasingly difficult to attend to them all.

¶ The rubricated pilcrow became a ghost: its brief reign as the de facto paragraph mark was over, usurped by the indented paragraph.[45]

* * *

Even after this ignominious relegation from mainstream use, the pilcrow refused to be done away with. Robbed of its raison d'être, it nevertheless survives as a proofreading symbol (where, aptly enough, it signifies a point at which a paragraph should be split in two), in legal documents, and as a boutique character used to bring a historical or typographical flourish to a work.[46]

One of the pilcrow's most intriguing appearances in this capacity came in *An Essay on Typography*, a book written by the famed English sculptor Eric Gill.[47] Born in 1882 and brought up the son of a Protestant minister, at thirty-one Gill converted to Catholicism and led an increasingly ascetic life as a monkish, artistic polymath.[48] His charisma and trenchant views attracted a retinue of like-minded contemporaries to a series of rural communities—communes, almost—with Gill at their center.

By the time Gill and his printing partner René Hague published *Essay* in 1931, Gill's suspicion of industrial society had cohered into a philosophy very much in the vein of the Arts and Crafts movement of the time, celebrating hand craftsmanship and reviling the uniformity of mass production. *Essay* was as much a manifesto as an educational textbook, its very genesis a canonical example of that same philosophy: Gill wrote the text, set it in a typeface of his own design, and, with Hague, printed the first edition by hand.[49]

Essay's bold use of the pilcrow stands out to the modern reader from its very first line, as Gill sets out his stall in a forthright manner:

> ¶ The theme of this book is Typography, and Typography as it is affected by the conditions of the year 1931. The conflict between Industrialism & the ancient methods of handicraftsmen which resulted in the muddle of the nineteenth century is now coming to its term.
> ¶ But tho' Industrialism has now won an almost complete victory, the handicrafts are not killed, & they cannot be quite killed because they meet an inherent, indestructible, permanent need in human nature. (Even if a man's whole day be spent as a servant of an industrial concern, in his

> spare time he will make something, if only a window box
> flower garden.)[50]

¶ *Essay* made creative use of the pilcrow, simultaneously recalling
its medieval heyday and introducing a subtle extra level of semantic
meaning: a pilcrow at the start of a line introduced a new thread of
discussion, whereas a pilcrow in running text separated paragraphs
within that discussion.[51] The result is text that appears haphazard
at first (why does the pilcrow jump from the start of one line to the
middle of another?) but which echoes the Arts and Crafts ideology
in its marriage of simplicity of expression and richness of meaning. ¶ Gill's book abounds with other hints of that same philosophy.
Whereas many books "justify" text (in other words, they align it to
both left- and right-hand margins) to provide a uniform appearance,
Gill used a "ragged right" setting to mimic a handwritten manuscript.
Abbreviations such as "&," "tho'," and "sh'ld" evoked medieval scribal
tradition and, providing narrower alternatives to the full words they
represent, could be judiciously employed to prevent *too* ragged a right-
hand margin. Illustrations were all taken from engravings cut by the
author himself. ¶ The abiding impression, when confronted with one
of the five hundred first edition copies of *Essay*, with its ragged hand-
cut pages and the fading ink of Hague & Gill's signatures on the final
page, is one of a labor of love.

Gill's Joanna, the blocky yet elegant typeface in which *Essay* is
set, was based in part on his earlier Perpetua type and was described
by the artist himself as "a book face free from all fancy business."
This is not the whole truth, however, and Joanna bears a number of
idiosyncratic touches that defy its supposed plainness. Unlike traditional roman typefaces, Gill used horizontal and vertical strokes
of similar width, married to square serifs that had been fashionable
a century earlier.[52] Perhaps most noticeably, the narrow italics slope

¶ Gill Sans *italic*

¶ Joanna italic

¶ Perpetua *italic*

Figure 1.6 Gill Sans, Joanna, and Perpetua: Eric Gill's most famous typefaces.

at a shallow three-degree angle and forgo the traditional italic forms for the letters *f, k, v, w,* and *z*.[53] Joanna lends *Essay* a distinctive air and an easy readability.

Although today Gill's typefaces are most visible of all his works, his chief occupation was as a sculptor, and his prodigious output as such seemed positively calculated to bait the prurience of his day. His first major commission was to carve the Stations of the Cross (a traditional Catholic depiction of Christ's final hours) for Westminster Cathedral, and churchgoers were shocked by their unspiritual directness.[54] While working on the Stations in the cathedral, a woman approached Gill to tell him that she did not think they were nice carvings; he responded, in characteristic form, that it was not a nice subject.[55]

Another of his works, a near-life-size carving of a couple entwined in a sexual embrace that Gill carved in 1910–11, posed problems both in creation and exhibition. Gill was forced to post an apprentice outside the modeling sessions in which his sister Gladys and her husband Ernest posed for the sculpture. Initially sold to a local private collector with a penchant for racy works of art, tastes had become liberal enough by 1949 that the sculpture could be sold at auction.[56] Even then, Gill's original title for the piece (as recorded in his private diary) was still considered too brazen. For public consumption, the cheerfully direct *They (big) group fucking* became the rather more circumspect *Ecstasy*.[57]

Despite frequent forays into then-taboo subjects, after his death Gill remained well known mainly for his artistic successes and staunch Catholicism. The Eric Gill known to his close-knit family and followers, however, was a startlingly different man. In 1961, twenty-one years after his death, the BBC broadcast an hour-long radio documentary about the artist, and in it could be discerned the first hints of the extraordinary gulf between Gill's public façade and the reality of his private life. Interviewed for the program, Gill's partner René Hague—now married to Gill's daughter Joan—spoke about his father-in-law's attitude toward evil:

> I wonder whether Eric really believed in evil. He would
> talk about the evils of industrialism, he would talk about
> things going wrong, but he certainly didn't believe that
> there was any "bad thing." He didn't believe in evil in that
> sense, that anything in nature could be evil. That was
> one of the reasons why he was willing to try anything,
> anything at all, but quite literally. Either right or wrong,
> or supposed to be right or wrong, he'd say "Let's try it, let's
> try it once, anyway."[58]

The awful truth behind Hague's musings became clear in 1989 when an unflinching biography revealed adultery, incest, child abuse, and even bestiality within the Gill household.[59] The artist's posthumous reputation was rocked by these revelations, yet despite this (or perhaps partly because of it), Gill remains a resonant name within the typographical world and *Essay* one of his most enduring contributions to it.

* * *

D espite occasional celebrity appearances as a paragraph mark
(such as in *An Essay on Typography*), the pilcrow remains largely
alienated from its traditional role. As compensation, perhaps, it has
since acquired a sort of talismanic power for those in the know, especially in the worlds of typography, design, and literature. Jonathan
Hoefler of the type design firm Hoefler & Frere-Jones (the company

Figure 1.7   Modern pilcrows, as tucked away in the dark recesses
of modern digital typefaces. All set at 72pt and equalized in height.
At top are a number of revivals of much older typefaces; *left to right* are
Linotype Didot, Adrian Frutiger's 1991 interpretation of Firmin Didot's
late eighteenth-century French typefaces; Big Caslon (Carter & Cone
Type), a display face by Matthew Carter based on William Caslon's early
eighteenth-century designs; Hoefler Text, a book face designed for Apple by
Jonathan Hoefler in 1991 and inspired by Garamond and Janson's typefaces
of the seventeenth century; and lastly the odd one out, Linotype Zapfino
by Hermann Zapf, a digital font based on a calligraphic alphabet of Zapf's
own design dating from 1944.[60] *At bottom,* modern fonts with well-defined
missions in life; *left to right* are the quintessentially modern Helvetica
(Linotype); Skia, designed by Matthew Carter to show off a new Apple
rendering technology; Courier New, designed as a typewriter face for IBM,
updated by Adrian Frutiger, and now used primarily in Microsoft Windows;
and finally Museo Slab, a modern slab-serif font by Jos Buivenga.[61]

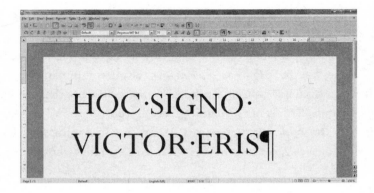

Figure 1.8   Hidden characters revealed in a word processing program. The typeface used here is Eric Gill's Perpetua.

is perhaps most famous for its **Gotham** typeface, as used for Barack Obama's distinctive 2008 presidential campaign posters) penned an essay about the joys of designing pilcrows; the Pilcrow Lit Fest takes its name from the character, and the eponymous protagonist of Adam Mars-Jones's second novel takes "Pilcrow" as his pseudonym, comforted by its status as an outsider.[62]

Hints of the pilcrow's former lives do still crop up in unexpected places. The Church of England's *Book of Common Worship* employs pilcrows as section markers and bullet points, recalling the medieval capitulum.[63] Clicking on that innocuous, pilcrow-labeled button in your word processor turns otherwise invisible spaces and line breaks into dots and yet more pilcrows, lending the average computerized document a dignified medieval appearance.

If the pilcrow is ever to be fully rehabilitated, its best chance lies with another, rather more significant, computer-based innovation. The Internet has fostered a new burst of interest in typography: amateur typographers design countless new fonts on inexpensive computers; personal web pages have democratized typesetting in a way unimaginable to Gutenberg or Gill, and disused characters have been rescued from obscurity to add spice and dignity to the everyday exchange of information. The pilcrow among them has once again carved out its niche as a paragraph mark, and is returned to its former glory in the glow of the computer screen.

Chapter 2 ✺ The Interrobang

The year 1962 was a momentous one for the United States of America. John Glenn became the first American, and only the second human, to reach orbit; the Kennedy administration successfully negotiated the nuclear tightrope of the Cuban missile crisis, and NASA launched AT&T's *Telstar*, the world's first telecommunications satellite, ushering in a new era of instantaneous global communications.[1] Consumer society, too, was reaching new heights: advertising ruled, and the ad men were at the peak of their game.

Amid this turmoil of Cold War and technological revolution, one Madison Avenue executive turned his attention to loftier matters. Martin K. Speckter was the head of his own New York advertising agency with no less than the *Wall Street Journal* account on his books; a keen hobbyist typographer, he also edited *Type Talks*, a bimonthly journal that explored the use of typography in advertising.[2] Frustrated with the growing tendency of copywriters to combine the exclamation mark and question mark to yield a surprised or rhetorical question— "Who would punctuate a sentence like that?!"—Speckter penned an article for *Type Talks* to offer a solution. "Making a New Point, or, How About That . . ." appeared in the March–April 1962 issue and argued for a single punctuation mark to replace this ugly, jury-rigged construction. As the article went on to explain, this putative symbol was intended to convey a particular mixture of surprise and doubt:

> To this day, we don't know exactly what Columbus had in mind when he shouted "Land, ho." Most historians insist

that he cried, "Land, ho!" but there are others who claim it
was really "Land ho?". Chances are the intrepid Discoverer
was both excited and doubtful, but neither at that time
did we, nor even yet, do we, have a point which clearly
combines and melds interrogation with exclamation.[3]

Speckter presented a set of speculative designs for his creation, as rendered by Jack Lipton, his agency's art director, and tentatively named his new mark the "exclamaquest" or "interrobang." At the article's close, he invited readers to "join the exalted ranks of Aldus, Bodoni et al" by supplying their own graphic interpretations of the symbol, as well as new names to compare with his own suggestions.

Response to the article was immediate and enthusiastic, and within weeks various newspapers had reported on the genesis of the new mark. On April 6, for instance, the *Wall Street Journal* published an editorial introducing the new symbol, displaying an immediate

Figure 2.1 Proposed interrobangs from *Type Talks*, March–April 1962, drawn by Jack Lipton of Martin K. Speckter Associates, Inc.

comic mastery of its intended usage with the example: "Who forgot to put gas in the car?"[4] Another mention came in the *New York Herald Tribune*, where advertising correspondent Joseph Kaselow devoted an entire column to Speckter's new symbol, hailing it as "true genius."* This welcome publicity was not entirely without hiccups: Kaselow's article was published on April 1—whether this was an unfortunate coincidence or the deliberate act of a misinformed editor is not recorded—and this predictably raised questions as to the interrobang's authenticity.[6]

Submissions of alternative names and sketches from other advertisers and graphic designers flowed in to *Type Talks* over the following months. Emboldened by the response to his first article, Speckter published a follow-up in the May–June '62 edition of *Type Talks*, taking the opportunity to firmly but genially rebuke suggestions that his newly minted symbol was less than serious:

> Well, *Type Talks* favors just about everything that makes
> for more effective communication, so our proposal
> is more than half-way serious. [...] more people read
> advertising than read books; is it too far-fetched to
> hope that advertising can successfully introduce a new
> character for our punctuation system?[7]

This second article put forward some of the alternative names submitted by readers. Portmanteaux abounded, giving rise to "emphaquest," "interrapoint," and the tongue-twisting "exclarogative." In other suggestions, the mark's application to rhetorical questions was addressed by "rhet," and its intentional ambiguity by the slyly humorous "consternation mark." However inventive these suggestions were,

---

* The *New York Herald Tribune* is now defunct, but international readers may recognize the title of its descendant, the *International Herald Tribune*.[5]

Figure 2.2   Alternative interrobangs submitted to *Type Talks*, May–June 1962.

one of Speckter's own terms had already gained traction in the news-paper stories that had reported on his original article. "Interrobang," formed from the Latin *interrogatio*, translating roughly as "a rhetorical question," and the English "bang," a slang word for exclamation mark, would prove to be the favorite.[8]

The second article also reproduced some of the designs sent in by graphic designers and typographers. As with the suggested names, some were abstract, others direct; more than anything else, though, they were all *fashionable*. These were, after all, the creations of an industry that simultaneously reflected and defined contemporary culture: Frank Davies's hot-air balloon and Larry Ottino's angular, inverted question mark (as shown in Figure 2.2) seem custom-made for a Saul Bass movie poster or glossy magazine cover. In the end, however, mirroring the popularity of "interrobang" over the other suggestions for its name, Jack Lipton's simple superposition of a ques-tion and exclamation mark (‽) would prevail, becoming the model for most future interpretations of the symbol.

Popular as it was with writers and admen, the interrobang faced a struggle for mainstream acceptance. Simulating an interrobang on a typewriter was possible, if clumsy—type "?" and then overstrike it with "!"—but for typesetters creating a printed document, there was no such shortcut. Those advertisements, brochures, and books that actually honored the writer's use of the character* had to be set using handcrafted interrobangs, either drawn by an illustrator or sculpted from rubber cement with a razor blade.[10] Speckter's mark was hobbled from the start.

The first breakthrough came four years after the interrobang's creation. With an eye on the upcoming US Bicentennial, the type conglomerate American Type Founders commissioned graphic designer Richard Isbell to create a new typeface marking the occasion. Released in 1966, Isbell's hand-set metal font was called Americana, and for the first time in a mass-produced typeface, it included among its accompanying marks of punctuation an interrobang.[11] Isbell's elegant interpretation of Jack Lipton's design was given pride of place in Americana type specimens and its introduction was significant enough for *Time* magazine to print an article on the subject in July 1967.[12] Providing a potted history of the character's creation, *Time* went on to declare that "Delighted by its possibilities, the A.T.F. plans to include [the interrobang] in all new types that it cuts."[13]

The circumstances of the interrobang's addition to Isbell's typeface were surrounded by misinformation and muddied facts, and led to a minor ruckus between Speckter and ATF. A September 1968 article in the trade publication *Publishers' Auxiliary*, for example, erroneously claimed that Speckter lobbied ATF to include the symbol; instead, as *Time* magazine had explained the year before, Isbell had simply chosen to include the symbol on a whim, most likely after encountering it elsewhere.[14] Not only that, but despite the interrobang's prominent placement on ATF's promotional materials, its

---

* In an illustrative collision of authorial intent and technological shortcomings, the 1982 book *Will That Be on the Final?*, bravely titled with an interrobang, is still listed in digital catalogues with a bipartite "!?".[9]

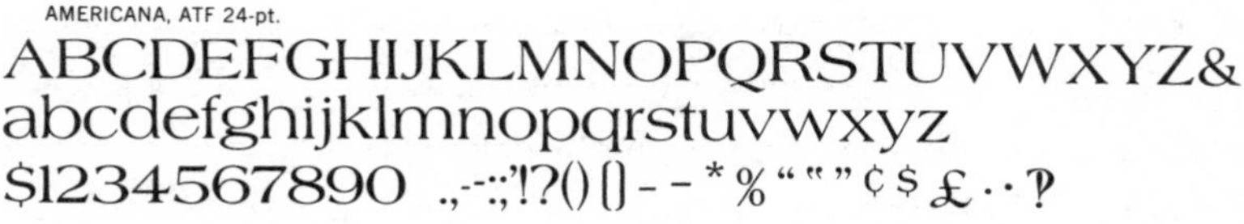

AMERICANA, ATF 24-pt.

ABCDEFGHIJKLMNOPQRSTUVWXYZ&
abcdefghijklmnopqrstuvwxyz
$1234567890 .,-:;'!?()[] - - * % " " " " ¢ $ £ ·· ‽

Figure 2.3 Specimen of Americana, by Richard Isbell, taken from *American Typefaces of the Twentieth Century* (1993) by Mac McGrew. An interrobang is visible at bottom right.

inventor's name was curiously absent, as was his own term for the character, passed over in favor of ATF's alternative "interabang."[15] The spat was defused only when the type foundry took out a full-page advertisement in *Art Direction* magazine that attributed the character's creation to Speckter and grudgingly acknowledged his preferred spelling of its name.[16]

Despite the contretemps, the provision of the interrobang in a commercial typeface was a positive step if the character was ever to succeed in the mainstream press. Another step toward that goal occurred in the autumn of 1968, as reported by the *Wall Street Journal*. Remington Rand, a prominent typewriter manufacturer, had an announcement to make:

> Remington Rand offers the new punctuation mark, the Interrobang (a combination of "?" and "!"), as a special type face for its Model 25 Electrics.[17]

Perhaps as a result of the symbol's increasing familiarity, the news warranted only a single line in a roundup of miscellaneous business reports, but the brevity of this mention belied its significance. A path had been cleared all the way from the copywriter's desk to the printing presses, and a new wave of enthusiasm for the interrobang was in the offing.

* * *

The interrobang's appearance on the keyboard of Remington Rand's Model 25 typewriter gave the mark a new legitimacy and ease of use overnight, and spurred renewed interest in the character. As with its appearance in Richard Isbell's Americana, the mark's jump from hot-metal type to the typewriter keyboard was the result of a happy coincidence: a Remington Rand graphic designer saw an ATF brochure for the font and lobbied in turn for its newest character to be made available on his company's typewriters.[18] The Model 25's replaceable key and type head allowed different characters to be installed as required, providing the perfect test ground for this as-yet-unproven mark of punctuation.[19] Remington Rand entertained ideas of a revolution in punctuation with its new interrobang key, and said as much in an internal newsletter, explaining that "[the] Interrobang

Figure 2.4 The monospaced interrobang designed by Kenneth Wright for Remington Rand's Model 25 electric typewriter and released in 1968. Its roots in Jack Lipton's 1962 interrobang are evident.

is already receiving favorable comments from typographers who are said to commend it for its ability to express the incredibility of modern life."[20]

Grandiose as this might sound, feverish interest in Martin Speckter's invention followed the release of Remington's interrobang key. That the typewriter was the era's dominant method of text entry, with offices echoing incessantly to the clacking report of ranks of typists, was not lost on the American media; for months during the autumn and winter of 1968–1969 newspapers and magazines across the country devoted column inches to the character and its new accessibility. Articles varied in length and tone: the *Wall Street Journal*'s matter-of-fact one-liner contrasts with *Newsweek*'s cautiously optimistic paragraph hedged by the disclaimer "the Interrobang symbol is not fully approved by grammarians and lexicographers."[21] William Zinsser, a literary critic, was moved to pen a half-page essay for *LIFE* magazine that ranged from incredulity ("Look at Spanish. ¿I mean, do they need all that stuff just to ask a question? ¡Ridiculous!") to plaintive nostalgia ("We need plain words to express plain truths. [...] The only trouble is that nobody uses them any more.")[22] One suspects that for Zinsser, who considered that "writing improves in direct ratio to the number of things we can keep out of it," the interrobang was merely a convenient contemporary target for a long-simmering cultural critique.[23]

Not all stories were qualified by caveats or tainted with polemic. Don Oakley, writing for the *Kansas City Kansan*,* considered that "the interrobang is a welcome addition to the writer's arsenal," and the

---

* Some of these newspaper articles contain unsubtle clues of the age in which they were written. Alluding to the fact that the typing pools that could now make use of the interrobang were populated almost exclusively by women, Don Oakley's article bore the blithely misogynistic title "Look, Girls, a New Key on Typewriter."[24] Another story on the subject, this time in the notoriously conservative *Richmond News Leader,* contains the example "'What do you mean, you've overspent your allowance (interrobang),' asked by the man of the house when the lady of the house asks for a supplemental appropriation to tide her over until payday."[25]

Globe of Joplin, Missouri, declared that "We can hardly wait for it to be installed on the regular typewriter keyboard, for it fits the times and comes none too soon when there's a new crisis or calamity almost every day."[26] Most fittingly, *Type Talks* itself covered the return of the character first aired in its pages six years earlier: for the November–December 1968 issue, Martin K. Speckter contributed an interview with Kenneth Wright, the designer of Remington Rand's interrobang glyph.[27]

Whether or not it had occurred to Speckter that he himself might "join the exalted ranks of Aldus, Bodoni et al" as he had exhorted his

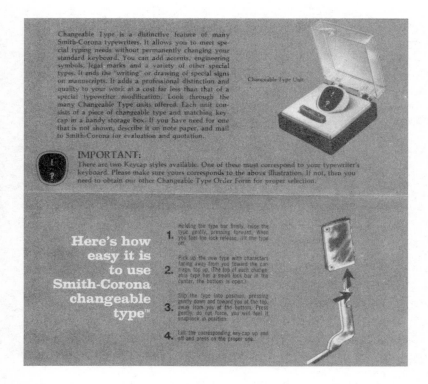

☞ *Figure 2.5*   A 1969 brochure from Smith-Corona showing their interchangeable interrobang key, a competitor to that of Remington Rand.

readers to do in 1962, he had succeeded—in the minds of some observers at least—in creating the first new mark of punctuation for centuries.[28]

* * *

U nfortunately, the interrobang's status as a cause célèbre during the late 1960s and early 1970s proved ephemeral, and its popularity reached a plateau even as Remington Rand's interrobang key let the average typist make use of it. A creation of the advertising world—and considered by some an unnecessary one at that—the interrobang faced resistance in literary and academic spheres and was beset by more prosaic technical difficulties at almost every turn.[29]

As demonstrated by the appearance of the interrobang in ATF's Americana, cutting a new punch for the casting of metal type was eminently possible, and the only real barriers to including a new character in such a font were ones of familiarity and usage. More problematic at the time were the automated typesetting machines that dominated the printing of newspapers and books. The Linotype machine, a baroque keyboard-driven device that cast lines of type from a "magazine" of individual letter molds,* accommodated only ninety different characters; the similar Monotype machine supported only thirty more, for a total of 120.[32] And despite the flexibility in letter placement and size brought by the "cold type" machines that succeeded them—the Linofilms and Monophotos that projected letters optically instead of casting them in lead—the new devices were little more than crude adaptations of their predecessors, and inherited the same limited character sets.[33] Faced with evicting an existing character to make room

---

* The metal block on which an individual letter is engraved for use in a Linotype machine is termed a "matrix," with lines of embossed type cast from rows of such matrices.[30] In hand-set type, an embossed letter punch is carved first, an indented matrix is struck from that punch, and individual letters, or "sorts," cast from the matrix are manually assembled into lines.[31]

for the upstart interrobang, more often than not a type foundry would choose convention over innovation; however infrequently it might be used, a comforting ae-ligature (æ), dagger (†), or section sign (§) had tradition on its side, and the newcomer did not. For this reason, the interrobang was slow to appear in automatically set typefaces.

The evolution of Isbell's Americana, from hand-set, hot-metal type to phototypesetting and beyond, illustrates the technological upheaval then under way in the printing industry and the compromises that came with it.[34] Hand set as it was, Americana could include an interrobang without having to displace an existing character, but the laborious nature of setting type by hand made it unsuitable for the kind of day-to-day printing carried out for newspapers and magazines.[35] Not only that, but by the 1960s metal type itself was becoming an anachronism, and ATF was suffering because of it; the 1968 extra-bold version of Americana was the last new typeface to be released by the company, whose ebbing fortunes would result first in acquisition and finally in bankruptcy.[36] In the strictest of senses, *Time* magazine's declaration that the interrobang would appear in all new ATF typefaces had been correct—Americana Extra Bold *did* carry an interrobang—though it proved to be a hollow promise.[37]

Years later, the phototypesetting company Compugraphics stumbled upon Isbell's interrobang and produced variants of it for their new, optical versions of Americana, but the familiar pressures of the fixed character set meant they never left the drawing board.[38] Even today, when digital fonts can contain near-limitless numbers of characters, Americana's software incarnations still have no interrobang.[39] Its loss in the transition from hand-set, hot metal printing to phototypesetting seems permanent.

This combination of factors—the six-year delay in getting the new character from composition to printing; the sheer inertia of punctuation practice; doubt as to the grammatical need for a new symbol—sent the interrobang to an early grave. By the early 1970s it had largely fallen out of use, and the chance for its widespread acceptance seemed to have been missed.

* * *

The interrobang's rise and fall is not without precedent in the world of punctuation. Before the advent of the printing press, the imprecision of manual copying meant that punctuation evolved as it passed from scribe to scribe, encompassing both bright new avenues and dark cul-de-sacs along the way. Many once-important marks (the pilcrow not least among them) were created, mutated, and killed off on the road from Aristophanes's three dots* to today's system.[40]

A most uncanny parallel actually occurs a hundred years after the printing press had imposed a degree of standardization on language and punctuation. Sometime around 1575, a curiously reversed question mark (⸮) began to appear in works of both printed and handwritten origin: this was the "percontation point," invented by an English printer named Henry Denham who so doubted the acuity of his readers that he decided to furnish them with a way to punctuate rhetorical questions.[41] Though trivial to write by hand (percontation marks appear in contemporary holographs from the poet Robert Herrick and playwright Thomas Middleton, both notable literary figures of the era), few other printers took the trouble to carve a new punch for the character and instead relied on italic (?) or blackletter (?) question marks to convey the same meaning.[42] This use of differently styled question marks (but question marks nonetheless) sometimes made it difficult for readers to be entirely sure that the author had in fact intended to use a percontation mark. This muddle aside, Denham's experiment came to an end within fifty years and the percontation

---

* See chapter 1, "The Pilcrow (¶)", for more on Aristophanes's early system of punctuation.

mark was relegated to the status of typographic curio. But as one modern commentator suggests, with the development of digital printing technology, "Those [percontation marks] that certainly exist [...] now can and should be reproduced, and post-metal printing offers the percontation mark a true second chance."[43]

Not only does this echo the predicament of the interrobang, edged out of typefaces because of the technical costs of including it, but in a more fundamental way the percontation mark and the interrobang represent two sides of the same linguistic coin. In formal rhetoric, *percontatio* is the asking of an open-ended question, where any answer may be given, whereas *interrogatio* attempts to confirm or deny a previous argument.[44] Certainly, anyone who has cause to pose the *Wall Street Journal*'s exasperated question—"Who forgot to put gas in the car⸮"—almost certainly knows the answer already.[45] It is not hard to imagine that had it been known to him, Martin K. Speckter would have seized upon the percontation mark's cause with enthusiasm.

* * *

D espite its failure to gain lasting approval after its initial foray into the public eye, Speckter's invention may yet enjoy a happy ending. It has become, if such a thing is possible, a cult punctuation mark.

Some seed of fascination with the word or the symbol itself has lodged in the collective consciousness of the world of typography, so that the old debates over its utility continue to this day. Opposing typophiles seek to bury or praise the interrobang, presenting new interpretations of its shape, cursing the difficulty of creating them, and arguing all the while over its grammatical correctness.[46] It has quietly made its way into Unicode, the standard computer character set, even if it is not yet present in many digital fonts.[47] Harking back to Martin Speckter's own printing endeavors, the artisan printers of Interrobang Letterpress have adopted his character's name while the

Figure 2.6   Interrobang cufflinks, made from vintage typewriter keys with the addition of printed interrobang glyphs.

design agency Interabang UK has instead chosen ATF's rebellious misspelling as a conversation piece.[48]

The interrobang also thrives beyond the boundaries of the typographical world as a name (and sometimes an emblem) for a diverse range of artifacts such as punk records, limited-run 'zines, and student newspapers.[49] One can buy cufflinks made from vintage typewriter keys with screen-printed interrobangs laid over their original letters, and Facebook boasts at least five distinct interrobang revival groups, with memberships ranging from the tens to the thousands.[50]

More visible still is the interrobang's starring role in the visual identity of the State Library of New South Wales, Australia. As it approached its hundred-year anniversary, the library was in need of a makeover. Tasked with rejuvenating the public face of this venerable Sydney institution, Vince Frost, of the city's Frost* Design agency, cast about for a logo that would capture the curiosity and delight of a simple visit to the library.[51] Frost's "eureka moment," as he recalled it, came when he lit upon the interrobang: though Frost did not expect library customers to recognize the mark, its intertwined

Figure 2.7 The logo of the State Library of New South Wales, created by Frost* Design.

question-and-answer nature fit the brief perfectly, and today the interrobang takes center stage in the library's logo.*

Martin Speckter died in 1988, too early to see this latest resurgence in his creation's fortunes. For his widow Penny, though, the most encouraging sign of the interrobang's continuing relevance is its adoption into *Merriam-Webster's Collegiate Dictionary*: as of its tenth edition, her husband's invention appears alongside commas, colons, and periods under the coveted heading of "punctuation."[53] The interrobang may yet win us over.

---

* The interrobang-like logo of National Museums Scotland, also recently updated, is sadly unrelated to Martin K. Speckter's mark of punctuation. The logo is intended to represent "answers, discovery, delight, surprise," and consists of question marks and explanation marks "combined [...] to form a symbol with a hint of the Scottish flag. Some see the flag, and others see a propeller, crossed swords, a scythe, hooks and eyes, even a knife and fork for our café manager!"[52]

Figure 2.8 Logo of National Museums Scotland. Tantalizing though the prospect is, this is not a pair of interrobangs.

Chapter 3 ❧ The Octothorpe

The # is something of a problem child. It seems at first to be quite innocuous, a jack-of-all-trades whose names and uses correspond in a pleasingly systematic manner: in the USA "#5" is read "number five" and "5#" as "five pounds in weight," giving "number sign" and "pound sign" respectively, while in Britain the cross-hatching suggested by its shape leads to the commonly used "hash sign."[1]

Dig a little deeper, though, and this glyph can be a frustratingly slippery beast. Its manifold uses encompass the sublime and the ridiculous in equal measure, and its many competing aliases have singularly failed to resolve into a single, internationally accepted name for the character.[2] The ranks of those names have recently been swollen by a grandiose new arrival: coined for reasons more frivolous than practical, the whys and wherefores of the term "octothorpe" continue to elude even the most studied experts. The simple # is not nearly as simple as it seems.

* * *

Unlike the pilcrow, whose lineage of Greek *paragraphos* and Latin *capitulum* is witnessed plainly by a succession of ancient manuscripts, and unlike the interrobang, whose creator thoughtfully provided the definitive explanation of its etymology, solid clues to both the # symbol's appearance and its various names prove elusive.

The most credible story behind the evolution of the symbol, and the only one to be corroborated by tangible evidence, springs once again from ancient Rome.

The Roman term for a pound in weight was *libra pondo*, where *libra* means "scales" or "balances" (from which the constellation takes its name) and where *pondo* comes from the verb *pendere*, "to weigh."[3] The tautological flavor of this pairing is borne out by the fact that both *libra* and *pondo* were also used singly to mean the same thing—one pound in weight—and it is from these twin roots that the # gets both its form and its oldest name.[4]

Sometime in the late fourteenth century the abbreviation "lb" for *libra* entered English,* and according to common scribal practice it was accessorized with a line—known as a "tittle," or "tilde," and for which the modern "~" is named—drawn just above the letters' x-height to denote the use of a contraction.[6] The barred form of "lb" was originally so common that some early printers cut the paired letters onto a single, combined punch, but it has since been overtaken by both its predecessor and its descendant: jotted down in haste (as seen in Isaac Newton's elegant scrawl in image 3.1), ℔ was transformed into # by the carelessly rushing pens of successive scribes, while the naked "lb" soldiers on to this day.[7] The ℔ has become a missing link, a vital evolutionary step buried out of sight in the paleographic fossil record.†

In tandem with the development of the # symbol, *libra*'s estranged partner *pondo* was also changing. Whereas *libra* had become "lb" and then # through the urgency of the scribe's pen, *pondo* was instead

---

* The corresponding abbreviation "oz," for "ounce," has a similar genesis. The Latin *uncia,* or "twelfth" (used in the sense of twelfths of a Roman pound), became the medieval Italian *onza* and was subsequently abbreviated to "oz."[5]

† ℔ does still survive as a character in its own right, lurking in Unicode as the "L B BAR SYMBOL."[8] I have never seen it used in print.

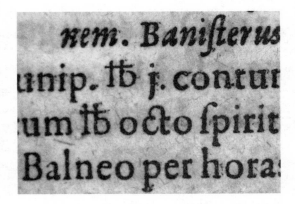 *Figure 3.1* ℔ as an abbreviation for *libra*, or "pound in weight," from the pen of Isaac Newton. Courtesy of the Roy G. Neville Historical Chemical Library, CHF.

subjected to the vagaries of spoken language. The Latin *pondo* became first the Old English *pund* (sharing a common root with the German *Pfund*) and later the modern word "pound."[9] *Libra* and *pondo* were reunited: #, the "pound sign," was born.

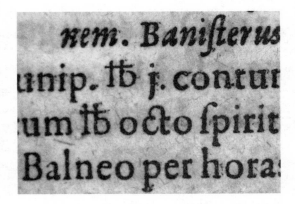

 Figure 3.2 A detail from Johann Conrad Barchusen's *Pyrosophia* (1698) showing printed ℔ symbols crossed by a tittle to show that they are abbreviations. Courtesy of the Roy G. Neville Historical Chemical Library, CHF.

* * *

T he # is but one of the relics of the phrase *libra pondo*, which spawned a dynasty of intertwined signs, words, and concepts that are still evident today. Most enduring of all are the weights, values, symbols, and terminology that have defined Western coinage and currency for more than a millennium—not least among them another "pound sign" with a rich Roman heritage.

Until relatively recently, the fall of the Western Roman Empire to barbarian invaders in 476 AD was held to mark the start of the medieval period, a benighted age of depopulation, superstition, and conflict sandwiched between glorious antiquity and the enlightened modern era heralded by the Renaissance.[10] Now, though, scholars consider this so-called Dark Age an oversimplification, and the dire overtones of "barbarian invasion" have softened to that of a general migration into the vacuum left by a rapidly disintegrating Empire.[11] The true state of Europe in medieval times was far more complex.[12]

Chief among the successors to the Roman Emperors were the eighth- and ninth-century kings of the Carolingian dynasty. Named for Charles Martel, his much-fêted grandson Charles the Great, and their many similarly christened successors, the Carolingians knitted Europe into a new empire inspired by their Roman antecedents.[13] The reign of Charles the Great, or "Charlemagne," was the very antithesis of a Dark Age, ushering in a mini-Renaissance of cultural and artistic endeavors: the study of classical works was revived, the largely illiterate clergy were educated, and disparate religious practices unified.[14] Though the king himself was famously illiterate (his toadying biographer Einhard described how Charlemagne kept writing implements under his pillow and on sleepless nights tried in vain to learn the letters of his name), he was shrewd enough to direct the monk Alcuin to develop a standardized lowercase script, or Carolingian minuscule, and carried out other reforms to the more prosaic machinery of government and the state.[15] In particular, a gradual standardization of currency begun under the earlier Carolingians was capped in 794 AD, when Charlemagne issued an edict fixing the coinage of his realm to the silver standard: he decreed that the coin called the *denier*, its name derived from an old Roman coin called the *denarius*, was to be minted at the rate of 240 coins per *livre*, or pound, of silver.[16] An existing convention held that twelve *deniers* were equal in value to an archaic gold coin of the Byzantine Empire named the *solidus*, and the ratios established by the combination of these two standards—240 *denarii* to 20 *solidi* to 1 *livre*—defined Western monetary culture for more than a thousand years.[17]

Thus the *libra pondo*, the venerable Roman pound weight, found itself enthroned at the head of a monetary dynasty of its own. Its name and value passed to the Frankish *livre*, the Italian *lira*, the British pound, and the German *Pfund*; the *solidus* in turn preceded the Frankish *sol*, the French *sou*, the British shilling, and the German *Schilling*, and the *denarius* gave rise first to the Frankish *denier* and later the *dinar*, *dinero*, penny, and *Pfennig*.* Until decimalization overtook them each in turn from the 1700s onward, the names and relative values of Western Europe's main coinages can all be traced back to the *libra pondo* and its Carolingian divisions.[19]

Ultimately, this transmission of *libra pondo* via the medium of coinage gave rise to another "pound sign": this time £, for pounds sterling. Mirroring its Carolingian ancestors, the British unit of currency was named for the 240 Norman pennies called "sterling" minted from each pound of silver.[20] In absolute terms, the British pound sign has

---

* The name of the *solidus* and its descendants give rise to the word "soldier," whose pay was measured in that same unit of currency.[18]

not traveled quite so far from its origins as its sibling the hash mark: it is, quite simply, a stylized *L* for *libra* with a tittle added to denote an abbreviation or symbol.[21] Unlike the similarly abbreviated ℔ of the fourteenth century, however, the £ sign is a relatively modern invention. The eponymous narrator of Daniel Defoe's ripping 1722 novel *Moll Flanders*, with her laserlike focus on the getting and keeping of money by any means necessary, still used a simple *l* for *libra* to list her ill-gotten fortune as "700 *l*. by me in Money, besides Cloaths, Rings, some Plate, and two gold Watches."[22] Some carelessly typeset modern editions have reinterpreted "700 *l*." as "#700," confusing pounds sterling, pound weights, and their respective symbols in a tangled etymological car crash.[23]

Even once £ had come into common use, the traditional abbreviation for pounds, shillings, and pence was still derived from the Latin *librae*, *solidi*, and *denarii*.[24] Though one might have said aloud "three pounds, four shillings, and fivepence," when writing down the same sum one would take care to render it as "£3.4s.5d."*

Neatly coincidental though all this appears, nailing down the exact definition of a so-called pound is remarkably tricky. The Roman *libra*, for example, was divided into twelve *unciae*, or ounces, and weighed about 327 grams.[28] Though he sought to re-create his own Holy Roman Empire, Charlemagne's reformed *livre* was instead a hefty 489.6 grams, while one pound sterling is closer to the "troy pound" named for the French town of Troyes, weighing in at roughly 373 grams.[29] Like the *libra pondo*, Charlemagne's *livre* and the troy pound are both divided into twelve ounces, though these "troy ounces" are

---

* There is yet another intriguing tangent to all these marks for currency and coinage. The slash-like mark called the "solidus" (/), often used to set fractions such as "¼," owes its existence to the £sd convention for pre-decimalization British currency. *S* for "shilling" was often rendered as an elongated "long s," or ſ; written out hurriedly, ſ became the attenuated /.[25] Thus it is that wartime British concertgoers might have shelled out a princely "two and six," or "2/6," to see a show.[26] And today's discerning beer drinker can still enjoy a pint of "80/-," or "80 shilling" ale.[27]

commensurately weightier than their Roman equivalents.[30] Finally, the modern "international pound"—formalized from an older unit named the *avoirdupois* pound—comprises sixteen ounces rather than twelve and is defined to be exactly 0.45359237 kilograms.[31] Little wonder the metric system is now mandated by law in all countries except the USA, Liberia, and Burma.

* * *

D espite boasting Latin roots of noble purpose, the # symbol is now used so promiscuously as to be completely dependent on its context. In addition to its most prominent uses as a weight or ordinal sign, in chess notation a # signifies checkmate; for the less pedantic typographer it may serve as a stand-in for the musical sharp symbol, or ♯,* and in many programming languages it indicates that the rest of the line is a comment only, not to be interpreted as part of the program.[33] Proofreaders wield the # to denote the insertion of a space: placed in the margin, an accompanying stroke indicates where a word space should be inserted, while "hr #" specifies that a dainty "hair" space should be used instead.[34] Perhaps most obscurely, three hash symbols in a row (###) are used to signal the end of a press release.[35]

The # has names almost as varied as its uses, and aside from the prosaic "number," "pound," and "hash" sign, it is or has been variously termed a "crunch," "hex," "flash," "grid," "tic-tac-toe," "pig-pen," and "square."[36] The origins of most of these names can be inferred from the character's shape or its function in a particular context, but its most elliptical alias does not give up its secrets so easily. The story of

---

* Microsoft took this path of least resistance when rendering the names of their programming languages C Sharp and F Sharp as "C#" and "F#," attracting a certain amount of derision in the process.[32]

how the # symbol came to be known as the "octothorpe" is entirely more tortuous.

* * *

W orks such as Robert Bringhurst's *Elements of Typographic Style* (widely acknowledged as the modern bible of typography), the *American Heritage Dictionary*, and the mighty *Oxford English Dictionary* have all weighed in with explanations for the origins of the # mark's most striking nickname. The fourth edition of the *American Heritage Dictionary*, for instance, says of the word "octothorpe":

> Alteration (influenced by **octo–**) of earlier **octalthorpe**, the *pound key*, probably humorous blend of *octal, an eight-point pin used in electronic connections (from the eight points of the symbol)* and the name of James Edward Oglethorpe.[37]

Unfortunately for this particular definition, the *AHD* appears to be its sole proponent. Oglethorpe, founder of the American state of Georgia as a refuge for inmates of English debtors' jails, seems an improbable candidate to be granted such an honor; his name is little known outside the state he founded, and there is no real evidence to suggest a link between Oglethorpe's haven for alleged financial miscreants and the character itself.[38] The *AHD* provides no details of the provenance of this theory, and it has a strong whiff of speculation about it.

Bringhurst's *Elements of Typographic Style*, an encyclopedic and otherwise reliable typographic reference work, takes a different tack:

> In cartography, [#] is a traditional symbol for *village*: eight fields around a central square. That is the source of its name. *Octothorp* means eight fields.[39]

A picturesque theory, and one with an apparent historical significance: the suffix -*thorp(e)* is an Old English word for village and still
occurs in British place names such as Scunthorpe.[40] Nevertheless, it is
unusual to find a Greek prefix such as *octo-* wedded to an Old English
word in this manner, and the true derivation of the symbol as a cor-
ruption of ℔ rather gives the lie to Bringhurst's definition.

Lastly, the *OED* gamely advances two similar but separate etymologies, both of which emanate from the unlikely linguistic wellspring
of AT&T's hallowed research subsidiary, Bell Telephone Laboratories.
First cited is the industry journal *Telecoms Heritage*, which alleges that
a Bell employee named Don MacPherson needed a suitably distinctive
name for the age-old # symbol:

> His thought process was as follows: There are eight points
> on the symbol so *octo* should be part of the name. We
> need a few more letters or another syllable to make a noun.
> [...] (Don Macpherson [...] was active in a group that was
> trying to get Jim Thorpe's Olympic medals returned from
> Sweden). The phrase *thorpe* would be unique.[41]

The question of who exactly Don MacPherson was, and why he needed
to find a name for the # symbol was not broached. The *OED*'s second
attempt, however, goes a little further, quoting a 1996 issue of *New
Scientist* magazine:[42]

> The term 'octothorp(e)' [...] was invented for '#', allegedly
> by Bell Labs engineers when touch-tone telephones were
> introduced in the mid-1960s. 'Octo-' means eight, and
> 'thorp' was an Old English word for village: apparently the
> sign was playfully construed as eight fields surrounding a
> village.[43]

Again a cartographic theme is invoked, though because it takes the shape of the symbol as the starting point, it might be lent more credence second time around.

In short, the only commonality to be found between these three sources and their four claimed etymologies is the agreement that "octothorpe" is formed from *octo-* plus "thorp(e)". Discounting the *American Heritage Dictionary*'s fanciful invocation of James Edward Oglethorpe, and ignoring Robert Bringhurst's charming but flawed explanation, two sources remain, both of which mention Bell Labs. Why, exactly, did the engineers at America's premier telecommunications laboratory feel the need to give this centuries-old symbol a new name?

* * *

B ell Labs, the one-time research arm of telecom giant AT&T, produced some of the twentieth century's most influential developments in science and technology. It boasts seven Nobel Prizes in Physics awarded for, among other things, a demonstration of the wave nature of matter, the invention of the transistor, and the discovery of background cosmic radiation. Other notable products include the laser, radio astronomy, the first communications satellite, and the UNIX operating system,* a key component of the Internet and of modern computing in general.[45]

Most relevant in terms of punctuation, though, is a small linguistic innovation that emerged in the wake of a much larger technological one. Engaged in the 1960s in reinventing the world's ageing telephone

---

* In certain UNIX programs, the hash symbol is forced into a shotgun marriage with the exclamation mark—the "bang" in printers' parlance—to yield #!, the "hash-bang" or "shebang."[44]

dialing system, one of the many Bell Labs engineers working on this mammoth task was almost certainly responsible for coining the term "octothorpe." And though the octothorpe's birthplace is well recorded, the question of exactly *who* created it remains contentious.

Since the arrival in the late nineteenth century of the earliest automated exchanges, telephone calls had been routed from caller to recipient by a method known as pulse dialing. Each digit of the recipient's number was transmitted to the exchange by interrupting the line a number of times equal to the desired digit, producing a series of characteristic "ticks" as the telephone's rotary dial was released. At roughly ten pulses per second, dialing a number tied up expensive call routing equipment for too long, and the problem was compounded as telephones became more and more widespread.[46] Pulse dialing was overdue for replacement.

Devised in the late 1940s and refined a decade later with the advent of affordable transistors, Bell Labs' new system consisted of a grid of buttons, each of which transmitted an audible tone when pressed.[47] Named the "dual-tone multi-frequency" system, or the friendlier "Touch-Tone" for public consumption, the design was simple but ingenious.[48] Its frequencies were selected to avoid confusing human voices with button presses, while by transmitting tones in the normal range of human hearing, the new system could be used over existing copper wiring without the need for costly upgrades.[49] Lastly, unlike pulse dialing, where the tick-tick-tick of each digit traveled no farther than the local exchange, the audible notes of a Touch-Tone handset reached all the way to a call's recipient, allowing callers to control systems such as voice mail or telephone banking.[50]

Though the underlying system supported a four-by-four grid of sixteen buttons, the first consumer handsets had only ten: the first three rows carried the digits 123, 456, and 789 respectively, with 0 orphaned at the center of a fourth row.[51] This layout was controversial. Accountants, whose calculator keypads were numbered from 9 down to 0, complained that the proposed out-of-order placement of the zero was an affront to mathematical consistency. The (winning) counterargument pointed out that on rotary dial phones, each number doubled as a set of letters for mnemonic purposes—2 = ABC, 3 = DEF, 4 = GHI, and so forth—and that reversing the buttons' proposed positions would ruin their corresponding alphabetical order.[52]

The next problem faced was linguistic rather than mathematical, when, in 1968, the two unused buttons either side of the zero were finally made available for public use in controlling menus and other

Figure 3.3   A Touch-Tone keypad as shown on a US military telephone. Visible here is the full four-by-four DTMF layout, with the fourth column of keys used to indicate increasing levels of precedence. "FO" denoted "Flash Override," the highest level, and was reserved for the President, the Joint Chiefs of Staff, and a select group of other high-ranking officers.[53]

special services provided by the exchange.[54] There were two questions to be answered: what symbols should these buttons carry, and what should they be called? Here the plot thickens.

* * *

E arly in the development of the new keypad, a number of test handsets had been produced with, respectively, a five-pointed star and a diamond symbol on the two new keys. These characters did not appear on standard typewriter keyboards, which proved problematic when documenting the design. Doug Kerr, a Bell engineer working on the new system, was tasked with selecting more suitable characters to replace them.[55] Kerr was Bell Labs' representative on the committee responsible for creating the nascent American Standard Code for Information Interchange, or ASCII, the verbose title given to a standard character set to be adopted by computer manufacturers.[56] Despite the *A* in its name, ASCII was intended to be an international standard, and with this in mind Kerr selected the asterisk and the hash symbol, satisfied that they both existed within the ASCII character set *and* appeared on the ubiquitous typewriter keyboard.

Once selected, the new characters needed names. "Asterisk" was considered too difficult to pronounce and spell, and the # sign, as we have seen, had no widely agreed name. Kerr suggested carrying over the names of the earlier test figures: "star" was an obvious choice, being both easier to pronounce than "asterisk" and descriptive of the character's visual appearance, while "diamond," explained away with a rather tenuous allusion to the center of the # symbol, would avoid any confusion over "pound" or "number" symbol.

But two of Kerr's peers were not to be swayed. Howard Eby and Lauren Asplund had been involved in testing the original star-and-diamond keypad and were mildly piqued by the rejection of what, to their minds, had been perfectly reasonable symbols.* As Kerr recounted, the pair sent him a memo explaining how they had decided to help "solve" this problem:

> They told me that they had read with interest the part of my report in which I regretted the absence of a unique typographical name for the character "#", and said they had solved my problem by coining one, "octatherp". [...] They said they were irritated that I had rejected some candidate characters they thought were good on the basis of lack of compatibility with emerging international standards (with which the Bell System had a tradition at the time of little interest). Thus, they said, as a way of getting even, they had included in the name the diphthong "th", which of course does not appear in German and several other languages and thus might be difficult for users of those languages to pronounce, which would serve them right.[58]

According to Kerr, then, the entirely artificial "octatherp," rather than "octothorpe," was the original form of the pound sign's new name. Kerr joined Asplund and Eby's lighthearted crusade and incorporated the word in his own documents, adding footnotes to the effect that # was "sometimes called *octatherp*."[59] "Octatherp" and its relatives started appearing throughout Bell literature and eventually made the leap into the wider world; as AT&T's new telephones became commonplace in the 1970s, newspaper stories about the new handsets

---

* Doug Kerr's 2006 essay on the subject names two different engineers—John C. Schaak and Herbert T. Uthlaut—as the originators of the word "octatherp." However, in personal correspondence with the author, Kerr quotes a message from Lauren Asplund that gives credit instead to Asplund and Eby.[57]

often included asides about the # symbol's distinctive appearance and name.[60]

As the *Oxford English Dictionary*'s alternative etymologies for the word "octothorpe" reveal, the picture is complicated by a competing backstory. A decade earlier than Kerr's 2006 account, another Bell Labs engineer had come forward with his own recollection. Writing in the journal of the *Telephone Heritage Group*, Ralph Carlsen averred that * and # had been chosen because of their presence on the typewriter keyboard and that again the # symbol's multitude of names had proved problematic.[61] Carlsen told the story of Don MacPherson, a Bell Labs supervisor sent to train customers in the use of the new system, who decided to create an unambiguous name for the symbol and inject some levity into his presentations at the same time.

Having selected the self-evident prefix *octo-*, MacPherson was in need of a second syllable to form a more convincing complete word, and his selection of "thorpe" was almost as leftfield as Asplund and Eby's thin-air conjuration of "therp." The Native American athlete Jim Thorpe, who had died in 1953, was considered by some to be one of the best American athletes of all time. Having won both the decathlon and pentathlon at the 1912 Olympic Games, Thorpe was stripped of his medals after officials discovered that he had played baseball professionally during 1909 and 1910, a violation of the Games' strict rules about amateur atheletes.[62] MacPherson, an avid supporter of the campaign to have Thorpe's medals posthumously restored, chose Thorpe's name to form the second part of his new word, and began to include "octothorpe" in his customer presentations and memoranda. Just as in Kerr's account, MacPherson's term made its way first into AT&T literature and then more broadly into the outside world.[63]

Carlsen's account is seemingly not authoritative enough for the *Oxford English Dictionary*, which also cites a *third* possible origin at Bell Labs, that of some anonymous wag's shoehorning together of *octo-* for "eight" and *thorpe* for "village."[64] Created to address the ambiguities of naming the # symbol, the word "octothorpe" has instead spawned its own obfuscated etymology. Whatever the true origin of its name, though, all this is to miss an important point. By selecting # for use on the telephone keypad, Bell Labs likely caused it to be seen by more people than ever before in its history. Without the Touch-Tone telephone, there is every chance that # would have labored on in obscurity; instead, with 85 percent of the world's population owning a cell phone, the humdrum octothorpe is familiar to billions.[65]

* * *

More recently, with the adoption of the octothorpe by the social messaging service Twitter to identify "hashtags"—terms used to group messages together according to common themes—the spotlight has returned to the #.[66] Just as Remington Rand's interrobang key gave Martin K. Speckter's character a new lease on life, so Twitter's hashtag has thoroughly invigorated the octothorpe.[67] Not for nothing did *GQ* magazine declare the octothorpe to be "Symbol of the Year 2010": the hash is enjoying a level of interest not seen since

Nimble Books LLC
@nimblebooks

all about the octothorpe from shady characters ... let's use hashtag #octothorpe #circularreference http://goo.gl/l13EM

Figure 3.4   Nimble Books creates the recursive hashtag "#octothorpe."

Doug Kerr, Don MacPherson, et al first got to grips with it on their telephone keypads.[68] Even if it does not quite match the scope of their achievements in physics and technology, Bell Labs' oddly named mark goes from strength to strength—even if, so far, a Nobel Prize in Tweeting has yet to be inaugurated.

Chapter 4 ☙ The Ampersand

I n contrast to some of the other symbols explored here, the ampersand seems entirely unexceptional. Another of those things the
Romans did for us, the symbol started life as the Latin word *et*, for
"and," and its meaning has hewed to its origins ever since. Even the
word "ampersand" itself manages to quietly hint at the character's
meaning, unlike the conspicuously opaque pilcrow or octothorpe.
Dependable and ubiquitous, the ampersand is a steady character
among a gallery of flamboyant rogues.

Things were not always thus, however. Today's ampersand might
take pride of place in the elevated names of Tiffany & Co. and Moët
& Chandon, but its Roman ancestor was a different beast. Born in
ignoble circumstances and dogged by a rival character of weighty
provenance, the ampersand would spend a thousand years of uneasy
coexistence with its opponent before finally claiming victory.

* * *

T he first-century-BC politician, philosopher, lawyer, and orator
Marcus Tullius Cicero belonged to that pantheon of Roman
personalities who, in the manner of the most prominent of today's
celebrities, could go by a single part of his tripartite name and yet still
be instantly recognized. Cicero, as he was and is invariably known,
was alternately immersed in and exiled from Roman politics at the
highest levels. His life and works are a microcosm of a republic groan-
ing under its own weight.

Born in 106 BC to an aristocratic but hitherto undistinguished family, on the face of it Marcus Tullius Cicero was an unlikely candidate to succeed within the Republic's rigidly hierarchical society. Political office in Rome had been the preserve of a wealthy elite since its very founding, and as the scion of a family possessing neither notable wealth nor patrician ancestry, Cicero faced an uphill struggle for acceptance.[1] Running afoul of another traditional Roman prejudice, Cicero was not a native of the city itself but rather a small provincial town named Arpinum to its south. Most unfortunate of all, though, his very name counted against him: his now-famous *cognomen*, or personal surname, meant "chickpea"; apparently inherited from a cleft-nosed ancestor, it was not the most stirring name for an aspiring politician.[2] The insecurity he felt at these disadvantages left the young Cicero with a fierce desire to succeed. Adopting the Homeric epithet "Always to be best and far to excel the others," he would live up to it in spectacular fashion.[3]

A lawyer by his mid-twenties, Cicero used wisely the opportunities afforded by his vocation, becoming a practiced orator, cultivating political contacts, and coming to public notice at the head of high-profile cases.[4] Making the leap from law to public service, he scaled the political ladder known as the *cursus honorum*, or "honors race," with almost indecent haste, elected at the first try and the youngest legal age to the successive offices of quaestor, aedile, and praetor.[5] His meteoric rise culminated in 63 BC with his election to the Republic's highest office, that of consul, one of two equal partners who served a one-year term and who held the power of veto over each other's actions. With a deal in place guaranteeing his corrupt and inept co-consul, Gaius Antonius Hybrida, a lucrative provincial governorship in exchange for his quiescence, Cicero was the de facto civilian leader of the Republic.[6] At the age of forty-three, this provincial lawyer from Arpinum sat at the head of the ancient world's preeminent superpower.

Early in his year of office, Cicero learned of the prospect of a coup orchestrated by Lucius Sergius Catilina, one of his defeated opponents for the position of consul, and the protégé of a cabal of reformists seeking to reduce the Senate's power. By then a shrewd politician, Cicero had cultivated a network of informants in the slippery world of the ruling classes, and was thus warned of the impending attempt on his life. Posting guards at his house to thwart the assassins, he stood before the Senate the very next day to deliver a scathing speech that turned popular opinion against Catiline and his cronies.[7] Its opening words are well known to scholars of Latin:

> *Quo usque tandem abutere, Catilina, patientia nostra? quam diu etiam furor iste tuus nos eludet? quem ad finem sese effrenata iactabit audacia?** [How far, finally, will you abuse our patience, Catiline? For how long will your frenzy still elude us? To what limit will your unbridled brazenness flaunt itself?][10]

Exposed, Catiline fled first the Senate and then Rome itself, hoping to muster his army and seize power by force, while his accomplices remained in the city only to be discovered and imprisoned. Cicero pressed his advantage, delivering another impassioned speech to persuade the Senate to have the conspirators put to death without trial.[11]

---

* Cicero's words had—and still have—a habit of insinuating themselves into the world of typography. The "Lorem ipsum" boilerplate text used by printers and designers is a deliberately jumbled extract from Cicero's *On the Ends of Good and Evil,* while the Catiline Orations themselves have traditionally provided material for type specimens.[8] As Daniel Berkeley Updike wrote in his 1922 manual *Printing Types,*

> No doubt the familiar opening of Cicero's oration, *'Quousque tandem abutere, Catilina,'* has had (since Caslon's time) considerable influence on the shape of the capital letter Q; for this sentence became so consecrated to type-specimens that most eighteenth century type-founders felt it necessary to employ it, and in order to outdo one another, they elongated the tails of their Q's more and more. I do not say that Q's have long tails because Cicero delivered an oration against Catiline; but that the tails of some Q's would not be as long as they are if the oration had begun with some other word![9]

The conspiracy was ended, but it would cost Cicero his political career. By flouting the due process of law he had given the reformists (not least among them a certain general named Gaius Julius Caesar) the means to persecute him in the courts; four years after the conspiracy, an embattled and conspicuously isolated Cicero fled to Macedonia.[12]

Cicero's turbulent life could have filled any number of books, and being an ardent self-promoter, he made a game attempt to write at least a few of them himself. He published his speeches as pamphlets to promulgate his views; he wrote a variety of philosophical treatises during his time in exile, and his voluminous correspondence was hoarded by his closest friend, Atticus, and later published by Cicero's indispensable secretary, Tiro.[13] Most apposite to this story, though, is the *manner* in which Tiro recorded his master's spoken words.

Born a slave of Cicero's household (but later freed, styling himself Marcus Tullius Tiro), Tiro was a gifted scribe who became Cicero's secretary, biographer, and confidant, making himself, as Cicero wrote to Atticus, "marvelously useful [...] in every department of business and literature."[14] After a tour of Greece some years earlier, Cicero had come away impressed by Greek shorthand and directed Tiro to create a similar system for Latin.[15] In response, Tiro devised a system composed of Latin abbreviations supplemented with existing Greek shorthand symbols, modifying and expanding it by degrees to yield a unique cipher. Romans were no strangers to scribal abbreviations: the letters "SPQR"—*Senatus Populusque Romanus*, or the "Senate and People of Rome"—were everywhere inscribed on monuments, buildings, and other paraphernalia of the state, and everyday correspondence was peppered with examples such as the salutation "SVBEV" for *si vales, bene est, valeo*: "if you are well, all is right; I am well."[16] The so-called *notae Tironianae*, however, were in a different league altogether. As Cicero boasted to Atticus in one of his regular letters, Tiro could record not only words but entire phrases and sentences in shorthand, and it was in this manner that the famous Catiline Orations were

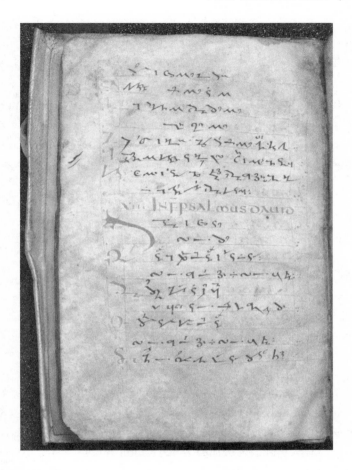

Figure 4.1   Psalm 68 written in Tironian notes, circa ninth century.

recorded for posterity.[17] Posterity, of course, would have to be content
with Cicero's massaged versions of Tiro's original transcription.

Among Tiro's *notae* was an innocuous character representing the
Latin word *et*, or "and."[18] Though this was only one symbol among
many (in their most elaborate medieval form, a system descended from
Tiro's original cipher comprised some fourteen thousand glyphs), the

utility of Tiro's system ensured that his *et* sign would considerably outlive both its creator and its sponsor.[19] This was not, however, the storied ampersand: when Tiro created his so-called Tironian *et*, or ⁊, the ampersand was still more than a century away.[20]

Recalled from exile after only a year, Cicero returned to public life by degrees. Enjoying a renaissance after Caesar's assassination, the veteran orator finally fell victim to the shifting sands of Roman politics in 43 BC, proscribed by the newly ascendant Mark Antony and assassinated by his soldiers.[21] Legend has it that Antony's wife Fulvia was so glad to be free of Cicero's oratorical powers that she pulled the tongue from his severed head and skewered it with hairpins.[22] Meanwhile, Tiro's career blossomed after his former master's death; in the increasingly bureaucratic Empire his secretarial skills earned him a comfortable retirement on a farm of his own, where he would die peacefully at one hundred years old.[23] His eponymous shorthand, and his *et*, would remain common currency for a further millennium after that.

* * *

When the ampersand first came to light a century after Cicero had delivered the Catiline Orations, it emphatically did not issue from the grandees of the Roman establishment; instead, it came quite literally straight from the streets. If the Tironian *et* was Tiro's brainchild, the ampersand was an orphan: its creator is not known,* and the closest it comes to a parent is the anonymous first-century graffiti artist who scrawled it hastily across a Pompeian wall.[25]

---

* The myth of Tiro as creator of the ampersand is a persistent one. In *Imperium*, the first part of his fictionalized life of Cicero, the author Robert Harris has his narrator Tiro humbly (and erroneously) declare: "I can modestly claim to be the man who invented the ampersand."[24]

Figure 4.2   Graffiti from Pompeii, circa 79 AD. Taken from
Formenwandlungen der &-Zeichen (1953) by Jan Tschichold.

Exactly when this first recorded ampersand was written is not known,
but the eruption of Mount Vesuvius in 79 AD, which suffocated the
town of Pompeii and preserved it under a layer of volcanic ash, does
impose a rather hard upper limit on the possible range of dates.[26]

This first-century ampersand is an example of a "ligature," a single
glyph formed by the combination of two or more constituent letters.
Modern-day ligatures, found in metal type or digital typefaces, are
used where two or more adjacent letters are difficult to "kern," or space
correctly, and are often subtle enough to escape notice unless the reader
is alert to their presence.[27] The ligatures most often used in English are
"fi," "ff," "fl," "ffi," and "ffl," which avoid awkward collisions between
overhanging *f*'s and the letters following them—compare these ligatures with their discrete counterparts "fi," "ff," "fl," "ffi," and "ffl". Type
designers may also choose to provide additional pairings such as the
purely decorative "st," the archaic "fb,"* or, as in the case of Hoefler &

---

* The "fb" ligature employs the archaic "long s" letterform, *f*, whose unfortunate resemblance
to *f* caused it to fall out of common use by the end of the eighteenth century.[28] The most popular
account of the character's demise relates to Shakespeare's *Tempest*. For his 1788 edition of the
play, the editor John Bell is alleged to have taken one look at Ariel's line "Where the bee fucks,

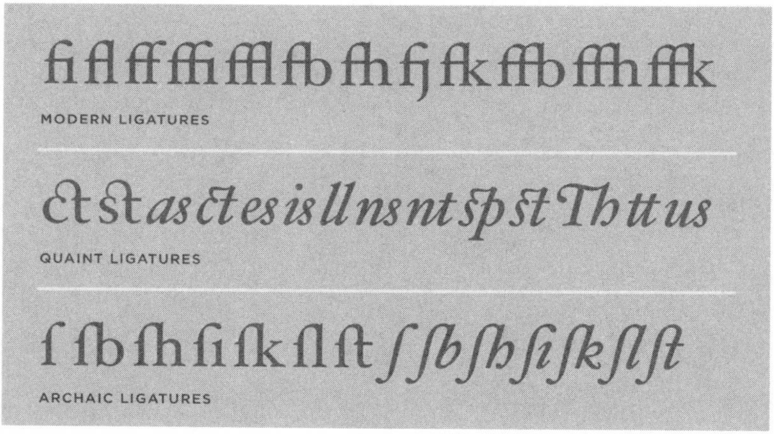

fi fl ff ffi ffl fb fh fj fk ffb ffh ffk

MODERN LIGATURES

&ct st as ct es is ll ns nt sp st Th tt us

QUAINT LIGATURES

ſ ſb ſh ſi ſk ſl ſt ſ ſb ſh ſi ſk ſl ſt

ARCHAIC LIGATURES

Figure 4.3   A representative set of modern, quaint, and archaic ligatures in Hoefler Text by Hoefler & Frere-Jones.

Frere-Jones's typeface Requiem, the extravagant "*ffl*," employed solely in the German word *Sauerstoffflasche*, or "oxygen tank."[30]

Coming from an era before type, the *Et* ligature that formed the embryonic Pompeian ampersand simply saved a writer time, the result of happy coincidence where the final stroke of one letter led neatly to the first of the next. Still clearly recognizable as the word *Et*, this first ampersand only barely qualifies as a ligature at all, with the middle arm of the *E* touching the stem of the *t* in a suspiciously coincidental manner. It is tempting to imagine that this Pompeian ampersand is in

---

there fuck I" and decided to employ the "short" or "round s" in place of the impious *ſ*. The real reason, however, is not quite so lurid. As Bell wrote in his introduction:

> [I have] ventured to depart from the common mode, by rejecting the long f in favor of the round one, as being less liable to error from the occasional imperfections of the letter f and the frequent substitution of it for the long ſ; the regularity of the print is by that means very much promoted, the lines having the effect of being more open, without really being at any additional distance.[29]

fact the result of an accidental slip of its doubtlessly nervous writer.*
Whatever its origins, the scrappy ampersand would go on to usurp
the Tironian *et* in a quite definitive manner.

* * *

From its ignoble beginnings a century after the debut of Tiro's
scholarly *et*, the ampersand assumed its now-familiar shape with
remarkable speed even as its rival remained immutable.

The ampersand's visual development is best documented in a
formidable piece of typographic detective work carried out by Jan
Tschichold, a graphic designer born in Leipzig in 1902.³² Famed as an
iconoclastic rule-maker and -breaker, Tschichold swung from one
extreme to another in a career that rewrote the rules of book design
and typography. His 1928 manifesto *Die neue Typographie* [The New
Typography] urged the abandonment of traditional rules of typesetting in favor of rigorous Modernism, championing asymmetric
layouts and sans-serif typefaces.³³ Then, arrested by the Nazis in 1933
as a "cultural Bolshevik," Tschichold reacted strongly to his ill treatment at the hands of the Third Reich and repudiated his earlier work,
detecting "fascist" elements in the strictures of Modernism.³⁴ In the
process, he earned the ire of his contemporaries as a betrayer of his
own principles.³⁵ Nevertheless, his work remains influential even
today.

Tschichold's masterly contribution to the study of the ampersand
came in 1953 in the form of a short booklet named *Formenwandlungen der &-Zeichen*, or *The ampersand: its origin and development*, as its
English translation would have it.³⁶ Drawing on earlier works by the

---

* It is suggested that the mathematical plus sign (+), often co-opted as an ampersand substitute,
is also derived from an *et* ligature.³¹ Unfortunately, the plus sign has attracted rather less attention from paleographers than has the ampersand, and this must remain conjecture at best.

calligrapher Paul Standard and the type designer Frederick Goudy, Tschichold collected hundreds of ampersands to chronicle the character's evolution from first-century Pompeii to nineteenth-century printing.[37] Even a single page of Tschichold's menagerie of & signs contains a surfeit of typographical riches:

☞ *Figure 4.4* Collected ampersands in Jan Tschichold's *Formenwandlungen der &-Zeichen* (1953). Notable here are (1) Pompeian graffiti; (8) an insular majuscule ampersand from the seventh-century *Book of Kells,* and (13) an eighth-century Merovingian ampersand, already recognizable as the modern ampersand form.

In its serried ranks of ampersands, Tschichold's paper traces the dozens of forms in which the sign appeared until the invention of the printing press in the fifteenth century led to the fittest among them being embossed permanently in metal. Each of the main families of type that have arisen since then—roman, italic, and blackletter—now boasts its own unique version.

So-called roman type—the familiar upright letterforms used almost universally to set long-form texts such as books, newspapers, and websites—brings with it the most regular and recognizable ampersand (&). When refugees from Johannes Gutenberg's hometown of Mainz first brought the technology of printing to Italy in the mid-1460s, they created type that matched the prevailing local handwriting, and in doing so, they unwittingly set a historical blunder in stone.[38] Obsessed with the classical world, fashionable Renaissance writers had revived what were erroneously thought to be *lettera antica*—the "ancient letters" of Rome—but their "roman" script was, in fact, the much later Carolingian minuscule* of the monk Alcuin.[39]

Nevertheless, the marriage of Alcuin's elegant lowercase alphabet to the square, chiseled capitals beloved of ancient stonemasons yielded type that imbued texts with a lightness and readability absent from the dense blackletter of earlier printed documents.[40] Like its officious Roman capitals, the ampersand that accompanies the roman alphabet is solid, well defined, and recognizable.†

The ampersands that accompany *italic* typefaces, on the other hand, are often very much more playful devices. Commonly thought of as ancillary to roman characters, italics originally comprised an entirely separate script modeled on the fluid, informal handwriting—the *lettera corsiva*—of a Renaissance scribe and copyist named Niccolò

---

* See chapter 1, "The Pilcrow (¶)," for more on Carolingian minuscule.
† The lowercase initial *r* in the term "roman type" serves to distinguish it from matters relating to the ancient city of Rome.

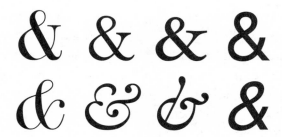

☞ *Figure 4.5*   Roman (*top*) and italic (*bottom*) ampersands compared. *Left to right*: the subtly different ampersands of Linotype Didot; the stylized *Et*- and *et*-ligatures of Monotype Baskerville and Hoefler Text respectively, and lastly Helvetica's simple oblique ampersand (Linotype).

Niccoli.[41] First cut for the famous Venetian printer Aldus Manutius, the sloping, condensed letterforms of italic script were narrower than their roman equivalents, and Aldus produced a pioneering (not to mention commercially successful) series of compact books set entirely in this new alphabet.[42]

Strange as it may seem now, the earliest italic fonts came with lowercase letters only; Aldus's early books, as well as those of his contemporaries, simply combined *Italic Lowercase Letters With Roman Capitals*.[43] Even after italics had acquired proper uppercase letterforms, courtesy of the French printers at Lyons who first pirated Aldus's lowercase italic alphabet and later embellished it with sloping capitals, the mixing of roman and italic type for emphasis did not become widespread until the seventeenth century.[44]

Italic letterforms diverge from their roman counterparts in small but noticeable ways: compare "*aefkpvwz*" with "aefkpvwz," for example. Though not all these variations exist in all italic typefaces, true italics (as opposed to sloping roman, or "oblique" letterforms) always display at least some of these distinguishing features. Similarly, the italic ampersand has become something of a playground for typographers: many italic ampersands are intricately designed works of art when compared with their roman siblings, and display their *et*-ligature heritage proudly.[45]

Lastly, and somewhat aberrantly, scribes working in blackletter, the Gothic script characterized by angular forms and densely packed text, largely forwent the ampersand altogether. Displaced from roman and italic lettering by the sensuous ampersand, Tiro's angular *et* found refuge in more apt surroundings.

While the scribes of the Italian Renaissance rediscovered and incorporated Carolingian minuscules into roman script, blackletter represents the centuries-long evolution of those very same minuscule letters as they continued in daily use throughout northern Europe.[46] Blackletter was peculiarly time-consuming both to write and to read;

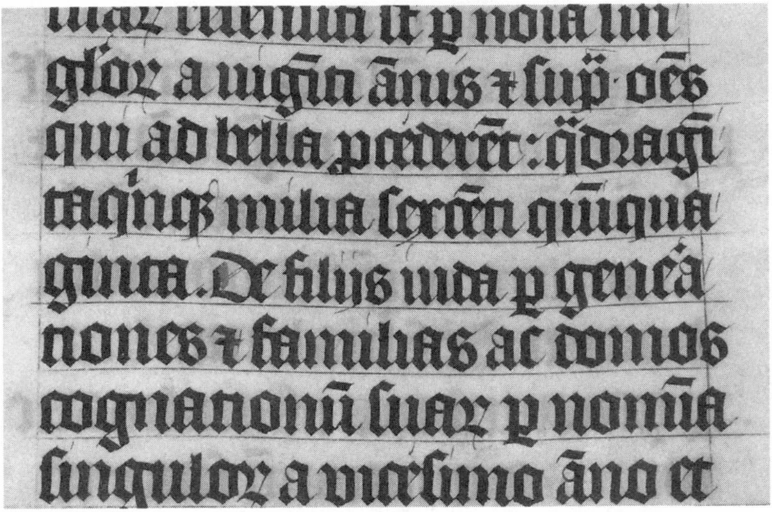

Figure 4.6 A Bible written in Belgium in 1407, with the Tironian *et* visible in the second and sixth lines. Curiously, the word *et* itself is used in full at the end of the final line.

many of its letters required several individual pen strokes to draw, and deciphering the closely packed letterforms, with their extreme contrasts between light and heavy strokes, was an exercise in perseverance. For many readers, blackletter was inextricably linked with the Church: not only was its architectural regularity redolent of the vaulted cathedrals at Rheims and Nôtre-Dame, but the painstaking effort required to create and consume blackletter works may actually have been welcomed by its most ardent practitioners.[47] As one modern commentator suggested:

> When writing, monks were not in a hurry. They wrote in honor of God. This is the only explanation of the forms of textura [a type of blackletter], so difficult to read but so decorative.[48]

Thus, when Johannes Gutenberg first printed his forty-two-line Bible in the mid-1450s, blackletter was the obvious alphabet in which to set it.[49] And though the first competing roman type was cut only a few years later by printers from Gutenberg's own hometown, blackletter type continued to dominate German books for centuries.

Among the different families of handwritten scripts and printed alphabets, the Tironian *et* was embraced in blackletter as no other. Though it garners a scant forty-eight entries in Tschichold's taxonomy, compared with more than two hundred ampersands, almost all are rendered with telltale Gothic blockiness.[50]

Though the Tironian *et* prospered in the blackletter manuscripts of the Middle Ages, the rest of Tiro's system of shorthand fared poorly. The medieval offspring of Tiro's system, modified somewhat from the original, still held to his ancient blueprint: common words were represented by a single symbol each, while those with a common stem but different suffixes were rendered using one symbol for the stem and a smaller one for the suffix. In short, each word was composed

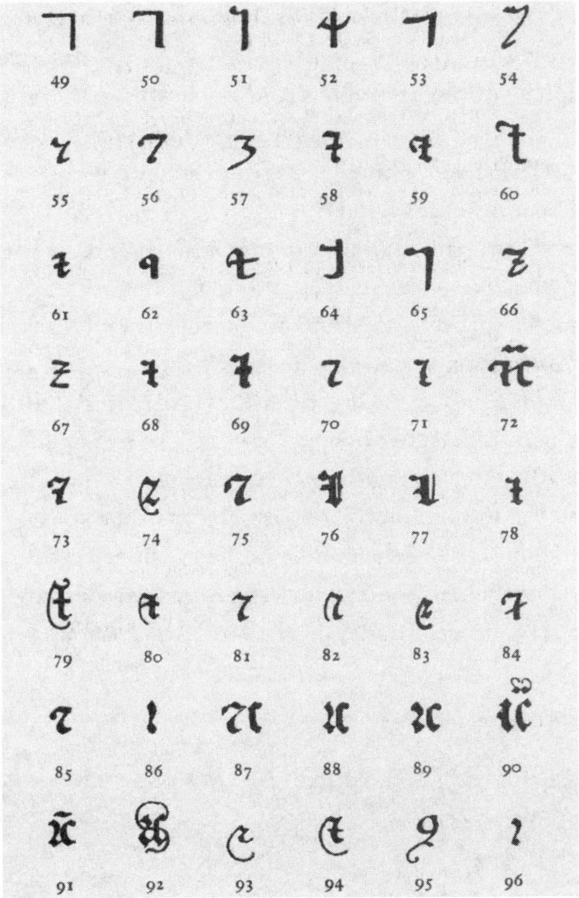

Figure 4.7 Collected Tironian *ets* in Jan Tschichold's
Formenwandlungen der &-Zeichen (1953).

of a distinct graphical unit—a single symbol, or an obvious pair of
symbols—and delivered much of the ease of reading that would later
be conferred by spaces between words. In some cases entire books
were written in Tironian notes, and the diligent Isidore of Seville

chronicled the ongoing use of Tiro's "common shorthand signs" in his encyclopedic seventh-century *Etymologies*.[51] As the practice of word spacing spread during the eighth century, however, the advantage of this "virtual" word spacing was nullified; the *notae Tironianae* were literally marginalized, pushed to the edge of the page and reduced to serving as a note-taking hand.[52]

Medieval shorthand in general found itself subject to a curious linguistic witch hunt. The secrecy and cipherlike nature of both traditional runic writing and shorthand did not coexist well with the distrust of witchcraft and magic prevalent in those times, and Tiro's system was further stigmatized as a result.[53] Briefly revived in the twelfth century, and later inspiring a series of copycat notations in English and other languages, the *notae Tironianae* were nevertheless a spent force.[54] The Tironian *et* was the sole survivor, soldiering on in blackletter type until it, too, fell out of use in the middle of the twentieth century.[55] Ironically, these supremely Germanic letterforms were finally banished by a 1941 Nazi decree condemning them as *Judenlettern*, or "Jewish

☞ *Figure 4.8*   A road sign showing the use of the Tironian *et* and ampersand in Irish Gaelic and English respectively.

Figure 4.9 A mailbox in Eire, labeled with "P⁊T" for "Posts and Telegraphs."

characters," and today blackletter appears mainly in newspaper mast-heads and documents where a Teutonic flavor is in order.[56]

Battered by changing writing practices and flighty typographic fashions, today the Tironian *et* survives in the wild only in Irish Gaelic, where it serves as an "and" sign on old mailboxes and modern road signs. Tiro's *et* showed the way, but the ampersand was the real destination.

The ampersand, all the while, went from strength to strength, providing a canvas for calligraphers and typographers to indulge their artistic proclivities, and ultimately earned a permanent place in type cases and on keyboards. It is undoubtedly the world's most respectable piece of graffiti.

* * *

The ampersand's hasty Pompeian creator did not stop long enough to caption his or her creation, and the term "ampersand" is a relatively new label applied to a thoroughly ancient symbol.

Modern folk etymology of the word "ampersand" supposes that it is derived from "Amper's and," after the symbol's alleged creator. Mentions of this derivation come from sources as diverse as an 1883 book entitled *Personal and Family Names* ("To him we trace the abbreviation, etc., called by English rustics Hampersand, *i.e. Amper's and*") and the collaborative online *Urban Dictionary*, which suggests that the symbol was both invented by and named for an elusive seventeenth-century typesetter called Manfred Johann Amper.[57] At the time of writing, Wikipedia claimed a similar etymology, but instead attributed the character's name to André-Marie Ampère, the Napoleonic-era French polymath for whom the "amp," the unit of electrical current, is already named.[58] These claims all lack corroborating evidence, and the truth is more prosaic: the ampersand is not named after anyone at all.

During the nineteenth century, the ampersand was routinely taught as the twenty-seventh letter of the alphabet. In common with those other letters that form words by themselves—*A* and *I*, for example—when spoken aloud, *&* was prefixed by the Latin *per se*, or "by itself."[59] Schoolchildren would recite "X, Y, Z, and *per se* and," with the second "and" being the name of the *&*. Especially bored pupils would not so much recite as slur the final syllables, and from this verbal mangling the "letter" *&* gained a dazzling variety of slang names. An entry from the 1905 *Dictionary of Slang and Colloquial English* records some of them:

> Ampersand. 1. The posteriors. 2. The sign &; ampersand. Variants: And-pussy-and; Ann Passy Ann; anpasty; andpassy; anparse; apersie (a.v.); per-se; ampassy; am-passy-ana; ampene-and; ampus-and; am pussy and; ampazad; amsiam; ampus-end; apperse-and; empersiand; amperzed; and zumzy-zan.[60]

Figure 4.10   The ampersand as twenty-seventh letter of the alphabet, in *My Own Primer, or First Lessons in Spelling and Reading* (1857) by Rev. John P. Carter.

The ampersand's position at the end of the alphabet led not only to its name but also to its contemporaneous double meaning of "the posterior," or "bottom."[61] Perhaps—who knows?—the lewd snickering that must have mingled with "and *per se* and" is partly responsible for the symbol's enduring name. Still, "and-pussy-and," "ampazad," "zumzy-zan," and their ilk have since fallen by the wayside, leaving "ampersand" alone to tell a tale of rote learning and enervated schoolchildren.[62]

Chapter 5 ❧ The @ Symbol

L ike the ampersand, the @ symbol is not strictly a mark of punctuation; rather, it is a logogram or grammalogue, a shorthand notation for the word "at." Even so, it is as much a staple of modern communication as the semicolon or exclamation mark, punctuating e-mail addresses, announcing Twitter usernames, and appearing in marketing copy. Unlike the ampersand, whose journey to the top took two millennia of steady perseverance, the "at" symbol's current fame is quite accidental. It can, in fact, be traced to a single keystroke made just over four decades ago.

* * *

I n 1971, Ray Tomlinson was a twenty-nine-year-old computer engineer working for the consulting firm Bolt, Beranek and Newman (BBN).[1] Founded just over two decades previously, BBN had recently been awarded a contract by the US government's Advanced Research Projects Agency to undertake an ambitious project to connect computers all over America.[2] The so-called ARPANET would provide the foundations for the modern Internet, and quite apart from his technical contributions to it, Tomlinson would also inadvertently grant the network its first global emblem in the form of the @ symbol.

The ARPANET project had its origins in the rapidly advancing state of the art in computing and the problems faced in making best use of this novel resource. In the early days, leaving a ruinously expensive mainframe computer idle even for a short time was a cardinal sin, and a so-called batch-processing mode of operation was designed to minimize downtime. Each computer was guarded by a priesthood of operators to whom users submitted their programs (often carried on voluminous stacks of punched cards) for scheduling and later execution.[3] The results of a "batch job" could arrive hours or days later, or sometimes not at all: a single error in a program could ruin an entire job. As time wore on, however, processing power grew and costs fell—by the mid-1960s, room-sized mainframes had been joined by newly compact "minicomputers" measuring a scant few feet on a side.[4] Soon the productivity of users themselves, rather than of the computers they programmed, became the main bottleneck. As such, the one-in, one-out pipeline of batch processing was gradually replaced by a "time-sharing" model wherein many users could interact with a single computer at once, each one typing commands and receiving immediate feedback on his or her personal terminal.[5]

The most common terminal design of the era was the so-called teletype,* a combined keyboard and printer on which a user could type commands and receive the computer's printed reply.[7] There were terminals that used other means to display input and output—notably cathode-ray tubes, or CRTs—but teletypes were near-ubiquitous, spawning hardened military versions and seventy-five-pound "portables."[8] Unlike today, where a keyboard and display normally occupy the very same desk as their host computer, teletypes were routinely separated from their hosts by hundreds of miles; a teletype might as easily be in the next city as the next room, communicating with its host computer via a squawking modem and a telephone line.

---

* This kind of combined keyboard/printer terminal device is more correctly called a "teleprinter" or "teletypewriter."[6] "Teletype" is an example of synecdoche, named for a prominent teleprinter manufacturer of the time.

Despite this facility to be geographically distant from its host, each terminal was still inextricably tethered to a single computer. Robert Taylor, the head of ARPA's Information Processing Techniques Office, was well acquainted with this problem: his office contained three teletypes connected to three different computers, in Santa Monica, Berkeley, and MIT respectively, each of which lived in ignorance of the others. Taylor said of the situation:

> For each of these three terminals, I had three different sets of user commands. So if I was talking online with someone at S.D.C. [of Santa Monica] and I wanted to talk to someone I knew at Berkeley or M.I.T. about this, I had to get up from the S.D.C. terminal, go over and log into the other terminal and get in touch with them.[9]

Thus, despite their utility, for the most part computers still lived in splendid isolation. It was this combination of factors—the attractions of ever-increasing power and flexibility, impeded by a frustrating inability to share information between computers—that spurred ARPA to investigate a network linking many computers together. As Taylor concluded:

> I said, oh, man, it's obvious what to do: If you have these three terminals, there ought to be one terminal that goes anywhere you want to go where you have interactive computing. That idea is the ARPANET.[10]

In 1968, the agency solicited bids from 140 interested parties to build the experimental network.[11] Although it would not be the first computer network, it was by far the most ambitious: not only would it span the continental United States (and, eventually, cross the

Atlantic via satellite link) but it would also be the first to use a novel and untested technique called "packet switching" on a grand scale.[12] Packet switching relied not on a direct connection between sender and recipient, but instead sent messages from source to destination by a series of hops across the network, fluidly routing them around broken or congested links.[13]

Some of the technology heavyweights of the time did not even bid. IBM, firmly wedded to the traditional (and profitable) mainframe computer, could not see an economically viable way to build the network, while Bell Labs' parent company, AT&T, flatly refused to believe that packet switching would ever work.[14] In the end, an intricately detailed two-hundred-page proposal submitted by relative underdogs BBN secured the contract, and construction of the ARPANET began in 1969. The project was a success, and by 1971 nineteen separate computers were communicating across links that spanned the continental United States.[15]

Working in BBN's headquarters, Ray Tomlinson had not been directly involved in building the network but was instead employed in writing programs to make use of it.[16] At the time, electronic mail already existed in a primitive form, working on the same principle as an office's array of pigeonholes: one command left a message for a named user in a "mailbox" file, and another let the recipient retrieve it. These messages were transmitted temporally but not spatially, and never left their host computer. Sender and recipient were effectively tied to the same machine.[17]

Taking a detour from his current assignment, Tomlinson saw an opportunity to combine this local mailbox system with some of his previous work. He used CPYNET, a command that sent files from one computer to another, as the basis for an improved e-mail program that could modify a mailbox file on *any* computer on the network, but the problem remained as to how such a message should be addressed.[18]

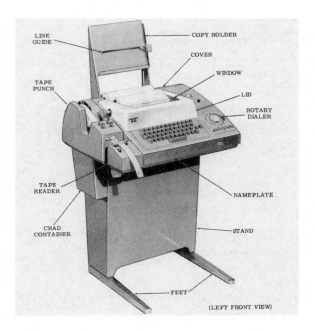

Figure 5.1   The ubiquitous Teletype model ASR-33 teleprinter.

The recipient's name had to be separated from that of the computer on which his or her mailbox resided, and Tomlinson was faced with selecting the most appropriate character for the job from the precious few offered by the keyboard of his ASR-33 teletype.

Looking down at his terminal, he chose @.

With four decades of e-mail behind us, it is difficult to imagine anyone in Tomlinson's situation choosing anything *other* than the @ symbol, but his decision was still inspired in several ways. First, @ was extremely unlikely to occur in computer or user names; second, it had no other significant meaning for the TENEX operating system on which the commands would run, and last, it was equally

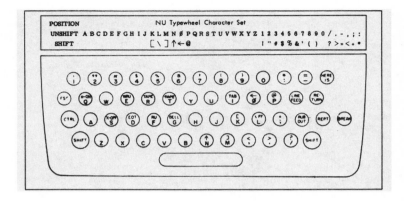

Figure 5.2 ASR-33 keyboard. Unlike modern QWERTY keyboards, the @ symbol shares a key with the letter *P*.

readable—"user *at* host"—to both humans and computers.* Tomlinson's own e-mail address, written using this newly formulated rule, was tomlinson@bbn-tenexa, signifying the mailbox of the user named "tomlinson" on the computer named "bbn-tenexa," the first of the company's two mainframes running TENEX.[20]

With the modifications to his mail program completed and an addressing scheme decided, Tomlinson typed out a brief message on the second machine and sent it to his mailbox on the first. The message was broken down into packets as it entered the ARPANET, which then routed each packet individually to its destination and reassembled them into a complete message at the other end before it was finally appended to his mailbox on bbn-tenexa. In real terms, the two machines occupied the same office, and the first network e-mail

---

* The @ symbol did have some unfortunately incompatible uses for other operating systems. Perhaps the most infamous was its use on Multics, the predecessor to UNIX, as a signal to "erase all preceding characters on this line." The problem was only resolved a decade later with a modification to Multics.[19]

traveled a physical distance of only around fifteen feet.[21] Perhaps apropos of this anticlimactic first step, Tomlinson has since forgotten the contents of the message:

> I have seen a number of articles both on the internet and in print stating that the first email message was "QWERTYUIOP". 'Taint so. My original statement was that the first email message was something like "QWERTYUIOP". It is equally likely to have been "TESTING 1 2 3 4" or any other equally insignificant message.[22]

Half-fearing the wrath of his superiors were they to discover his pet project, Tomlinson initially kept quiet about his invention. As a colleague recalled, "When he showed it to me [...] he said, 'Don't tell anyone! This isn't what we're supposed to be working on.'"[23] His concern was misplaced: e-mail became the fledgling network's first "killer app," gaining influential converts such as ARPA director Steve Lukasik. Lukasik took to traveling with a portable teletype so that he could check his mail even when out of the office, and his managers quickly found that e-mail was the only reliable way to keep in touch with him.[24] This viral quality led to an explosion in the use of e-mail across the network, and by 1973, only two years after the first e-mail traveled from one side of Tomlinson's office to the other, it accounted for three-quarters of all traffic on the ARPANET.[25]

Tomlinson's makeshift programs were replaced many times over as the ARPANET expanded and ultimately evolved into the modern Internet, but the use of the @ symbol remained a constant. As one half of an indivisible double act with the World Wide Web, e-mail became synonymous with the Internet as a whole, and the @ symbol's place in history was assured.

How, though, did @ find its way onto the keyboard of Ray

Tomlinson's ASR-33 teletype and so pass into Internet history? Moreover, where did it come from in the first place?

* * *

B efore its accidental ascent to stardom, @ went unremarked for centuries. Widely used to mean "at the rate of"—for example, "3 apples @ $1 each"—the symbol lived out a useful but mundane existence in the world of commerce, rarely warranting a second glance from paleographers or philologists.[26] Even now, propelled into near ubiquity by the meteoric rise of e-mail, credible accounts of the @ symbol's visual appearance and meaning remain surprisingly thin on the ground.

Emblematic of this lack of scholarly interest prior to e-mail is the sign's treatment at the hands of Berthold L. Ullman, a prominent twentieth-century professor of Latin. Ullman's otherwise comprehensive 1932 treatise, *Ancient Writing and Its Influence,* dismisses the character with a single perfunctory line: "There is also the sign @, which is really for *ad*, with an exaggerated uncial *d*."[27] *Ad* is Latin for "to," or "toward," and the "uncial" script to which Ullman referred was a family of rounded, uppercase alphabets used after the decline of Roman majuscules and before the creation and adoption of Carolingian minuscules.[28] Unfortunately, inviting though it is to imagine that "ɑð" might have given rise to @, Ullman's confidence in his pronouncement did not extend to providing any evidence for it.

There is a different theory (and one similarly lacking in documentary proof), that @ comes from the French *à* for "at," or "at the rate of," where the scribe would write the letter *a* and then add the accompanying *accent grave* without lifting his pen.[29] Although this usage is not in question—in at least some French manuscripts, @ was used in place of *à*—there is no evidence to suggest that this is the *source* of the symbol's shape as opposed to simply another use of the character to mean "at the rate of."

Perhaps the least outlandish suggestion is that @ emerged from the old scribal practice of marking abbreviated words with a tittle, or bar, placed over a letter.* Words beginning with the letter *a* were commonly abbreviated as *ā* to save precious space on the page and to speed the writing process. Thus accessorized, *ā* became @ as scribe after scribe sloppily combined the letter and its overbar. Influenced perhaps by the @ symbol's modern meaning of "at the rate of," the writer Keith G. Irwin suggested in 1961 that the abbreviated word in question must be the Greek preposition *ana*, or "treating all alike," but a recent discovery points to a rather more obscure candidate.[30]

* * *

Though the origins of the @ symbol's visual appearance are speculative at best, its use as shorthand for "at the rate of" is better attested. One scholar in particular saw his work reach an audience far greater than the norm for an otherwise minor piece of paleographic research: in 2000, a number of national newspapers reported on the work of one Giorgio Stabile, an Italian academic who had finally unearthed documentary evidence of the symbol's meaning, if not its visual appearance.[31]

Stabile's search for the birth of @ started with an analysis of the symbol's various names. An online survey conducted in 1997 revealed that the symbol went by a multitude of names across thirty-seven different countries, many of them inspired by its shape: *snabel-a*, or "(elephant's) trunk-a" in Danish and Swedish; *apestaart*, or "monkey's

---

* See chapter 3, "The Octothorpe (#)," for another application of this practice.

tail" in Dutch; *zavináč,* or "rollmop herring" in Czech and Slovak; *Klammeraffe,* or "spider monkey" in German; *strudel,* or a roll-shaped bun, in Hebrew; *kukac,* or "worm" in Hungarian; *grisehale,* or "pig's tail" in Norwegian, and *gül,* or "rose" in Turkish. French and Italian have both formal terms—respectively *arobase,* an archaic unit of weight, and *anfora,* or "amphora"—and also the more whimsical *escargot* and *chiocciola,* both meaning "snail." English deploys the cheerlessly direct "commercial at" or, simply, "at sign."[32]

Stabile observed that despite the symbol's many figurative aliases, only a few names were unrelated to its shape: the English "commercial at," the French *arobase* (also rendered in Spanish and Portuguese as *arroba*), and the Italian *anfora,* or "amphora." "Commercial at" evidently described the character's typical usage, but *arobase, arroba,* and "amphora" bore further investigation.[33]

Amphorae were long-necked pottery storage jars with tapered bases, used for centuries by the Greeks and Romans to transport cereals, olives, oil, and wine, and the word referred not only to the vessels themselves but also related units of volume and weight.[34] The standard Roman amphora, embodied in the *amphora Capitolina* kept securely in Rome itself, had a volume of a cubic foot, or about twenty-six liters.[35] The Spanish and Portuguese *arroba,* on the other hand, was a customary unit of weight *and* volume, representing either a quarter of a *quintal,* or hundredweight,[*] or, alternatively, a volume of around sixteen liters of liquid.[37] The word *arroba* itself came from the Arabic *al-rub´,* or "one-fourth," a term absorbed into the languages of the Iberian Peninsula under Moorish rule, and which later made its way into French as *arobase.*[38]

The key to Stabile's discovery was a letter sent from Seville to

---

[*] The Spanish and Portuguese units of weight are actually slightly different: the Spanish *arroba* was around twenty-five pounds, while the Portuguese unit was thirty-two pounds.[36]

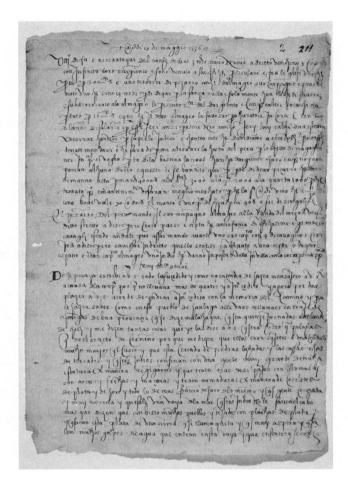

Figure 5.3   @ for *amphora* in Francesco Lapi's letter of May 4, 1536.

Rome on May 4, 1536, by a merchant named Francesco Lapi, in which Lapi discussed the arrival in Spain of three trading ships from the New World. Writing that an amphora of wine sold there for seventy or eighty ducats, he used the familiar @ symbol as an abbreviation for the word "amphora."[39]

Consulting a contemporaneous Spanish-Latin dictionary, Stabile found that *arroba* was synonymous with *amphora*; the Spanish, Portuguese, and Latin units of measure might have differed in their exact definition, but the @ was their common shorthand.[40] In those southern European countries, then, the @ symbol is named for and embodies a link to its ancient roots: *arroba*, *anfora*, and *arobase* are perhaps the character's truest names, abbreviated in turn to *ā* and then @.*

* * *

From this starting point as a unit of measure in southern Europe, by the eighteenth century the @ symbol had entered English as mercantile shorthand for "at the rate of," and by the late nineteenth century the symbol was known by the flatly descriptive appellation "commercial a."[42] Prospering in commercial circles, noted but not dwelled upon by printers and typographers, and rarely warranting much interest from the general reader, the stolid @ symbol nevertheless came close to extinction in the face of two of the nineteenth century's greatest innovations.[43]

Throughout 1867, the Kleinsteuber Machine Shop in Milwaukee attracted a steady trickle of spectators who left amazed at the speed and precision of a novel mechanical writing device being fabricated there. The shop had been retained by an unheralded inventor named Christopher Latham Sholes to produce prototypes of a machine designed to write "with types instead of a pen": Though not the first to try, the frail, self-deprecating Sholes, together with his partners Carlos Glidden and Samuel W. Soulé, had developed what would become the first commercially successful typewriter.[44] With

---

* Giorgio Stabile's discovery was corroborated by Jorge Romance, who in 2009 uncovered an even earlier use of the @ symbol in a Castilian document from 1445.[41]

a minimal amount of training, anyone could use Sholes's patented machine to rapidly produce regular, legible documents; the typewriter revolutionized clerical work and became the default method of text entry for more than a hundred years.[45]

The @ symbol, however, was absent from the keyboard of Sholes's first prototype. The pianolike keyboard of his 1867 machine bore two rows of keys, with capital letters arrayed along the lower row and the upper keys occupied by the numbers 2–9 (the letters *O* and *I* stood in for zero and one) and a few miscellaneous glyphs (; $ - . , ? /).[46] The inclusion of the dollar sign suggests that Sholes was aware of his machine's commercial applications, though Sholes himself largely failed to profit from his invention and in 1873 he was driven to sell out to the Remington Arms Company.[47] The first Remington model bore an improved four-row keyboard of Sholes's design with an arrangement close to the modern QWERTY layout, but still without an @ symbol.[48] Despite its practical utility, @ would have to wait until 1889, when it was finally admitted onto the keyboard of the competing Hammond 12; from there the @ spread rapidly onto other machines, and within a couple of decades the character had been adopted as part of the increasingly standardized typewriter keyboard.[49]

The next innovation to shake the world of information processing, such as it was in the late nineteenth century, came only a few years later. In 1890, for the first time, the results of a US census were collated using a baroque new electromechanical device designed and built by a statistician named Herman Hollerith.[50] Hollerith's "Tabulator" processed data collected on punched cards to tabulate the 1890 census far more rapidly than had been possible for its 1880 predecessor, for a population that had grown by 25 percent in the interim, all the while saving $5 million.[51] Like Sholes, Hollerith was not the first in his field, but he was the most successful by far: his Tabulator foreshadowed the programmable computer, and his use of punched cards to provide it with data would persist until the 1970s.

🖙 *Figure 5.4*   The @ symbol on early typewriters. *Top row, left to right*: the distinctively curved layout of an "Ideal" model Hammond (undated but produced from 1884); a Franklin 7, produced from 1892; and a portable Blickensderfer 5 (1893). *Middle row, left to right*: Pittsburgh 10, 1898; an 1889 Hall; and a Postal (produced from 1902–1908). The Hall, at center, is an "index" typewriter, where the operator uses one hand to select a letter and the other to actuate a mechanism that impresses that letter. *Bottom row, left to right*: a 1907 Royal Bar-Lock, a 1911 Royal 5, and a 1921 Corona 3.

Hollerith's cards held twenty-four columns of twelve rows each and were specifically designed to record census information for a single person.[52] When later repurposed for general data entry, each column was used to represent a digit in the range 0–9, along with two optional "control" positions, used to indicate special conditions such as a credit balance.[53] With only numeric characters supported, the @ didn't have a chance, and despite its status as standard character for text input, the symbol was rendered useless by the text storage methods of the era. A typist could easily enter an @ on his or her keyboard, but to a computer that did not understand it, the "at" sign did not even exist.

Little by little, the repertoire of characters that could be represented on a punched card grew larger. By 1932, for instance, a "Hollerith card" punched according to the Binary Coded Decimal Interchange Code (BCDIC) could draw from a set of forty characters: the digits 0–9, the letters *A–Z*, the minus sign, the asterisk, the ampersand, and a space. BCDIC grew again in the 1950s to encompass forty-eight characters, and with this expansion the @ was finally brought into the fold alongside other symbols such as the octothorpe, dollar sign, and percent sign.[54] The @ began to appear in other coding schemes too. The civilian version of the United States Army's 1960s FIELDATA code gave it pride of place as character 0, the first symbol in the code, while IBM, descended from Herman Hollerith's original Tabulating Machine Company, used the character in its influential 1961 "Stretch" supercomputer.[55]

1	2	3	4	CM	UM	Jp	Ch	Oo	In	20	50	80	Dv	Un	3	4	3	4	A	E	L	a	g
5	6	7	8	CL	UL	O	Mu	Qd	Mo	25	55	85	Wd	CY	1	2	1	2	B	F	M	b	h
1	2	3	4	CS	US	Mb	B	M	O	30	60	O	2	Mr	O	15	O	15	C	G	N	c	i
5	6	7	8	No	Hd	Wf	W	F	5	35	65	1	3	Sg	5	10	5	10	D	H	O	d	k
1	2	3	4	Fh	Ff	Fm	7	1	10	40	70	90	4	O	1	3	O	2	St	I	P	e	l
5	6	7	8	Hh	Hf	Hm	8	2	15	45	75	95	100	Un	2	4	1	3	4	K	Un	f	m
1	2	3	4	X	Un	Ft	9	3	i	c	X	R	L	E	A	6	O		US	Ir	So	US	Ir	So
5	6	7	8	Ot	En	Mt	10	4	k	d	Y	S	M	F	B	10	1		Gr	En	Wa	Gr	En	Wa
1	2	3	4	W	R	OK	11	5	l	e	Z	T	N	G	C	15	2		Sw	FC	EC	Sw	FC	EC
5	6	7	8	7	4	1	12	6	m	f	NG	U	O	H	D	Un	3		Nw	Bo	Hu	Nw	Bo	Hu
1	2	3	4	8	5	2	Oo	O	n	g	a	V	P	I	Al	Na	4		Dk	Fr	It	Dk	Fr	It
5	6	7	8	9	6	3	O	p	o	h	b	W	Q	K	Un	Pa	5		Ru	Ot	Un	Ru	Ot	Un

Figure 5.5   Layout of the original Hollerith punched card, circa 1895, highlighting the census-specific information carried by each position.

The year 1963 saw the introduction of the American Standard Code for Information Interchange, or ASCII, an internationally recognized character set designed in part to curtail the proliferation of coding schemes.[56] A regular in many other coding schemes, the @ was an obvious candidate for inclusion.* Now named "commercial at" (the term was first attested in 1969), by the time Ray Tomlinson was looking down at his teletype in 1971 and mulling over the symbols available to him, the combination of a standard keyboard and a standard character set ensured that the fateful @, or "at" key would be there to meet his gaze.[58]

* * *

As e-mail (and the Internet as a whole) arrived in the public consciousness, @ came to symbolize not just the Internet itself but also a sort of generic modernity, or progress. At the turn of the twenty-first century, the symbol could be found in the names of everything from Internet service providers (Excite@Home) and Internet "c@fés" to plays (F@ust, Version 3.0).[59] In 2000, the city of Barcelona, Spain, abandoned its existing planning code for the bohemian Eixample district and replaced it with a forward-looking designation: the industrial area once labeled "22a" now became "22@," where "the most innovative companies co-exist with research, training and tech transfer centers, as well as housing [...], facilities [...] and green area."[60] And in a conceptual move worthy of the most modern of artists, in 2010 the Museum of Modern Art "acquired" the ethereal concept of the @ symbol. As Paola Antonelli, MoMA's senior curator of architecture and design explained,

---

* Ironically, the @ symbol was only inducted into Morse code—the granddaddy of encoding schemes—as recently as 2004.[57]

> [The acquisition] relies on the assumption that physical
> possession of an object as a requirement for an acquisition
> is no longer necessary, and therefore it sets curators free
> to tag the world and acknowledge things that "cannot
> be had"—because they are too big (buildings, Boeing
> 747's, satellites), or because they are in the air and belong
> to everybody and to no one, like the @—as art objects
> befitting MoMA's collection.[61]

At present, years after the dot-com bubble knocked the wind out
of the first wave of Internet entrepreneurs, the @ has lost some of its
luster, and an ever-expanding roster of replacements are assuming its
mantle as a sign of the future. No longer is there a universal symbol of
connectedness or modernity, and this survivor from the first days of
the Internet is giving way to unthreateningly generic *e-* and *i-* prefixes
owing more to marketing departments than technical innovation.
The @ is once again common currency—to borrow Paola Antonelli's
expression, it belongs to "everybody and to no one"—and though it is
little remarked upon, it rightly retains an importance rather greater
in scope than purchase orders and grocers' chalkboards.

Chapter 6 ❧ The Asterisk and Dagger

The asterisk (*) and dagger (†) have performed a punctuational double-act for millennia. Today they appear most often when pointing the reader toward a footnote* or endnote, but the asterisk and dagger are far older than the footnotes they adorn; they are among the oldest of all the textual marks and annotations, in fact, and spring from that second-oldest of literary professions, the editor.

* * *

Nowadays it seems natural to consider the asterisk the senior partner and the dagger its subordinate. Most obviously, the asterisk appears before the dagger when used to label footnotes, but it takes the lead in other contexts too: in European typography, dates of birth are marked with an asterisk and deaths with a dagger—"Albert Einstein (*1879)," or "Herman Melville (†1891)"—and in the specialized musical notation of Gregorian chant, the asterisk and dagger indicate long and short pauses respectively.[1] The typographer Robert Bringhurst goes as far as to declare that the asterisk is a staggering five thousand years old, which would make it not only the dagger's elder sibling but also by far the oldest mark of punctuation of any stripe.[2]

---

* In honor of their role as footnote reference marks, I plan to fill this chapter with numerous lengthy and entirely tangential footnotes so as to take full advantage.

The reality is not so simple. Five millennia ago the cuneiform alphabet of the Sumerians *did* contain a starlike character called the *dingir*, or *an* (✳), which stood for the idea of "heaven" or "deity," but though it shares an apparent visual connection with the later asterisk, there is no evidence to link the two. Instead, and perhaps counterintuitively, the dagger is the older of the two marks, though it started life in a wholly unrecognizable form.[3]

As with many other innovations of the ancient world, the intertwined stories of the asterisk and dagger begin at the great library of Alexandria in Egypt. Founded in the fourth century BC and encompassed by a larger institution called the Mouseion (literally, "temple of the Muses"; the modern word "museum" comes from the same root), the library was the heart of an ancient university whose scholars studied literature, mathematics, anatomy, astronomy, botany, and zoology.[4] The Mouseion was the Bell Labs of its era: It was there, in the third century BC, that the astronomer Aristarchus of Samos first posited that the Earth orbited the sun, and where the institution's third librarian Eratosthenes calculated the diameter of the Earth to within fifty miles.[*] It was at Alexandria that Euclid wrote *Elements*, his seminal treatise on mathematics, and where Archimedes invented the screw-shaped pump later given his name.[6] Punctuation itself got its start here,[†] as did the practice of accenting letters to alter their pronunciation—both innovations attributed to the fourth librarian, Aristophanes—and the asterisk and dagger were soon to follow.[7]

The first librarian at Alexandria was the grammarian Zenodotus of Ephesus, appointed in the third century BC by the Alexandrian king Ptolemy II and was assigned the task of revising Homer's epic poetry.[8]

---

[*] It was 1,800 years before Nicolaus Copernicus succeeded in reviving Aristarchus's ideas of heliocentricity. Copernicus was so piqued at having been beaten to the punch that he pretended ignorance of the Alexandrian's earlier theory so as to give more weight to his own work.[5]
[†] See chapter 1, "The Pilcrow (¶)," for more on Aristophanes's system of punctuation.

Legend has it that in times past, Homer's works had been lost to some unnamed disaster, and, endeavoring to make a name for himself by reconstituting these fabled texts, an Athenian official named Peisistratus offered to pay by the line anyone who could bring some Homeric verse to him.[9] Many crafty supplicants used Peisistratus's scheme to enrich themselves, and the resultant text was a distended shadow of the original, sprinkled with many spurious lines and verses. Addressing himself to the text, Zenodotus took the simple step of drawing a straight line (—) in the margin alongside each superfluous line: quite literally at a stroke, he had invented the field of literary criticism.[10]

Though its shape was not yet recognizably daggerlike, the name given to Zenodotus's literary skewer was a clear sign of the direction in which it would evolve. Named for the Greek *obelos*, or "roasting spit," the striking image of the obelus transfixing erroneous text was echoed later by Isidore of Seville, who said of the mark that "like an arrow, it slays the superfluous and pierces the false."[11]

Zenodotus's invention of the obelus and his textual criticism of Homer's works were expanded on by later Alexandrian scholars, and it was one of his successors who first paired the obelus with a new mark called the asterisk. Succeeding Eratosthenes and then Aristophanes as librarian, Aristarchus of Samothrace* sought to update Zenodotus's pioneering work.[12] Finding the obelus necessary but not sufficient to the task at hand, Aristarchus introduced an array of additional symbols to aid his work. The most basic of these was the *diple*, a simple angle (>) used to indicate any one of a number of noteworthy features in the text, with the related *diple periestigmene*, or dotted *diple* (⸖) used to mark passages where Aristarchus disagreed with Zenodotus's changes. The obelus reprised its traditional role of marking spurious

---

* As distinct from Aristarchus of Samos, the astronomer. Our adoration of mono-named Greeks and Romans becomes problematic when more than one person with a given name aspires to greatness.

lines, but Aristarchus allied it with a new symbol called the *asteriskos*, or "little star."[13] Used alone, the dotted, starlike glyph (⁂) denoted genuine material that had been mistakenly duplicated, and the two characters were occasionally deployed together to mark lines that belonged elsewhere in the poem.[14] Zenodotus might have been the first editor, but it was Aristarchus's approach that stuck: his expanded palette of asterisk, obelus, and *diple* are still known to classical scholars as the Aristarchean symbols.

* * *

E ven as it suffered variously from fire, invasion, and religious tur-moil, Alexandria continued on into the Christian era as the Hellenic world's preeminent seat of learning, and it was an Alexandrian Christian who would take the asterisk and dagger from their classical roots into a long association with the new religion.[15]

Unlike Zenodotus, Aristarchus, and company, who had been lured to the Mouseion by promises of free accommodation and exemption from taxes, Origen Adamantius (literally, "Man of Steel," named for his iron constitution) was a native Alexandrian.* Born in 185 AD, by the age of seventeen Origen had seen his father martyred at the hands of the pagan Romans† and only a year later was installed as head of Alexandria's Christian school.[18]

Devout and fiercely ascetic, Origen fasted twice weekly, exercised vigorously, and took little sleep. Rumors abounded of why these privations were necessary. Eusebius, his contemporary biographer, held that Origen had castrated himself in response to a disastrously literal

---

* Origen was also described, somewhat less romantically, as "brazen-boweled."[16]
† Origen was prevented in joining his father in martyrdom only because his mother hid his clothes. He contented himself with writing a stern letter to his imprisoned father, exhorting him to embrace death for his faith.[17]

interpretation of Matthew 19:12 ("There are eunuchs who have made themselves such for the sake of the kingdom of heaven") and that he was attempting to hold at bay the creeping flabbiness that would have identified him as such. Other, more apocryphal, stories suggest that Origen himself spread the rumor of his own castration to hide his homosexuality, or even that he "invented a drug to apply to his genitals to dry them up" to suppress his carnal appetites for winsome female students.[19]

Whatever the motivation behind his legendary abstemiousness, Origen's greatest contribution to Christian scholarship was his painstaking reconciliation of the Hebrew Old Testament, or Pentateuch, with its original Greek translation. Much like Peisistratus's cash-for-Homer wheeze, the reputed origin of this first Greek Bible is viewed with raised eyebrows in academic circles. Allegedly, seventy translators (or seventy-two, in some tellings) were assembled on the island of Pharos, just off Alexandria, and presented with the Hebrew text; retiring to consider it separately, they emerged from seclusion to find that all seventy-odd translations were identical. Taken as proof of the miraculous nature of the translation, the resulting text came to be known as the Septuagint—from the Latin *septuaginta* for "seventy"—or simply by the Roman numeral LXX.[20]

Having moved from Alexandria in Egypt to Caesarea in Palestine in 232, Origen and his scribes toiled for a decade to juxtapose the Pentateuch and the LXX with three later Greek translations in a single massive volume.[21] Each of the three thousand or so leaves of the resulting "Hexapla," or "sixfold," was divided into six individual columns, into which Origen arranged the Pentateuch, its transliteration into Greek, the LXX, and the three alternative translations.[22]

Like Zenodotus before him, Origen's aim was not to create a canonical Greek text but instead to allow readers to understand the differences between the original Hebrew and the LXX, and as such he turned to Aristarchus's ancient signs. As before, the obelus marked spurious passages in the LXX that did not occur in the original Hebrew; where verses from the Hebrew were found to be missing from the LXX, he copied them from one of the other Greek translations and marked them with an asterisk.[23] Also, like Aristarchus, he occasionally placed the two characters together to indicate that the ordering of the LXX was at odds with the Hebrew.[24] Origen's sole addition to this system was the metobelus, or closing obelus: having marked a line as spurious or missing, he placed a metobelus to mark the end of the erroneous text.

The visual appearance of the asterisk and obelus, as used by Origen and his later copyists, varied over time. The asterisk took the familiar form of ※, though in later versions it was occasionally rotated to yield ⚹, and the Hexapla's obeli ranged from simple horizontal lines to dotted forms known as the lemniscus (÷) and hypolemniscus (⨪). Epiphanius, a fourth-century bishop and Bible scholar, espoused a theory that the Septuagint's seventy translators had been confined to cells in pairs while they carried out their work, and that the number of dots surrounding an obelus indicated how many of those pairs of translators had seen fit to introduce those new, explicatory words into the LXX.[25] Later scholars consider this convenient theory of two-man cells to be hogwash, and view the lemniscus and hypolemniscus as simple variant forms of the obelus. Lastly, the metobelus was variously represented as two vertically-aligned dots somewhat like a heavyset colon (:), a slash with an accompanying dot or dots (/. or ⫶), or, in later versions, a malletlike character (⟍).[26]

Unfortunately, rather than clarifying matters, Origen's grand work ultimately had the opposite effect. Unaware of the significance of the marks littering the text, later scribes tasked with copying out Origen's carefully annotated LXX either copied these critical signs incorrectly or omitted them altogether, causing the text to be transmitted in a form even more muddied and confused than when Origen

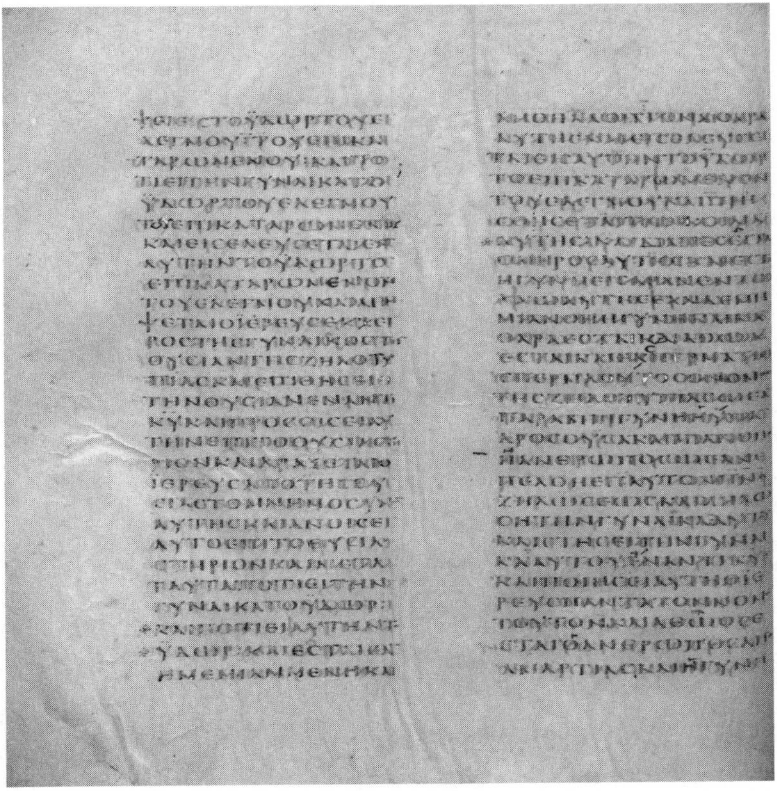

Figure 6.1 Asterisks in the Codex Colberto-Sarravianus, a fifth-century Greek Bible.

had taken up the project. The Hexapla's very fame—considered, as it was, to be the text that most closely matched the original Hebrew—caused these corrupted versions to be copied and recopied, sealing the fate of what had been a monumental work of scholarship.[27]

* * *

Figure 6.2 Double dotted obeli, or lemnisci, in a Graeco-Coptic psalter of the sixth century.

The asterisk and obelus next appeared on opposite sides of the biggest theological bust-up since the formation of Charlemagne's Holy Roman Empire. In 1517, Martin Luther, a hitherto obscure monk and theologian in the German town of Wittenberg, had had enough. The Vatican had dispatched a priest named Johann Tetzel to the neighboring region of Magdeburg to raise money for the construction of St. Peter's Basilica in Rome. To do this, Tetzel sold "indulgences"—letters granting absolution for sins that a buyer wished to have expunged from his or her spiritual record*—both to the local populace and to Wittenbergers enticed there by Tetzel's combination of doomsaying and redemption.[30] In a theological sense, indulgences commuted temporal rather than spiritual punishment, but Luther saw that Tetzel was slyly conflating the two and pushing them on congregations terrified for their immortal souls.[31]

Luther was incensed. Not only was the Church playing God, but it had the bare-faced cheek to charge for it. He wrote a letter to the archbishop of Magdeburg, enclosing with it a document entitled "Disputation on the Power and Efficacy of Indulgences," though it would later become famous as *The Ninety-Five Theses* after the number of propositions it contained. Ostensibly a call for a reasoned debate on the subject, Luther's *Theses* took on rather more of a polemic aspect when he nailed a copy to the door of Wittenberg castle church for all to see.[32] The Protestant Reformation had begun.

In the tit-for-tat of pamphlets and treatises that followed, the asterisk and obelus played a brief but prominent supporting role. In 1518, Luther's rival, Johannes Eck, published a refutation of the *Ninety-Five Theses* called *Obelisci*, or "Obelisks," its title taken from the diminutive for "obelus."[33] Luther countered later that year with *Asterisci*, or, "Asterisks."† Schooled in Latin and Greek, Eck and Luther could have had no doubt as to each other's intentions: Eck sought to show Luther's arguments to be false—to "obelize" them as Zenodotus had obelized dubious lines in the *Iliad*—while Luther's "Asterisks" highlighted defects in Eck's reasoning. This scholarly in-joke appears

---

* It is thought that Johannes Gutenberg, pioneer of printing with movable type, may have printed such indulgences for the Church before starting work on his forty-two-line Bible.[28] Luther, who hated to see the Church enriching itself at the expense of its adherents, would nevertheless have raised a wry smile at this; he himself knew the power of printing, and took full advantage of it to promote his own views with a series of pamphlets and books.[29]

† The *Cambridge Companion to Martin Luther* translates Eck's and Luther's *Obelisci* and *Asterisci* as "Skewers" and "Stars" respectively, catching Eck's meaning but rather missing Luther's.[34]

a welcome nod to civility amid the increasingly vehement rhetoric flying back and forth in the years after Luther's broadside against the Church.

Eck's *Obelisci* and Luther's *Asterisci* are now footnotes in the history of the Reformation, but the asterisk and obelus—especially in its modern form of the dagger (†), of which more later—continue to play a role in liturgical documents. In psalmody, for example, the musical recital of psalms, the dagger is used to mark a minor pause with the asterisk indicating a longer one.[35] In Roman Catholic services the dagger may act as a substitute for the more proper Maltese, or square, cross (✠) to indicate points at which the priest must make the sign of the cross.[36]

So strong is the resemblance between the typographic dagger and the Christian cross that the two are often confused. Some typefaces,

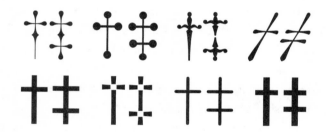

☞ *Figure 6.3*   Typographic daggers and double daggers, or "dieses" (singular "diesis"), set at 72pt and equalized in height. Using the same typefaces as Figure 1.7, these are *top row, left to right*: Linotype Didot, Big Caslon (Carter & Cone Type), Hoefler Text (Apple), and Zapfino (Linotype); *bottom row, left to right*: Helvetica (Linotype), Skia (Apple), Courier New (Microsoft), and Museo Slab (Jos Buivenga). The dilemma facing type designers is evident: should a dagger be just that, or is a cross an acceptable substitute? Whatever the decision, asterisks and daggers often bear artistic or architectural flourishes corresponding to the period with which they are most closely identified.

for instance, depict literal knives with pointed blades and ornate guards, whereas others have entirely more straitlaced crucifixes with blunt ends and square arms. Unicode, the standard computer character set, hedges its bets by including characters for both the dagger (†) and the "Latin cross" (✝); the majority of typefaces, though, provide only a dagger—either wicked or chaste, depending on their leanings.[37]

* * *

The passage of time saw the asterisk and obelus massaged into new shapes. Scholarly attention to the pair is maddeningly thin, however, especially with respect to life after their classical heyday; fewer in number than Aristophanes's mundane but ubiquitous points, and less exotic than outliers such as the pilcrow and manicule (☞), it is difficult to trace their journey through the Middle Ages and beyond. What little can be said for certain is that the great unifying influence of the printing press quickly gave rise to forms that persist even today. By the middle of the sixteenth century, the square, crosslike asterisks scattered throughout medieval manuscripts (examples of which can be seen in Figures 1.4, 6.4, and 9.2) had resolved into separate families of five- or six-pointed stars and Maltese crosses.[38] The various dotted, plain, and slanted obeli, on the other hand, combined into a single character—the cross, or dagger (†)[39]—with the lemniscus alone surviving intact as the mathematical division symbol (÷).*

---

* The lemniscus first appeared in this role during the same period of typographic consolidation that gave birth to the footnote. In the aftermath of the English Civil War, the victorious Republican leader Oliver Cromwell applied himself to creating a pan-European "Protestant League" with the new Commonwealth of England at its head.[40] One such mission saw the English mathematician John Pell dispatched to Switzerland with orders to reassure the Protestant cantons there of Cromwell's support, to discover any diplomatic intrigues that Charles I might attempt, and to encourage the Swiss to send their sons to English universities.

Five years earlier, a previous Parliamentarian ambassador named Isaac Dorislaus had been assassinated in the Hague by Royalist agents, and with this in mind Pell skulked incognito

The symbols' meanings changed too. Whereas Aristarchus's signs indicated spurious, missing, or disordered text, in medieval manuscripts the two marks took on a purpose closer to that of the ancient *diple* and were used simply to draw attention to interesting text. Later still, manuscripts and then early printed books began to employ the symbols in a more structured manner, using them to link marginal notes with the text to which they referred.[44] It is in this mode that the asterisk and dagger became part of the typographic establishment, and the story from this point on is intertwined with that of the humble footnote.

The footnote as we recognize it today attained its current form over the course of the sixteenth and seventeenth centuries. Notes in the margin and between the lines—so-called glosses—had featured in written documents since time immemorial. Just as readers punctuated tightly packed *scriptio continua* to ease its interpretation, so they populated the margins with their own observations, clarifications, and translations of the text.[45] The Renaissance, though, marked a change. The marginal note passed from the province of the reader to that of the writer; notes grew longer and more frequent as authors preemptively surrounded the narrative with their own, "authorized" commentary.[46] As might be expected, religious texts took this to

---

through Holland before carrying on to Zurich, where he subsequently spent four years carrying out Cromwell's orders.[41] While there, Pell met a prominent young official named Johann Rahn who acted as *Schützenmeister,* supervising shooting practice, and as *Zeugherr* responsible for military supplies and artillery. Tutored by Pell during 1657 but posted elsewhere a year later, Rahn wrote a mathematical textbook called *Teutsche Algebra* for publication in 1659. *Algebra* was a seminal work: it was arranged into three columns containing algebraic steps, line numbers, and proofs respectively so that the reader could easily follow Rahn's reasoning, and it contained the first known use of ÷ as a division symbol. Pell is widely considered to have suggested both the layout and the use of the obelus as a division symbol, but such was the Englishman's modesty he forbade Rahn from crediting him by name.[42]

Ironically enough, despite first appearing in a German language textbook, the obelus as division symbol never quite took off in Germany. Today, division is signified there by a colon (:), while Rahn's obelus, carried over to the English translation of his book (to which John Pell contributed), went on to become the standard notation in the English-speaking world.[43]

extremes: the dangers of an unauthorized interpretation of biblical language held a particular horror for the Church, and between the twelfth and eighteenth centuries the margins of the standard Bible, or "Vulgate," became congested with the Church's officially sanctioned *glossa ordinaria*.[47]

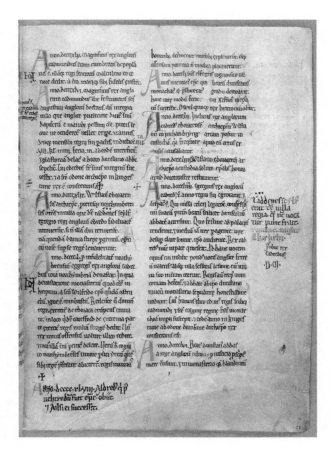

Figure 6.4 Crosslike asterisks (and a single dotted variant) in a twelfth-century manuscript, apparently used as reference marks. See Figure 9.2 for another twelfth-century asterisk used as a reference mark.

With the proliferation of notes in all forms of document, the problem of how to associate a note with the text to which it referred grew in importance. The solution was simple: embed a letter or symbol in the text, and label the corresponding note with that same character.

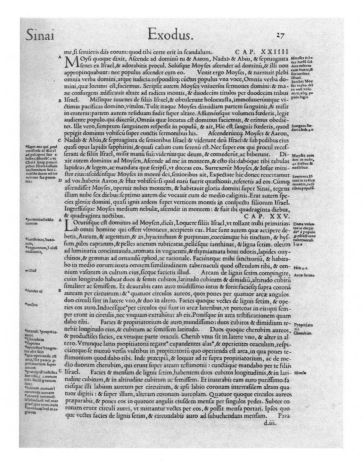

☞ *Figure 6.5*   A leaf from Robert Estienne's Latin Bible of 1532, with asterisks used to link notes to a specific location in the main text, and pilcrows used to provide explanatory translations of specified words.

Alphabetical labels, asterisks, daggers, and other typographic marks were all employed to link notes to text in this fashion.[48]

The first known footnote—that is, a note placed at the foot of the page, as opposed to in the margin, and linked to the main text by some special symbol—appeared in the "Bishop's Bible" of 1568, printed in London by Richard Jugge. Another victim of overzealous religious commentary, Jugge ran out of margin for the sixth and seventh notes on one particular page and so tucked them neatly below the main text. Sadly, the first footnote was labeled (f) rather than *.[49]

By the seventeenth century, notes were customarily placed at the bottom of the page and enumerated using an ordered sequence of symbols with the asterisk and dagger at their head. Despite more than three hundred years of use in the intervening period, however, the precise order in which footnote symbols should appear has never been settled. One sixteenth-century author blazed a meandering trail, adding notes labeled *d, e, f, *, d, *, e, f, g, h, i, *,* and *l* to a single page in a frenzy of marginalia, while a calmer eighteenth-century document might use *, †, ‖ and ∴.[50] Two centuries later, the English lexicographer Eric Partridge observed in 1953 that "the following are often used": *, †, **, ‡ or ††, *** or ** or **, and finally †††.[51] The 2003 *Oxford Style Manual* suggests *, †, ‡, §, ¶ and ‖, while the sixteenth edition of *The Chicago Manual of Style* recommends *, †, ‡ and §, having trimmed ‖ and ¶ from earlier editions.[52] The asterisk and dagger have taken their rightful places at the front of the queue.

The footnote gained respectability as the reader's scrawled marginal note gave way to the writer's authoritative printed block, and in the hands of certain authors the composition of footnotes was elevated to an art form. Perhaps the most famous footnote of all, and one that surely would have to be invented did it not already exist, occurs in the Reverend John Hodgson's magnum opus, his six-volume *History of Northumberland,* published between 1820 and 1840.[53] In a work already renowned for its thoroughness, the third volume further distinguished itself by dint of a mammoth 165-page footnote describing the history of Roman walls in Britain. This unprecedented marginal essay is, sadly, introduced by the letter *u* rather than an asterisk or dagger. It does, however, boast an abundance of child notes labeled alphabetically from (a) to (z) (and which are so numerous that they begin again at (a) twice more), and the *children* of these child notes, finally, are condescended to suffer conventional reference marks such as the asterisk and dagger.

Another work rightly lauded for its sublime mastery of the footnote is Edward Gibbon's *The History of the Decline and Fall of the Roman Empire*, published at the end of the eighteenth century. Maintaining an even-handed tone in the main text, Gibbon lets his true feelings run riot in a torrent of footnotes. He sniffily describes a fellow scholar, the Abbé le Boeuf, as "an antiquarian whose name was happily expressive of his talents"; dismisses Voltaire in a single sentence ("unsupported by either fact or probability, [M. de Voltaire] has generously bestowed the Canary Islands on the Roman empire"); and, lamenting Origen's act of self-mutilation in one note, muses in an adjacent one that "the praises of virginity are excessive."[54]

For all of the footnote's noble history, it has always had to contend with certain slights lobbed in its direction, and almost every profession that has cause to employ footnotes has at some point or another agonized over the proper use of this most polarizing device. The addiction to footnotes on display in legal documents, for example, which are often weighed down by references to related cases and explanatory asides, was castigated in a 1936 article in the *Virginia Law Review*. In "Goodbye to Law Reviews," Yale law professor Fred Rodell wrote:

> The explanatory footnote is an excuse to let the law review writer be obscure and befuddled in the body of his article and then say the same thing at the bottom of the page the way he should have said it in the first place.[...]

> The footnote foible breeds nothing but sloppy thinking,
> clumsy writing, and bad eyes.[55]

The legal establishment's love of complexity, however, militates against such reductionist thinking. Happily for the footnote, if not for legal writing, both Rodell's article and a similar 1986 plea entitled "Goodbye to Footnotes" were roundly ignored.[56]

The academic footnote, an essential component of a well-researched paper, has also come under attack. The *MLA Handbook*, a widely used style guide for academic works, states baldly that "comments that you cannot fit into the text should be omitted unless they provide essential justification or clarification of what you have written."[57] Seizing upon the MLA's excommunication of the footnote, a 1989 paper in the journal *College English* entitled "Elegy for Excursus: The Descent of The Footnote" was a virtual obituary for the form, opening with the line "The footnote, being dead, bears studying."[58] Once an exalted explicatory device, the footnote now required academic study to explain its own fall from grace.

More recently, a flurry of newspaper articles and books have reacted with dismay to the literary footnote's perceived status as an endangered species.[59] Chuck Zerby's 2003 book *The Devil's Details: a History of Footnotes*, for example, is partly an enthusiastic call for the revival of the form and partly an account of its history, should the patient in fact be beyond help.[60] The doomsaying that dogs the heels of the literary footnote may, however, be rather overstating the case: the footnote was a vital part of the novelist's toolbox throughout the twentieth century and continues to be so today, with some works notable for extraordinary uses of the form. Vladimir Nabokov's 1962 novel *Pale Fire*, for instance, consists solely of a 999-line poem augmented by copious notes, while J. G. Ballard's 1990 story "Notes Towards a Mental Breakdown" is told by a single sentence ("A discharged Broadmoor patient compiles 'Notes Towards a Mental

Breakdown,' recalling his wife's murder, his trial and exoneration.") annotated with a series of lengthy footnotes.[61] *The Mezzanine*, Nicolson Baker's 1988 debut novel* comprises in large part a series of "footnotes that include footnotes about the nature of footnotes."[62] And in Mordecai Richler's 1997 *Barney's Version,* the exaggerations and inaccuracies of the Alzheimer's-stricken narrator are amended in footnotes supplied by his son.[63] Perhaps most celebrated of all, David Foster Wallace's 1996 novel *Infinite Jest*, an already weighty book, is made weightier still by no fewer than 383 endnotes, some of which are further elucidated by footnotes of their own.[64] Rumors of the footnote's demise have been greatly exaggerated.

* * *

Outside the more rarefied literary professions, in recent times the presence of an otherwise innocuous asterisk or dagger is often read as a warning sign; the proverbial "small print" of advertisements and contracts has acquired a sinister aspect. A simple * may hide the exorbitant rate of interest to be charged on a bank loan, or a † may remind the reader that his or her house is at risk of repossession in the event of a default. Occasionally, though, the unwelcome footnote takes a bow on a larger stage.

Barry Bonds is by some measures the most successful baseball player the world has ever seen. With record-breaking totals of 71 home runs in a single season and 763 over his twenty-one-year career, Bonds was a sporting phenomenon; at least, that is, until his personal trainer pleaded guilty to distributing banned steroids in 2005. Bonds

---

* Baker is a veritable connoisseur of unusual typographic techniques. His essay *The History of Punctuation* is discussed in chapter 8, "The Dash (—)."

himself had testified in 2003 that he had never knowingly used such performance-enhancing drugs, but public opinion turned against him and Bonds found himself associated with the dreaded asterisk in an echo of a much earlier (though more genteel) baseball controversy.[65]

In 1961, the New York Yankees' Roger Maris and Mickey Mantle were competing to break George Herman "Babe" Ruth's record of 60 home runs in a single season. Hospitalized with a leg abscess, Mantle dropped out of the running late in the season leaving Maris to score a record-breaking 61st run, but the baseball establishment was not happy. Ruth's record was practically scriptural in its significance, and the sport's commissioner, Ford Frick, connived to downplay Maris's achievement. Noting that the earlier record had been set during a 154-game season, as opposed to the 162 games played by Maris that year, Frick called a press conference to announce that:

> Any player who has hit more than 60 home runs during his club's first 154 games would be recognized as having established a new record. However, if the player does not hit more than 60 until after this club has played 154 games, there would have to be some distinctive mark on the record books to show that Babe Ruth's record was set under a 154-game schedule.

In response, the *New York Daily News'* sportswriter Dick Young allegedly cried out, "Maybe you should use an asterisk on the new record. Everybody does that when there's a difference of opinion." Though at that time there *was* no official record book, and despite the fact Maris's record was never actually labeled with an asterisk, Young's off-the-cuff remark became part of baseball lore.[66]

Thus it was that when the news broke of Barry Bonds's alleged steroid use, journalists and fans alike invoked Maris's asterisk. While

Figure 6.6   Baseball fans brandish asterisks at a 2007 game between Barry Bonds's team, the San Francisco Giants, and the Milwaukee Brewers.

sports columnists agonized over whether Bonds's records ought to be singled out in this way, baseball fans had already made up their minds and took to waving banners printed with giant asterisks at his games.[67]

In 2011, Bonds was found guilty of obstructing justice, though the Baseball Hall of Fame refuses to rule out his nomination in future years and has not yet indicated how his records will be presented. Whatever happens, though, the asterisk will not be denied: the ball with which Bonds broke the all-time home-run record was bought by clothing designer Mark Ecko, branded with a laser-cut asterisk, and presented to a grudging Baseball Hall of Fame as a souvenir of the whole sordid episode.[68]

In an entirely different sphere of American life, George W. Bush, forty-third president of the United States, has also been dogged by an insinuating asterisk. Perhaps mindful of the *Chicago Tribune*'s infamous "Dewey Defeats Truman" gaffe a half century earlier, the *Boston Globe*'s headline on the 2000 presidential election read "Bush Wins Election*" and came with a damning caveat: "*Pending Gore Challenges, Possible Supreme Court Ruling."[69] Bush had lost the popular vote to his rival Al Gore and was hounded by allegations of voting irregularities in the key state of Florida, where a recount was under way that would decide the election.[70] A controversial Supreme Court ruling caused the Floridian recount to be halted, and Bush was awarded the presidency.[71] A letter published in the *New York Times* shortly after the affair caught the mood of Gore's supporters:

> Because we Americans are far more honorable than the
> United States Supreme Court and our politicians, we will
> accept George W. Bush as president. But because we know
> there were thousands of votes not counted, there will
> always be an asterisk and a question mark after his name.[72]

Garry Trudeau, author of the widely syndicated *Doonesbury* comic strip, had for some years reduced presidents and other senior politicians to graphic icons of their defining characteristics. Smooth-talking Bill Clinton was drawn as a waffle, the "lightweight" Dan Quayle as a feather, and hot-tempered Newt Gingrich as a bomb. When it came to selecting a symbol for the new president, Trudeau chose an asterisk surmounted by a Stetson hat, simultaneously invoking the disputed election result and echoing a criticism that Bush was "all hat and no cattle."[73] When Bush presided over military adventures in Afghanistan and Iraq, the cowboy hat was replaced by a Roman centurion's helmet; as American troops became bogged down in those remote wars, the helmet became increasingly tarnished and its crest threadbare.[74]

More than one journalist has drawn a comparison between Barry Bonds and George W. Bush* and the implied footnotes they have been unable to shake: the asterisk's innuendo is difficult to erase.[76]

* * *

The parallel trajectories of the asterisk and dagger, from the scrolls of ancient Alexandria to today's books, newspapers, and comics, are littered with typographic footnotes of their own. Along the way the asterisk has spawned the "asterism" (⁂), named for a constellation of stars and used as late as the 1850s to indicate a "note of considerable length, which has no reference," and also the descriptively named but enigmatic "two asterisks aligned vertically" (⁑) that lurks in Unicode's unplumbed depths.[77] The dagger, on the

---

* At the time of writing, the career of yet another American sporting hero has been tarnished by an accusatory asterisk. In August 2012, Lance Armstrong, seven times winner of the Tour de France, chose not to continue his fight against doping charges. George Vecsey of the *New York Times* opened his article on the affair with the headline, "Armstrong, Best of His Time, Now with an Asterisk."[75]

other hand, gave rise to a junior partner of its own in the form of the double dagger, or "diesis" (‡), originally used to indicate a small change in musical tone but that has now graduated to be an established reference symbol in its own right.[78] Few other marks have survived quite so long as this pair, and their marriage is as strong as ever. Our texts will continue to be illuminated by little stars and our hyperbole punctured by sobering daggers for years to come.

Chapter 7 ⁊⟜ The Hyphen

O ther than the irreducible period, the hyphen is about the simplest mark of punctuation it is possible to construct. Or rather, its *shape* is just about as simple as is possible, and even that is taking some liberties in describing the situation. Consider, for instance, the following characters: –, —, ——, -, -, -, and -. Which of these are hyphens? The first four are all dashes, the fifth is the mathematical minus sign, the sixth is an ugly chimera called the hyphen-minus—a hyphenated hyphen, no less—and only the last is properly considered a hyphen. And if we turn our attention from the shape to the usage of this one true hyphen (the others marks here are addressed next, in chapter 8) we are immediately presented with some fearsome accompanying baggage.

In the run-up to America's entry into World War I, both Theodore Roosevelt and Woodrow Wilson admonished "hyphenated" German- and Irish-Americans for their supposedly divided loyalties, while in 2007 bibliophiles were aghast when the *Oxford English Dictionary* dropped the hyphen from around 16,000 compound terms.[1] But all this is as nothing to the untold heartache and misery that has for centuries been visited upon grammarians, typographers, and printers by the simple act of hyphenating a word at the end of a line: for the past five hundred years the hyphen has literally shaped the words, lines, paragraphs, and pages we read.

* * *

The hyphen was first documented by another in the long line of overachieving, tax-evading scholars at the library of Alexandria. With punctuation already invented, the Earth's diameter measured, and Homer's epic poetry saved for future generations, the second-century-BC grammarian Dionysius Thrax was evidently left with precious little to do.* A student of the fifth librarian Aristarchus (he of asterisk and obelus fame), Thrax set to work on a short essay entitled "*Tékhnē Grammatiké*,"† or the "Art of Grammar," documenting the state of the art in grammatical practice.³ The *Tékhnē* concerns itself largely with morphology, or the construction of words, digressing briefly on the high, middle, and low points first created by Aristarchus's predecessor, Aristophanes, and in later supplements strays further into punctuation and other matters.⁴ Though some of the scribal practices Thrax described were employed patchily at best, the *Tékhnē* remains both the earliest known and the most important work on the ancient Greek language.

The first of Thrax's supplements addressed prosody, or the spoken delivery of a text, and catalogued the marks used to clarify the emphasis, intonation, and rhythms therein.⁵ Nestled between the familiar apostrophe ('), which clarified ambiguous syllable boundaries, and the commalike *hypodiastole* (‚), used to separate difficult words, lay the hyphen (‿)—a bowed line drawn under adjacent words to indicate that they should be understood as a single entity.⁶ In an age when texts were written entirely without word spaces, the hyphen, apostrophe, and *hypodiastole* were invaluable in interpreting an author's words. The conjoined words "littleusedbook," for example, are given quite

---

† Correctly attributing ancient manuscripts is not an exact science, and the authorship of the "*Tékhnē Grammatiké*" and its later supplements is a matter of some dispute.²

Figure 7.1 A sublinear hyphen (*line 6, center*) in a mid-second-century Homeric manuscript.

different meanings by the application of a hyphen or *hypodiastole* to yield "littleusedbook" and "little‚usedbook" respectively.

This "sublinear" hyphen (so called because it was drawn below the main line of text) maintained its form and function in Greek texts for centuries. Ironically enough, when its end did come—as it did in a roundabout and galling manner, like a boomerang returning to its oblivious thrower—it was courtesy of the dogged, Grecophile Romans.

* * *

As mentioned in chapter 1, "The Pilcrow (¶)," sometime in the late second or early third century the Romans adopted the Greek practice of writing without spaces between words, abandoning their previous style of separating·words·with·dots.[7] This was more a statement of fashion than practicality, and was finally reversed in the eighth century as frustrated Celtic monks pried apart unspaced Latin texts to make them easier for their nonnative brains to parse.[8] Eighth-century copyists struggling with these newfangled word spaces would sometimes place one where it was not required; rather than start again with a new page (parchment was so expensive that it was not unusual to wash, scrape, and reuse the pages of an old or unimportant text) or attempt to scrape off the mistake with the razor that formed part of every scribe's toolkit, a simple bowed, Greek-style hyphen could be used to close up an unnecessary gap without difficulty.[9] (Copyeditors today use a remarkably similar symbol, closing up incorrectly separated words with a sort of dou͡bled Greek hyphen.[10] Sadly, the lack of any evidence to the contrary means that the appearance of this modern mark is likely a happy coincidence rather than a consequence of its ancient forebear.)

When word spacing was imported *back* into Greek manuscripts in the ninth century, it became obvious to scribes that a judiciously placed space could separate words as surely as a *hypodiastole*, and equally, that a carefully omitted space was just as effective as a hyphen: hyphenated͡terms gave way to simple compound͡words.[11] Later still, when Gutenberg's regimented blocks of movable type appropriated the "airspace" above and below each character, the act of inserting a Greek hyphen below the baseline of the text required convoluted typesetting gymnastics.[12] Already under pressure from spaces between words, the sublinear hyphen disappeared; printing finally killed off the handwritten Greek hyphen, and its flight from Greek to Latin was complete.

With all this in mind, then, how did the modern compound-word hyphen make its way into English? The ancient Greek hyphen, which shared the modern mark's ability to join related words, had been made redundant by word spacing; its Latin doppelgänger was instead employed to fix mistakenly broken words, and remained stubbornly sublinear rather than inter-word. The answer may lie in the rise of the hyphen's other main form—the "marginal" hyphen, or "coupling stroke," placed at the end of a line of text to indicate a single word that has been broken across lines.

* * *

I n an eerie case of parallel evolution, the marginal hyphen appears to have come about entirely separately in Greek and Latin manuscripts. David Murphy, author of a helpfully self-describing paper entitled "Hyphens in Greek Manuscripts," holds that the practice of hyphenating words at the end of lines was a logical extension of the Greek sublinear hyphen. Confronted with a hyphenated word broken across lines, a scribe would place the hyphen at the end of the first line or the beginning of the second line, or sometimes both; it subsequently may have occurred to him that *any* word broken across a line could be hyphenated.[13] After all, what was the purpose of the hyphen except to indicate that two parts of a word belonged together?

The Latin backstory is provided by Paul Saenger, an authority on the introduction of spaces between words and the practice of silent reading that followed.[14] Saenger contends that the "graphic unity" of spaced-out words made scribes loath to split them across lines without some indication that they had done so. Latin hyphens first appeared in this role in tenth-century England, spreading to the Continent during the tenth and eleventh centuries.[15] By the twelfth century the Latin hyphen had acquired an oblique slant and could be found on (hy/phen), above (hy′phen), or below the line (hy͵phen), occasionally varying in position even within the same manuscript, with extravagant double hyphens (= and ⸗) following from 1300 onward.[16]

What is the relationship between the compound-word and marginal hyphens in Latin manuscripts? For his part, Saenger takes the opposite view to Murphy, hypothesizing that the marginal hyphen came first; already used to connect words split across lines, it later came

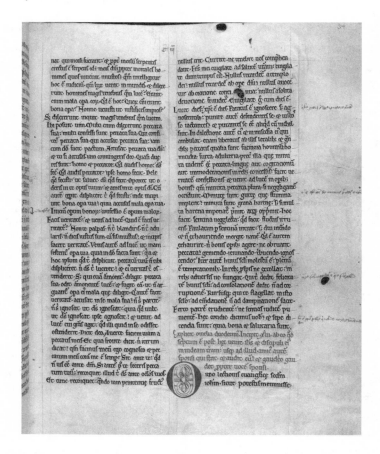

Figure 7.2   A bevy of line-end hyphens in an English monastic manuscript of 1167. The exceptional neatness of the scribe's layout and handwriting contrasts with the quality of the parchment, which is marred by four separate holes.

to be used to connect words split across spaces.[17] That tantalizing idea is the closest that the compound-word hyphen comes to a family tree or an authorized biography, but perhaps such a murky history is appropriate. The hyphen is, after all, an unstable mark of punctuation: like a radioactive isotope, over time, a hyphenated term will tend to shed its hyphen and fuse into a single word.[18] Wherever it came from, the compound-word hyphen never stays around for long. The marginal hyphen, on the other hand, consistently outstays its welcome.

* * *

B orn in 1401, by the middle of the fifteenth century the German cardinal Nicholas of Kues had built a reputation as something of a Renaissance man. "Cusanus," to give him his Latinized name, had dabbled in science (with indifferent results) and philosophy (to somewhat more acclaim), but his real talent lay in navigating the byzantine organization of the Catholic Church.[19] Fired by a philosophical belief in the essential unity of things, Cusanus set out to heal a fractured and squabbling institution: as a negotiator he brokered a settlement with the heretical Hussite sect of Bohemia, and later struck a power-sharing deal between the pope and the Holy Roman Emperor; as a reformer he forbade "undignified" organ music during services and demanded that priests give up their concubines.[20] It was in this latter role, during a visit to the German town of Mainz in 1451, that he threw his weight behind the campaign for standardization of the Church's daily manual, or "missal."[21]

One particular citizen of Mainz—a goldsmith named Johannes Gutenberg—was observing developments keenly. With a secret invention up his sleeve, Gutenberg was in a unique position to capitalize on any move toward a standardized missal, but, along with Cusanus, was frustrated by the archbishop of Mainz, who favored another, different, version of the missal. With no authorized version on the horizon, Gutenberg turned his attention to the one book guaranteed to be a bestseller: the Bible.[22] His invention was, of course, printing by means of "movable type," the setting of entire pages in pre-cast metal letters so that they could be impressed quickly, repeatedly, and consistently.

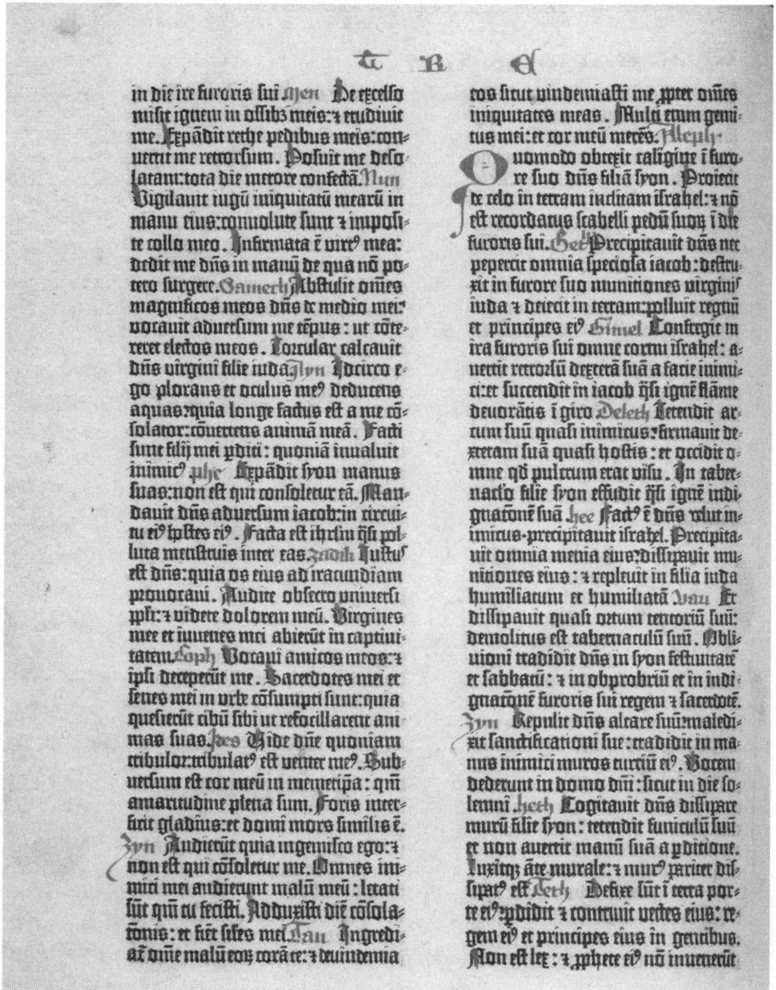

Figure 7.3   A leaf from Gutenberg's forty-two-line Bible showing a ladder of no fewer than eight consecutive hyphens (*right-hand column, lines 16–23*). Also visible is another of the contrivances used in the name of perfect justification: a Tironian *et* (*right-hand column, line 11*) is at odds with the fully spelled-out word "et" at the start of the line immediately below it.

With it, he sparked a revolution in the storage and transmission of information.

Revolutionary though Gutenberg's movable type was, the handsome forty-two-line Bibles that he printed in the mid-1450s presented anything but a novel aspect. So called because of the number of lines per page,* each copy was set in the ubiquitous, densely spaced blackletter script of the time, employed familiar scribal abbreviations such as the Tironian *et* (⁊), and was sprinkled with comforting, rubricated capital letters to guide the eye to new books and chapters.[24] (Gutenberg tried printing capitals in red but found that this slowed the production process. After a few attempts, he reverted to the usual practice of leaving empty spaces for a rubricator to later fill in.)[25] Aside from the pomp and ceremony of these *litterae notabiliores* and the steadfastly traditional presentation, the most arresting quality of Gutenberg's Bible is the sheer uniformity of the text. Each line is perfectly justified, the letters are closely and regularly packed, and word spaces are all of equal length. The regularity of the text still amazes modern typographers, as explained by Hermann Zapf, one of the doyens of twentieth-century typography:

> What we [want is] the perfect grey type area without the rivers and holes of too-wide word spacing. The general concept was not new at all. Our old hero Johannes Gutenberg in nearby Mainz also wanted the perfect line, to compete with the calligraphers of the fifteenth century. [...] How could Gutenberg get those even grey areas in his two columns without disturbingly wide holes between the words?[26]

---

* Gutenberg began printing his Bibles with forty lines, increasing to forty-one when he realized that he would otherwise run out of space, and further increased to forty-two lines for the bulk of the book.[23]

Zapf's "disturbingly wide holes" occur when a line of text cannot be stretched to meet both margins without unreasonably wide word spaces. This usually happens when a line contains many long words and consequently few spaces, which in turn may lead to unsightly, straggling "rivers" of white space meandering up and down the page: a string of short words is easier to justify than an interminable concatenation of polysyllabic sesquipedalianisms.

Gutenberg had an arsenal of techniques at his disposal—some subtle, others distinctly not—to combat this problem. At the finer end of the scale, Gutenberg used many different versions of the individual characters, each piece subtly different not only in appearance (which better mimicked handwriting) but also in width, providing a small but useful degree of flexibility in spacing a line. The same scribal abbreviations that helped give the Bible its traditional air allowed for shorter words, as did ligatures such as ꝏ, ꝫ, and ꝩ.[27] Perhaps the most obvious factor at the level of individual letters was the typeface itself:* the heavy, regular strokes of the *textura* (woven) blackletter script that Gutenberg used give the page a distinct evenness of color.[29]

By far the most potent weapon at hand in the battle against excessive word spacing was the hyphen—which, in the case of the forty-two-line Bible, was cut in the slanted, double form (⸗) common to blackletter texts of the time.[30] Gutenberg was decidedly unafraid to use it. Whereas the modern writer or compositor is hamstrung by a multitude of rules controlling where a word may safely be broken, in Gutenberg's day the first rule of Hyphenation Club was that there are no rules. The *Chicago Manual of Style*'s twelve-point plan for acceptable hyphenation in its sixteenth edition suggests that hyphenating more than three lines in a row is undesirable "for aesthetic reasons,"

---

* The word "minimum" is often held up as an example of both the evenness *and* illegibility of blackletter typefaces.[28]

Figure 7.4   The character variants, ligatures, and abbreviations that Gutenberg used to help achieve evenly justified lines; notice the Tironian *et* (*line 15, third from right*) and the double hyphen (*line 16, at end*). One study found that Gutenberg used 47 capitals, 63 lowercase letters, 92 abbreviations, 83 ligatures, and 5 punctuation marks.[31]

yet Gutenberg managed ladders of eight consecutive hyphens.[32] The *Oxford Style Manual* avers that one-letter fragments of hyphenated words are never acceptable and that fragments of up to three letters are frowned on, but the forty-two-line Bible happily slices "ɛ⸗go," "o⸗mne," and "ter⸗re" into obedient bits.[33] The fifteenth-century hyphen was a blunt tool, but an effective one.

Aside from Gutenberg's scattergun use of hyphenation, the

physical manner in which his hyphens were printed reveals the care with which his Bible was created. A glance at this or any other modern book will show that line-end hyphens are invariably printed inside the right-hand margin as part of the main block of text. Gutenberg's double hyphens, however, hang in the margin *outside* that boundary, and this apparently minor detail provides a clue to the single-mindedness with which he pursued perfection in his work.* For in order to place his hyphens in the margin, Gutenberg had to add an extra space to the end of each and every non-hyphenated line—that is, to satisfy his craving for this one typographic nicety he set an extra *36,000*† characters.[34] Although this is an extreme example, the pursuit of perfect hyphenation and justification—H&J, as they are called in the industry—has obsessed typographers since this very first printed book.

* * *

For a large part of its history, the quest for adequate hyphenation and justification was characterized by a one-sided struggle between the slow-moving technology of printing and the increasingly complex conventions of word division. For more than four hundred years after Gutenberg first plucked a character from a type case, printers continued to set books in almost exactly the same manner, placing characters by hand on a "composing stick" set to the width of the text and binding completed lines into a wooden "chase" ready for

---

* This prominent hyphen placement, combined with the forty-two-line Bible's status as the first major printed book, may have led to Gutenberg being erroneously credited as the "inventor" of the hyphen.

† The Gutenberg Bible was composed of just under 1,300 pages bearing (of course) forty-two lines of text each, and roughly a third of all lines are hyphenated. To hang his hyphens in the margins, then, Gutenberg or his compositors would have had to set somewhere around an additional 1300 × 28 = 36,400 space characters. This estimate is probably on the high side—it does not take into account the small number of forty- and forty-one-line pages, for instance—but it is not unreasonable.

printing. If a line was too short, word spaces were widened to pad it out; if it was too long, the final word had to be manually hyphenated and the line respaced accordingly.[35] When a line could not be justified to the compositor's liking, the author might even be called in to rewrite the offending text.[36]

Laying siege to this static technology were ever-changing tastes in typography and grammar. Though they had been integral to the Latin scribe's art, abbreviations in modern languages were fewer in number and were often discouraged altogether in running text; a drive to reduce the number of characters, or "sorts," required of a typeface caused a decline in ligatures and letter variants, and, other than within its German heartland, by the end of the nineteenth century blackletter had largely retreated to niche applications.[37] At the same time, the rules of hyphenation themselves grew ever more complex: published toward the end of the era of manual typesetting, the 1906 *Chicago Manual of Style* contained no fewer than fourteen separate rules for word division.[38] In other words, it was getting harder to hyphenate and justify lines, and the archaic composing stick was not helping.

The race to automate the composition process finally came to fruition in the closing decades of the Victorian era. Baroque mechanical contraptions had invaded every corner of nineteenth century life, from factories to homes: Joseph-Marie Jacquard's punch card–driven loom of 1801 made it possible to mass produce intricate fabric weaves; Charles Babbage's mathematical engines of the 1820s and '30s pioneered the automated solution of mathematical formulae, and even a visit to the bathroom was enlivened by the appearance of the flushing toilets popularized by one Thomas Crapper.[39] The ossified printing industry was long overdue for a similar shake-up.

The writer Samuel Clemens, known by his nom de plume, Mark Twain, understood the potential for a mechanical typesetter better than most. Exempted from the human condition, as he saw it, such a device would never get drunk, would work as diligently at three a.m. as three p.m., and was immune to unionization.[40] Unfortunately, for all his foresight, Clemens invested his faith—and his money—in the wrong man. James W. Paige fiddled in vain with the intricate and flawed "Paige typesetter" for a fruitless decade, bankrupting his sponsor even as they were overtaken by events outside their control.[41] First, in 1886 an immigrant German watchmaker named Ottmar Mergenthaler demonstrated his line-casting "Linotype" machine to an audience of delighted newspapermen, whereas Tolbert Lanston's "Monotype" system, unveiled a few years later, was similarly well received in the fine printing world of bookmaking.[42] The Linotype and Monotype may have lacked the novelty of Jacquard's loom or the legendary complexity of Babbage's difference engine, but their combined impact on the printing industry was earthshaking.

Mergenthaler's Linotype machine, the first to appear by a few years, was a ticking, whirring behemoth. So named because it produced a "line o' type" at a time, the Linotype combined composition, casting, and distribution (the tedious process whereby a compositor returned each letter to its appropriate compartment in the type case) into a single machine.[43] As an operator typed at the Linotype's keyboard, brass matrices carrying engraved characters were released from an overhead magazine and assembled into a line along with wedge-shaped "spacebands." Next, the automated justification system forced these spacebands simultaneously upward, widening the line until it abutted the ends of the desired column measure. From there, a molten alloy of lead, antimony, and tin was forced into the mold formed by the justified line to create a "slug," or line of type.[44]

Though the Linotype's automatic justification mechanism freed compositors from the laborious process of spacing and respacing lines, it was not without drawbacks. Other than the plaintive ring of a "hyphen bell" rigged to sound as the line neared completion, deciding where a line ended or when a word should be hyphenated remained a

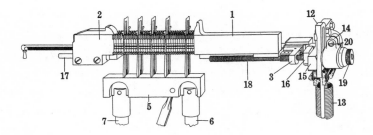

Figure 7.5   The Linotype justification mechanism. The jaws of the vise (1, 2) are set to the desired column width, and the justification ram (5) pushes the wedge-shaped spacebands upward to take up the slack.

stubbornly manual process.[45] Lines could not be edited before casting, so a badly spaced or badly hyphenated line had to be re-set in its entirety; conversely, a mistake discovered *after* a line had been cast could ripple down through the following lines and require all of them to be re-set. Perhaps the most egregious omission on early machines was that there was no easy way to set nonjustified lines; the operator had to manually fill the remainder of each line with blank matrices, or "quads," and then justify the line as normal to simulate the appearance of a ragged right edge.[46]

Mergenthaler's machine was soon competing with Tolbert Lanston's Monotype, which, in contrast to the all-in-one Linotype, comprised separate keyboard and casting devices. Echoing the use of punched cards by Jacquard's loom and Babbage's mathematical engines, as the operator typed in his or her copy, the Monotype keyboard emitted perforated paper tape that was then fed into the casting machine, allowing several keyboardists to simultaneously set copy for a single noisy, rapid-fire caster. Type cast by Monotype was generally considered to be of higher quality than that of its line-casting competitors: its individually cast letters permitted composition errors to be corrected by hand, and it was possible to mix machine-set type with more complex material such as mathematical equations and chemical formulae.[47]

Given that the Monotype composition and casting mechanisms were separate, justification was handled in a different but equally ingenious manner. As the operator entered his or her copy, the keyboard mechanically recorded the cumulative width of all characters in the line. When the end of the line approached (again signaled by a bell), a cylindrical scale, or "unit drum," informed the user of the word spacing required to justify the line; having pressed a pair of special keys to record this on the tape, the user carried on to key the next line. When the completed spool was fed into the caster, the operator took care to feed it in back to front: the entire document was processed in reverse order, so that the caster could read and set the word spacing for each line before casting it.[48] Clever though this was, the end result was that justification was no better or worse than that of the Linotype. The keyboardist had to play the same guessing game as to which letters or words could be shoehorned in at the end of the line, and hyphenation was still left entirely to the operator's discretion.

For all the speed gained over hand composition, there were dangers inherent in machines that required their users to work beside bubbling crucibles of molten lead.[50] The joy of mechanically setting line after line o' type came with the added frisson that a "squirt" might occur at any time: any detritus caught between two adjacent Linotype matrices would allow molten type metal to jet through the gap. And aside from the immediate dangers of seared flesh, operators of both Linotypes and Monotypes ran the more insidious risk of poisoning from the (highly flammable) benzene used to clean matrices, the natural gas that some machines burned to melt the type metal, and the fumes emitted by the molten type metal itself.[51]

* * *

☞ *Figure 7.6* A Monotype keyboard, with punched paper tape,
line-width gauge, and drumlike justification scale visible at top. Also shown
here are the various QWERTY keyboards used for roman, italic, bold, or
small capital letters as required. The red numeric keys (at the top left of the
keyboard) are used to punch the computed justification parameters at the
end of the line.[49]

For more than half a century, printing was dominated by Lino-types, Monotypes, and a host of copycat devices. Their monopoly was challenged first in the 1950s by optical, or "cold type" machines, and when fully digital composition arrived in the 1970s, hot metal typesetting's sunset had begun.[52]

The brief reign of the optical, or phototypesetter, was not a happy one. Rather than cast lead type that could be inked and printed many times over, phototypesetters instead exposed film negatives of letters onto photosensitive paper; master pages thus composed were then printed via other methods such as offset lithography. Early phototypesetters were hastily retrofitted versions of their hot-metal predecessors (Intertype, for example, produced a Linotype clone whose matrices carried tiny squares of film instead of engraved brass letters), with some devices producing different sizes of type by placing appropriate magnifying lenses between the film and the paper.[53] The results were often worse than their purely mechanical forebears: whereas each size of metal type could be subtly adjusted to account for its relative dimensions—the strokes of smaller sizes made heavier, and those of larger ones lighter, for instance—lens-based enlargement or reduction produced crudely distorted letterforms.[54]

In 1976, a computer science professor named Donald E. Knuth received proofs set using a phototypesetter for a new edition of his book *The Art of Computer Programming*. Knuth despaired at the drop in quality: some letters were oddly rotated; others were badly spaced, and the overall texture of the page—its "color"—was patchy. Then, in February 1977, Knuth was shown a purely digital typesetting machine—essentially a high-quality, computer-driven printer that composed shapes from an array of dots so tiny that the eye could not perceive them. Knuth saw immediately that the practice of typography had changed irrevocably.

> [...] the problem of printing beautiful books had changed
> from a problem of metallurgy to a problem of optics and
> then to a problem of computer science. [...] The future
> of typography depends upon the people who know the
> most about creating patterns of os and 1s; it depends on
> mathematicians and computer scientists.[55]

In March the same year Knuth wrote to his publisher, telling them that he was going to write a program to typeset the book and that new proofs would be ready in July.[56] As it turned out, it took two years to put in place the basics of TEX, as he called his program, and it was not until thirteen years later that he declared it complete.[57]

Until the arrival of computers in printing, the technology of hyphenation and justification had necessarily focused on the latter. Linotypes and Monotypes could mechanically justify a line, but knowledge of the interminable hyphenation rules set down by *The Chicago Manual of Style*, much less the tens of thousands of syllabified words present in a typical dictionary, was a fantasy for such devices.[58] Computer-based composition, however, presented an opportunity to redress the balance and to place hyphenation and justification on equal footings. Knuth's TEX, which contained 4,500 "positive" and "negative" hyphenation patterns (for example, *b-s*, *-cia*, *con-s*, and *-ment* are potential hyphenation points but *b-ly*, *-cing*, *io-n*, and *i-tin* are not) extracted from *Merriam-Webster's Pocket Dictionary*, along with a list of fourteen exceptional words, found 89 percent of all hyphenation points and placed almost none incorrectly.[59] Reliable hyphenation had finally joined justification in the computer age.

Computers enabled another innovation that even the most diligent of hand compositors would have been hard pressed to match. Whereas a Linotype operator focused exclusively on the single line at hand, and a hand compositor could jockey characters back and forth on the composing stick to adjust H&J over a few lines at a time, with the processing power of a computer behind it, TEX could try *every* possible paragraph layout* in the search for the best overall combination of word spacing, letter spacing, and hyphenation.[61] In order to compute the optimal paragraph layout, each decision made in setting a given text was assigned a "badness" score: marginal hyphens were bad, successive marginal hyphens worse; word and letter spaces were allowed to vary within a small range of values but excessive adjustment carried a penalty. Breaking of phrases that should normally be kept together (such as proper names and mathematical formulae) was penalized, as were widows and orphans (single lines left behind or carried over to a new page).[62]

Essentially, Knuth programmed TEX with knowledge of the same aesthetic decision-making process that a typographer would carry out; unlike that typographer, TEX could perform thousands of paragraph arrangements every second and pick the best among them. Knuth's optimistic experiment in typesetting had moved typography a step closer to Hermann Zapf's tantalizing "perfect grey type area."

Hermann Zapf himself raised the bar even further in the mid-1990s with the aid of a little shoulder-standing. Publishing a paper touting the benefits of his self-referentially named "*hz*-program," Zapf took TEX's paragraph-justification mechanism to extraordinary new lengths.

---

* Even a very short paragraph with ten possible line-break locations, including spaces between words, inter-word hyphens, and optional "soft" hyphenation points, can be arranged in 1,024 distinct ways. TEX, however, ignores some obviously unlikely cases (such as placing one word on the first line and all the rest on the second, and so forth); this, along with some clever computational tricks, reduces the typical number of configurations to be tested to around the same as the number of potential break points.[60] Adding in *other* parameters, however, such as word spacing and letter spacing, the permitted length of a paragraph's final line, and so on, redoubles the complexity of the problem.

> There now is your insu-
> lar city of the Manhattoes,
> belted round by wharves as
> Indian isles by coral reefs—
> commerce surrounds it with
> her surf. Right and left,
> the streets take you water-
> ward. Its extreme downtown
> is the battery, where that no-
> ble mole is washed by waves,
> and cooled by breezes, which
> a few hours previous were
> out of sight of land. Look at
> the crowds of water-gazers
> there.

Figure 7.7   Hyphenated and justified text with glyphs expanded or contracted by up to 2 percent, as set by Donald Knuth's TEX. The text is set in Computer Modern, one of the first typefaces Knuth designed specifically for use with TEX. (The right-hand margin is shown to highlight the "margin kerning" technique first employed in Hermann Zapf's *hz*-program.)

First, and most controversial, in a crude imitation of Gutenberg's use of alternative letterforms, the *hz*-program could squeeze or stretch individual characters by a few percentage points in width to achieve good word spacing.[63] Zapf's automatic letter scaling was a trivial operation in terms of the mathematics and computing effort required, but it represented a conceptual leap away from the physical immutability of metal type. No longer would the type designer's artistic vision for a character set be permitted to stand in the way of recapturing the perfection of the forty-two-line Bible; no longer was the typographic letter sacrosanct. Denizens of the typographic world were not amused, with Robert Bringhurst delivering a withering retort:

> [...] no typesetting software should be permitted to compress, expand or letterspace the text automatically and arbitrarily as a means of fitting the copy. Copyfitting problems should be solved by creative design, not fobbed off on the reader and the text nor cast like pearls before machines.[64]

Adding insult to injury, the *hz*-program also happened to letterspace text as required. Though the practice has a robust tradition of use in blackletter texts, where it serves to e m p h a s i z e words, adding space between letters has long been a bugbear of modern typographers.[65] As the American type designer Frederick Goudy is often misquoted as saying,* "Anyone who would letterspace lowercase would shag sheep."[67] Like it or not, however, Zapf's "micro-typographic" features have since been absorbed into Donald Knuth's TEX and many other standard typesetting programs.[68]

It is hard to escape the feeling that Zapf, Knuth, and company took up a sledgehammer to crack a nut. Employing the brute strength of computers to rearrange paragraphs and mathematically deform letters in an endless quest to avoid hyphens seems redundant when Gutenberg's elegant original solutions stare them in the face: hyphenate more often, not less; embrace abbreviations; and encourage type designers to provide alternative letterforms. One could even move

---

* Frederick Goudy's original quote actually related to blackletter text rather than lowercase letters, and was made in relation to his then-new Goudy Text blackletter typeface.[66] Goudy's quote has since been co-opted into decrying lowercase letterspacing wherever it happens to be found.

wholesale to left-justified, or ragged-right text,* given that study after study shows that it is easier to read than the obsessively justified lines present in almost all modern books.[70] What the typographer Ari Rafaeli called his profession's "loathing of hyphens" has a lot to answer for.[71]

---

* For all his faults, the ever-unconventional Eric Gill used almost all of these techniques in *An Essay on Typography*, employing a ragged-right setting, abbreviating words frequently, and hyphenating with abandon.[69]

Chapter 8 ❧ The Dash

As the introduction to the previous chapter suggested, to call this chapter "The Dash" is a little disingenuous. Having excluded the final three symbols—the minus sign, the "hyphen-minus," and the hyphen itself—from our list of dashes and dashlike marks (–, —, ——, -, -, -, and -), we are left with four others.* The "dash" is not so much a solo artist as a quartet where each member wears the same suit but plays a different instrument.

Of all the dashes, the "en dash" and its longer counterpart the "em dash"—named for corresponding typographic units of length—are most often seen in print. The en dash is used as a substitute for the word "to" in numerical ranges or relationships ("1939–1945," "Paris–Roubaix bicycle race"); acts as a kind of superhyphen to connect compound terms ("pre–World War II"); and is occasionally used to neuter offensive or sensitive w––ds by hiding individual letters.[2] Used singly, the longer em dash indicates an instance of "aposiopesis," an abrupt change or end to a thought or speech ("What the—?"); doubled up, em dashes censor entire ——— or portions of w——s.[3] To complicate matters, en and em dashes sometimes mean the same thing: American style guides advocate using unspaced em dashes to set off parenthetical clauses—like this—whereas most British texts prefer a spaced en dash – like this.[4]

---

* With reference to the *octo-* plus "thorpe" etymology of the term "octothorpe," in the computer industry the dash and its two-pointed siblings are sometimes jokingly called "bithorpes."[1] It was tempting indeed to appropriate this term to mean "all dashes and dashlike characters."

More exotic than the en and em dashes is the "quotation dash" used by some authors and in some non-English languages to denote spoken dialogue. Slightly longer again than the em dash, a quotation dash is used to introduce each new line of dialogue, as seen here in the opening lines of James Joyce's already fabulously opaque *Ulysses:*[5]

> Stately, plump Buck Mulligan came from the stairhead, bearing a bowl of lather on which a mirror and a razor lay crossed. A yellow dressinggown, ungirdled, was sustained gently behind him on the mild morning air. He held the bowl aloft and intoned:
>
> —*Introibo ad altare Dei.*
>
> Halted, he peered down the dark winding stairs and called out coarsely:
>
> —Come up, Kinch! Come up, you fearful jesuit![6]

Rarest of all dashes is the "figure dash," used to divide strings of digits, such as telephone numbers ("555‒4385"), that do *not* represent ranges.[7] Designed to match the width of a typeface's Arabic numerals— and by extension, present only in those typefaces with "tabular" digits of equal widths—the figure dash exists solely to maintain the regularity of appearance of numbers set in tables or lists.[8]

These subtle but prized typographic conventions find themselves under threat from the wretched "hyphen-minus," an interloper introduced to the dash's delicate habitat in the late nineteenth century. Too crowded to accommodate a full complement of dashes, the typewriter keyboard required a compromise; the jack-of-all-trades hyphen-minus was the result, and its privileged position at the fingertips of typists everywhere has led to it impersonating dashes and hyphens alike with alarming frequency. In print and online, the well-set dash is an endangered species.

* * *

C lues to the genesis of the dash, in any of its forms, are elusive. First, and perhaps most surprising, the dash and the hyphen seem to have precisely nothing in common except for their visual appearance; if what little *has* been written about the dash is anything to go by, its origins have more in common with the pilcrow—or at least its rudely vacant grave, the indented paragraph—than with any other written symbol.

As has been seen throughout this book, punctuation has been in a state of evolutionary flux ever since Dionysius Thrax first documented Aristophanes's ancient system of points, but that evolution was fragmented and haphazard until printing exerted its stabilizing influence in the fifteenth century.[9] Scholars punctuated one way, letter writers another, and even though they shared certain marks in common, individual authors could not resist promoting their own systems as the one truly correct way to punctuate.[10]

Buoncompagno da Signa, born near Florence around 1165, was such an author.[11] A practitioner of the *ars dictaminis*, his era's vogue for formal letter writing, da Signa advocated a system of punctuation composed of only two marks: his *suspensivus* marked a short pause and his *planus* indicated a final pause, or stop. Both marks were formed by single pen-strokes named *virgulae*, the diminutive of the Latin *virga* for "rod" or "staff," or even, in medieval slang, "penis."[12] In light of this, Buoncampagno's choice of symbols is suggestive to say the least: the *suspensivus* was drawn as an eagerly upraised *virgula sursum erecta*, or "upright virgule" (/), with the *planus* represented by a correspondingly exhausted *virgula plana*, or "level virgule" (–).

The cause of the *virgula suspensiva* was taken up by other dictaminists too, and by and by it came to be used for all pauses in a sentence except the final one.[13] By the fifteenth century, the "virgule" was so widely used that it had become interchangeable with the

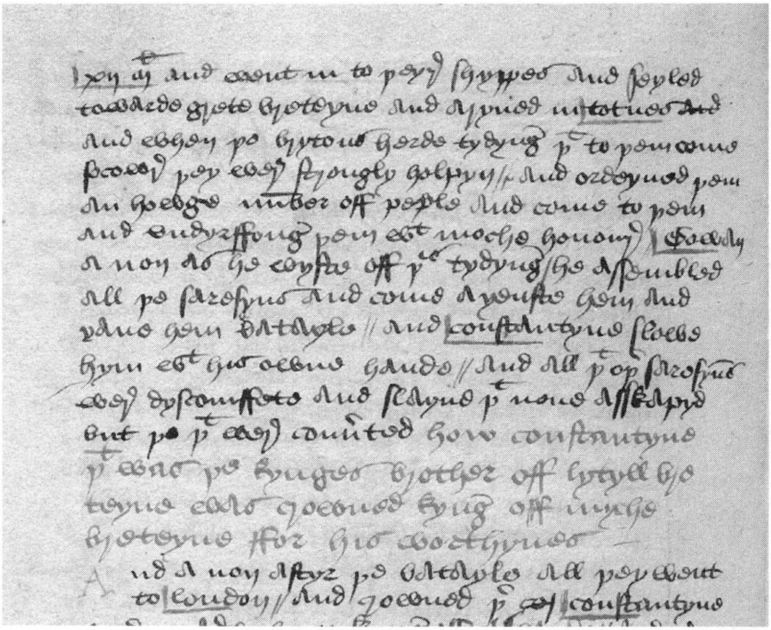

Figure 8.1 Double and single virgules in a late-fifteenth-century copy of the *Brut Chronicle,* a legendary account of the founding of Britain.

points that were also used to mark intermediate pauses and stops—the descendants of Aristophanes's ancient *distinctiones*, in fact—and which were now carelessly placed at varying heights in relation to the text.[14] Though the modern comma eventually superseded it, the virgule lives on in the French term for that mark of punctuation—*la virgule* is still with us.[15]

Frustratingly for our purposes, the enticingly dashlike *virgula plana* did not catch on, but rather conceded its role in marking the completion of a sentence to its oblique sibling. From the thirteenth century, scribes began to use a pair of virgules (//) to indicate that a pilcrow or other section mark should be inserted into the text; ignored

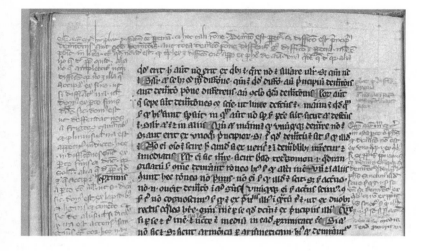

Figure 8.2   Double slashes, or virgules, are just visible behind the pilcrows in this heavily annotated copy of Aristotle dated to the second half of the thirteenth century.

by a harried rubricator, the plaintive // became a mark of punctuation in its own right rather than a piece of scaffolding in the manuscript-production process. Thus, the decline of the pilcrow went hand in hand not only with the rise of the indented paragraph* but also that of the double virgule, and during the fifteenth and sixteenth centuries / and // were customarily employed to mark minor and major pauses respectively.[16]

  Still, the *virgula plana* limped on, cropping up in manuscripts as disparate as fourteenth-century medical recipes and nineteenth-century plays.[17] Some modern treatises on punctuation do hint at a connection between the medieval virgule and the modern dash— Oxford University Press's *Poetry Handbook* nonchalantly mentions

---

* See chapter 1, "The Pilcrow (¶)."

that "the dash's Latin name is the *virgula plana*," and *The Visual Dictionary of Typography* says that in the *Fraktur* variant of blackletter text, "two virgules represented a dash"[18]—but they do so without supporting evidence.[*]

In comparison with the confused origins of the mark itself, the etymology of the dash's name is mercifully straightforward, arising as it does from the verb "to dash," in the sense of striking violently. *The Oxford English Dictionary* cites a 1552 suggestion that one might "[d]ashe or stryke with a penne," with a later document from 1615 exemplifying the use of the word in that same sense: "And thus by mere chaunce with a little dash I have drawne the picture of a Pigmey."[19] Having said that, the names of the modern dashes bear investigation: though the figure and quotation dashes are self-explanatory, the en and em dashes are cryptically terse.

An integral part of printing terminology, the "em" was originally a unit of length equal to the width of the letter *m*, though in modern use the em is defined to be equal to the body height of the type— thus, for a twelve-point typeface one em is equal to twelve points, and for a sixteen-point typeface the em is sixteen points in size.[20] (The "pica point" used in Britain and the United States is equal to $\frac{1}{72}$ inch; the "Didot point" used in continental Europe is slightly larger, at 0.3759 mm.)[21] The em dash, therefore, is a dash that is one em in length; two-em and three-em dashes are also seen on occasion, though it is rare for them to be cut as single characters and a series of adjacent em dashes serves just as well.[22] Also named for this unit of length is the "em quad,"[†] a square piece of lead used to add em-width

---

[*] Since it seems to be the done thing, let me throw in a similarly unsubstantiated theory of my own. I suspect that the *virgula plana* and the dash are one and the same mark, and that the *virgula plana*'s function as a major pause is the ancestor of the dash's modern use to surround parenthetical clauses, which, when spoken, warrant a pause on either side.

[†] In the printing industry, en and em quads are sometimes given the acrophonic nicknames "nut" and "mutton."[23]

spaces,   like   this,   and to pad out, or "quad," paragraph indents and partial lines like this one.[24]

The corresponding en dash is also named for its size; originally defined as the width of the letter *n*, the en has now been formalized to mean exactly half an em.[25]

This abundance of fussily named and proportioned dashes came into its own in the swirling melee of eighteenth- and nineteenth-century punctuation. Despite the superficial conformity that printing had imposed on all the jostling marks in circulation, the use of punctuation was still haphazard and excessive—and the dash was at the center of the melee.[26]

* * *

O n its publication in 1993, M. B. Parkes's *Pause and Effect: An Introduction to the History of Punctuation in the West* was recognized as the most comprehensive and authoritative book yet produced on the subject. *Shady Characters* owes an immense debt of gratitude to Parkes and his book: without his exhaustive survey of two millennia of punctuation, encompassing everything from Aristophanes to Virginia Woolf, this book—and no doubt many others besides—could not have been written.* In a review of *Pause and Effect* written for the *New York Review of Books*, though, the author Nicholson Baker chided Parkes for one particular omission: where, Baker wondered, was the commash?[27]

That writers and printers suffered at one time from a tendency— or more precisely, from an irresistible, overweening *need*—to burden the written word with unwonted punctuation first became apparent in the seventeenth century. Early symptoms can be discerned in the

---

* *Pause and Effect* is discussed again in Further Reading.

1622 edition of Shakespeare's *Othello*, where the comma, colon, semi-colon, and even the period collude with the em dash to add weight to otherwise standard pauses and semantic markers.[28] In the second act, for instance, Iago declares: "I'll tell you what you shall do, — our general's wife is now the general"; act III sees Desdemona reassure Cassio: "O that's an honest fellow: — do not doubt, Cassio," and in the climactic finale Othello spits, "O strumpet, — weepest thou for him to my face?"[29]

The comma-dash, or "commash" (,—), and its companions the "colash" (:—) and "semi-colash" (;—)* grew in status until they were almost ubiquitous, and the words of Captain Ahab, Fagin, and Elizabeth Bennet were liberally seasoned with such "dashtards," as Baker called them.[31] Given its comparative rarity, Baker understandably declined to acknowledge the stop-dash (.—); even in an era when the printed page fairly danced with extraneous commas, when dashes coupled promiscuously with other marks and " quotations " came with built-in safety margins, the contradiction inherent in such a pairing was too rich for the average writer.[32]

As with all good parties, this two-century-long festival of typographic excess had to come to an end. The passing of the Victorian era brought with it a general sobering-up of punctuation practice, and the commash and its ilk soon found themselves under threat. *The Chicago Manual of Style*, launched in 1906, ruled against the dash hybrids from the start—except, curiously enough, the stop-dash, which was permitted only to introduce notes or asides, as in the construction "NOTE.—", though this too had been expunged by the 1969 edition.[33] "Compound points" such as the commash were tolerated for slightly longer in British English, though by 1953 the British lexicographer Eric

---

* "Commash," "colash," and "semi-colash" are Nicholson Baker's terms. The novelist Will Self used the alternative spelling "comash" in a 2008 *Guardian* article.[30]

Partridge had also concluded "you [should] use compound points only when they are unavoidable."[34]

Assailed by punctuational Darwinism, the commash made one last attempt at salvation. As if disguising itself from the predations of eagle-eyed copyeditors, the occasional *reversed* commash (—,) survived into print until at least the 1960s; Baker identified such reversed marks in the works of Marcel Proust, in the memoirs of the famed Baltimorean journalist H. L. Mencken ("My father put in a steam-heating plant towards the end of the eighties—the first ever seen in Hollins Street—, but such things were rare until well into the new century") and in the novels of John Updike, but these were needles in a haystack of conformity.[35] Baker himself made a tentative effort at resurrecting the dashtards, slipping a semi-colash into a piece for *The Atlantic* in 1983. Unfortunately it did not pass muster: "The associate editor made a strange whirring sound in her throat, denoting inconceivability, and I immediately backed down."[36] For the time being at least, the day of the commash was over.

* * *

Even as dashes of a certain stripe dallied with commas, semicolons, and the like, the mark was pressed into service of a more serious kind—that of censoring individual l–tt–rs or even entire ———. This practice was known as "ellipsis," from the Greek *élleipsis*, "to fall short" or "to leave out," and occasionally by the related "eclipsis," hinting at the eclipsing of things better left unwritten.[37] One 1856 primer on punctuation explained that the point, asterisk, and dash could all be employed to such ends; evidently, the need to elide information was more than a single mark could handle. Anticipating the modern tendency to use the asterisk to decontaminate d*mn curses, the same book suggested that "[p]eriods are considered much less offensive to the eye than asterisks"; those same periods nowadays indicate a trailing-off of thought or narrative . . . though the dash remains very much the poster child for literary self-censorship.[38] For better or for worse, the dash is one of the few marks of punctuation used to deliberately *obscure*, rather than clarify, the meaning of a sentence.

The preponderance of ellipsis in the writing of times past is often blamed on Victorian prudishness—as W. Somerset Maugham wrote in his play *The Constant Wife*, "We have long passed the Victorian Era when asterisks were followed after a certain interval by a baby"—but this is not the whole story.[39] Ellipsis is both older and more nuanced than a simple reaction to nineteenth-century mores; it rose to prominence in the first half of the previous century.

Born in London sometime around 1660, Daniel Foe (he later took to prefixing his surname with an aristocratic "De," claiming descent from a landed family named De Beau Faux) lived in interesting times. Before reaching his tenth birthday, Defoe had experienced at first hand the plague that swept London in 1665, leaving 70,000 dead, and the Great Fire of the following year that razed four-fifths of the city's homes, while in 1667 he would have learned of the daring seaborne raid on the nearby town of Chatham that helped force the second Anglo-Dutch war to a humiliating conclusion for the English.[40]

A Presbyterian, the adult Defoe joined the ill-starred rebellion of 1685 against the Catholic king, the newly crowned James II of England, Scotland, and Ireland. Later, having obtained a royal pardon for his role in the affair (probably by paying the going rate of £60), he embarked on a career as a merchant, punctuated by periodic incarceration in debtors' jail.[41] Bargaining his way out of one particularly odious spell in Newgate Prison, Defoe finally found his métier as a political agent and propagandist, writing pamphlets to support the controversial Act of Union between Scotland and England and spying at the restive Parliament in Edinburgh.[42]

Thus, it was with a credible claim to a life well lived—to a possession of a certain degree of character, so to speak—that at the august age of sixty or thereabouts Daniel Defoe wrote what is often called the first modern, character-driven novel.[43] Published in 1721, *The Fortunes and Misfortunes of the Famous Moll Flanders** broke the mold of the "romances" prevalent at the time, whose archetypal heroes existed in a world of high adventure and recycled plots. Defoe's thieving, bigamist heroine was an edgy amalgam of some of the most notorious criminals of his time (Defoe may have interviewed the infamous pickpockets Moll King and "Callico" Sarah while visiting a friend in Newgate) who moved among bankrupt merchants, transported felons, and prostitution rings.[45] Defoe's contemporaries (and his competitors for the title of first novelist) also valued realism: the titular heroine of Samuel Richardson's *Pamela* exhibits something approaching Stockholm syndrome toward her aristocratic captor, while Henry Fielding's Tom Jones is both an orphan and a licentious fornicator.[46] Unlike their literary antecedents, these were fallible, plausible, and above all *realistic* characters.

Ironically, this emphasis on realism required new forms of artifice to maintain the reader's suspension of disbelief. It was with an eye on creating this illusion of reality that Defoe omitted the names of almost all the characters in *Moll Flanders*, either by explicitly declining to reveal them or, more expediently, by simply censoring them with a spearlike dash, so that they might better seem to refer to real people. As Moll declares in the very first line of the novel:

> My true name is so well known in the records or registers at Newgate, and in the Old Bailey, and there are some things of such consequence still depending there, relating

---

* Or, to give its full title, *The Fortunes & Misfortunes of the Famous Moll Flanders &c. Who was Born in Newgate, and during a Life of continu'd Variety for Threescore Years, besides her Childhood, was Twelve Year a Whore, five times a Wife (whereof once to her own Brother), Twelve Year a Thief, Eight Year a Transported Felon in Virginia, at last grew Rich, liv'd Honest, and dies a Penitent.*[44] And to think I argued for a shorter subtitle for *Shady Characters*.

> to my particular conduct, that it is not be expected I
> should set my name or the account of my family to this
> work[.][47]

Later, when Moll's mother explains to her the true disposition of some of the seeming gentlefolk at large in Virginia, Defoe makes reference to the brands received in punishment for past crimes and redacts the names of the branded as if to avoid offense:[48]

> "You need not think a thing strange, daughter, for as I told
> you, some of the best men in this country are burnt in the
> hand, and they are not ashamed to own it. There's Major
> ———," says she, "he was an eminent pickpocket; there's
> Justice Ba——r, was a shoplifter, and both of them were
> burnt in the hand; and I could name you several such as
> they are."[49]

When Samuel Richardson published *Pamela; or, Virtue Rewarded* in 1740, he chose to frame his narrative as a series of letters from the virginal Pamela Andrews to her God-fearing parents. The preternatural eloquence and copious free time possessed by this fifteen-year-old housemaid notwithstanding, *Pamela*'s epistolary form was intended to heighten the novel's realism, presenting the characters' subjective experiences directly to the reader without the distorting lens of a narrator.[50] For all this grandeur of vision, though, Richardson was not above employing the dash when discussing Pamela's lecherous suitor Mr. B——, implying that for such importunate advances to become public knowledge would surely have ruined the reputation of any real-life gentleman.[51]

Ellipsis by way of dashes continued to pepper eighteenth- and nineteenth-century fiction of all genres. Jane Austen saw fit to hide the name of the "———shire regiment," from which the rakish Mr.

Wickham elopes with Lydia Bennet, and Robert Louis Stevenson sought to lend *Treasure Island* an air of documentary reality by stating only that the adventure took place in "17——" and declining to give the longitude and latitude of the island in question.[52]

Throughout this period the desire for realism was tempered by strict attitudes toward blasphemy and cursing, and much as a character might wish to d—— someone to h——, writers and publishers could not afford to offend the reading public. Again, such modesty was in evidence well before the Victorians began cinching their moral corsets, as shown in 1751's *Adventures of Peregrine Pickle* by the Scottish author Tobias Smollett. The foulmouthed pronouncements of Peregrine's guardian, Commodore Hawser Trunnion, required judicious deployment of dashes:

> They make a d—d noise about this engagement with the
> French: but, egad! it was no more than a bumboat battle,
> in comparison with some that I have seen. There was old
> Rook and Jennings, and another whom I'll be d—d before
> I name, that knew what fighting was.[53]

Just as Trunnion will "be d—d" before he names the third man, Smollett will be d—d before he dares write the word "damned" itself. Anthony Trollope's epic account of *The Way We Live Now*—"now" being 1875, in the midst of a series of financial scandals—serves as a more typically Victorian example, and as such Trollope's bombastic financier Augustus Melmotte often finds his exclamations softened by censorious dashes in the same way ("The d—— you do!").[54]

By 1878, the librettist W. S. Gilbert (more famous as one half of Gilbert and Sullivan) could poke fun at the increasingly euphemistic use of "d——" for "damn," and had the captain of HMS *Pinafore* sing, "Bad language or abuse, / I never, never use [...] I never use the big, big D."[55] The use of the dash as a stand-in for various profanities was so common, in fact, that the word "dash" became a mild epithet in its own right; by 1883 the cumbersomely named Lord Ronald Charles Sutherland-Leveson-Gower, a member of Parliament, historian, and sculptor, could write in his *Reminiscences*, "Who the Dash is this person whom none of us know? and what the Dash does he do here?"[56] The dash had transcended punctuation.

* * *

While Richardson, Defoe, and other novelists were striking out words in the name of art, for certain other eighteenth-century writers the dash was less a literary device than a get-out-of-jail-free card. In 1737, a young journalist named Samuel Johnson joined London's monthly *Gentleman's Magazine*. Among his duties, Johnson was required to report on parliamentary proceedings, but herein lay a problem. Reporting "any votes or proceedings of the House" was illegal while Parliament was in session, though it was generally tolerated during the summer recess, when Johnson would reconstruct debates from notes taken by a cadre of reporters in the public gallery. Then, in 1738, all reporting was banned outright.[57]

Determined to circumvent the ruling, the magazine's proprietor, Edward Cave, directed Johnson to take his already part-fictional approach to its logical conclusion: Cave extracted summaries of important debates and the names of those involved from the door-keepers to the House of Commons, from which Johnson fabricated accounts of those debates. Publishing them as "Debates in the Senate of Great Lilliput"—Lilliput being the fictional land of tiny people described in Jonathan Swift's 1726 satire *Gulliver's Travels*—Johnson created Swiftian pseudonyms for the politicians and institutions involved.[58] Prime Minister Robert Walpole became "Walelop" and Lord Halifax "Haxilaf"; members of the Commons were "Clinabs"

To Mr URBAN, on his VOL. XI.

Prodesse & delectare.   *Omne tulit punctum, qui miscuit utile dulci.*

WHILE pleas'd thy length'ning Labour I peruse,
Accept this Tribute from the grateful Muse,
Who reads thy Page with still enamour'd sight,
And mixes mental *Profit* and *Delight.*

To plan with Judgment, and collect with Skill,
And one fair Whole with due Proportion fill;
With Truth to form the Mind, with Sense, to please,
Is not (however thought) a Work of Ease.

Thus rightly modell'd, thy instructive Page,
Or to improve the Reader, or engage,
On Learning's Basis fix'd, securely stands,
And monthly fills unnumber'd---wishing Hands.

When *Lilliputian* Patriots warm debate,
We see the Model of our *Free born* State;
Where *Reason* draws the Sword in *Truth's* Defence,
And *Liberty* is the Result of *Sense;*
Hear how A..G...LE.. in Independence strong
Pours the full Tide of Eloquence along!
Born in the Camp or Senate to excel,
In acting greatly, or in speaking well.
There C...T...P..E L..Y with attick Spirit shines,
And Dignity with sprightly Ease conjoins;
C...RT...T in Courts experienc'd long, sedate
Marks the impending Dangers of the State;
As the calm *Pilot* o'er the dubious Wave,
Forebodes the Storm,---- and stands prepar'd to save.
Honour from H---L---F---x new Worth receives,
And all the *Englishman* in B--TH--RST lives.
C---R E--- x asserts his long illustrious Name,
And T---L---E--'s patriot Bosom pants for Fame.
Not bolder breaks the Thunder from on high,
Than P..LT N--Y breathes the Voice of Liberty.
In B--EN--D blameless *Cato* lives confest,
Shines in his Speech, and animates his Breast;
And L-TT-L-N in Virtue's early Hour,
Begins to be---what *Wyndham* was before,
To Language, *these,* its noblest use impart,
And mend the Judgment---while they move the Heart.

Nor wants (to own the Truth) the pow'rful Court
Firm Advocates her Measures to support.
N-c--LE speaks with senatorial Grace.
And H--v-Y's solemn Periods sooth to Peace,
H-R DW-K's distinctive Pow'rs to these belong,
The Wit of Hor-E, with the Flow of Y-NGE.

C..H..LM..LY's impartial Views by Honour led,
And H..NT..N's Thought, in classic Learning read,
By W...NN..NGT...N the *Call to Order* spoke,
The Skill of P--H--M, and the Strength of C..K.E;
But chief *His* envied *Energy of Thought,*
Who never *spoke* (at least) but *as he ought.* †

Nor less, selected with judicious Care,
Thy Essays grave or gay amuse the Ear.
All Ranks, all Tempers Entertainment find,
Such Charms has Novelty with Truth combin'd.

But most (for most the Muse like Addison delight)
Thy tuneful Numbers tempt my eager Sight.
Pleas'd I behold a thousand Beauties shine,
And new Improvements grace thy fair Design,
While bright *Eliza* strikes the warbling strings,
What Heart but softens as the Seraph sings?
Or when afflicted *Caroline* complains,
E'en Pity listens at the melting Strains.
Not fonder mourns the Turtle for its Dove,
Than tender *Emma* wails her absent Love;
Those shew how Learning, join'd to Beauty, fools
The Pride of Man and Pedantry of Schools.

When *Chester* tunes th' *Anacreontic* Lyre,
The sportive Graces waken gay Desire;
Nor can he cheat us in a borrow'd Name;
We feel the Sun, tho' clouded, by his Flame.
If *Grenville* sage, produce th' instructive Plan,
And bid the reasoning Brute, direct the Man,
Improv'd we listen to the moral Tale,
"For oft Examples more, where Precepts fail
Savage with native Dignity can charm,
Oh may his Verse its int'r Inspirer warm!
These conscious feel the true poetic Flame,
Know to excel;---and brighten into Fame!
Nor yield thy moral Poems less Delight,
FRIENDSHIP * revives, and * POVERTY grows bright.
Nor blame the Muse---who views thy growing store,
If, prudent, she forbear to mention more;
'One Train of Light the *Gallaxy* appears,
'Tis Knowledge only shews it made of Stars.

Proceed successful then, each rolling Year
With added Excellence adorn'd appear;
All Malice scorn, all Artifice defy,
And see new Rivals, in Oblivion die.

† FARI QUÆ SENTIAT, Sir *Rob. Walpole's* Motto.
* Two Pieces sign'd Y, by the same Hand with those sign'd *Alcæus.*

Figure 8.3   The poem that opened the December 1741 issue of *The Gentleman's Magazine.* The names of contemporaneous political figures are obscured by a smattering of em dashes, en dashes, and periods. *Gentleman's Magazine,* December 1741. SC 1490. Courtesy of Edinburgh University Library, Special Collections Department.

and the Lords were "Hurgoes."[59] Incredibly, this blatant flouting of the law seemed to pass unnoticed by the authorities; at the very least, it was sufficiently tolerated that in 1741 Cave published a poem linking the magazine's Lilliputian proceedings to the lightly disguised names of prominent politicians.[60] Explaining that

> When *Lilliputian* Patriots warm debate,
> We see the Model of our *Free born* State;[61]

The poem continues in a cavalcade of ellipsis: "C...st...f...eld," "H—l—f—x," "P––ltn––y" and many others are pseudo–name–checked. The real-life personages of the Earl of Chesterfield, Lord Halifax, and the MP William Pulteney must have been galled by the magazine's impertinence.

Samuel Johnson continued his Lilliputian antics for *Gentleman's Magazine* until 1744, though as entertaining as his parliamentary reporting was he is now better remembered as Dr. Johnson, author of the renowned 1755 *Dictionary of the English Language*.[62] And despite having had Johnson's words put in his mouth for years on end, the earl of C...st...f...eld still had the goodwill to act as Johnson's patron (perhaps by way of revenge, he contributed rather more moral than financial support) during the dictionary's protracted, nine-year compilation.[63] The ban on parliamentary reporting was finally lifted in 1771, and with that, the dash's role as a rebel mark of punctuation striking at the heart of the British establishment was over.[64]

* * *

The painstakingly typeset commashes, colashes, semi-colashes, and censored w——s that characterized pre–twentieth century literature were dealt a cruel blow by the onward march of technology. The arrival of Christopher Latham Sholes's typewriter in the late

1860s sent shockwaves through the worlds of writing, office work, and publishing, counting Samuel Clemens and Friedrich Nietzsche among its early adopters, but trouble arrived along with it.[65] The limited set of characters that the typewriter could reproduce forced the "Great Typewriter Squeeze," as one blogger called it, the mass extinction of punctuation and other glyphs that accompanied the coming of the "machine to supersede the pen."[66] The typewriter would make a hash of the dash.

As mentioned previously, Sholes's original pianolike keyboard had room only for uppercase letters, the numbers 2–9, and a few non-alphanumeric marks—including one that bore more than a passing resemblance to the dash.* Although this might seem unremarkable, other marks, even those as essential to modern English as the apostrophe, colon, and exclamation mark had to wait years or even decades to finally gain permanent places on the typewriter keyboard.[67] The exclamation mark, for instance, was absent from both the original 1868 keyboard and the improved 1878 QWERTY layout, and typists had to construct them by typing a period, a backspace, and finally an apostrophe (!).[68] Dedicated exclamation-point keys were such a rarity, in fact, that *The Secretary's Manual* of 1973 still described how to construct them manually.[69]

The dashlike character that muscled its way onto the typewriter keyboard was, however, neither fish nor fowl. Sholes's nameless hyphen/dash/minus sign (-) had to carry the load for the em, en, figure, and quotation dashes and all their visual relatives. Typographic propriety had suffered an ignominious blow: from a suite of dashes for every occasion, writers were reduced to using and reusing this single character wherever any faintly dashlike symbol might ordinarily have appeared.

---

* See chapter 5, "The @ Symbol," for more on Sholes's original keyboard. See also chapter 2, "The Interrobang (‽)," for more on the typewriter's role in the interrobang's difficult birth.

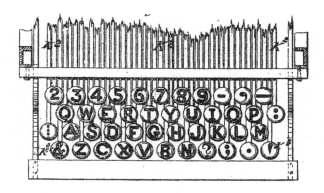

Figure 8.4   An illustration of an early QWERTY keyboard taken from Sholes's 1878 patent, with the hyphen-minus character third from the right on the top row. The dashlike character at top-right is actually an underscore.[70]

Still, though, typists adapted. Even before the nineteenth century was out, Isaac Pitman, inventor of Pitman shorthand, proponent of phonetic spelling, and a steadfastly unsentimental sort of chap, declared that a single, spaced hyphen - or preferably, two unspaced hyphens--would serve perfectly well in place of the absent em dash.[71] The practice was not universally admired: the dime novelist William Wallace Cook was one early voice of protest, writing in 1912 that he considered it "poor policy" to be forced into using two hyphens where an em dash should rightly be placed.[72]

Despite Cook's misgivings, Pitman's shortcut was persistent. The double hyphen became a familiar sight in typewritten documents, and though printers could still call upon a full complement of dashes, the occasional double hyphen sometimes slipped past an inattentive compositor to end up in print.[73] In one particular niche, the -- succeeded in displacing even handwritten dashes; among its many conventions, comic-book dialogue exclusively employs the double hyphen in preference to the dash.[74] Todd Klein, a comic-book letterer and logo designer, suggests that the change from dash to double hyphen occurred when writers moved from longhand to typewriters; though the letterers still inked their speech bubbles by hand, they were reading from typewritten scripts exhibiting all the quirks and limitations of that medium.[75]

Neglected for decades in everyday writing, the dash was treated little better by the digital computer. Freed from the fetters of the typewriter's mechanical keyboard, the gatekeepers of 1963's ASCII character set could not find space among their positively roomy set of 128 glyphs for more than a single dash or dashlike character.[76] The

Figure 8.5   A double hyphen stands in for an em dash in comic-book lettering. Taken from *Cerebex*, Planet Comics number 73 (1953). (Spoiler alert: Cerebex the "electronic brain" goes wild and is finally defeated by a wooden robot immune to Cerebex's powerful magnetic field.)

typewriter's ugly hyphen/en dash/minus chimera was adopted as the one-size-fits-all "hyphen-minus," and the em dash, en dash, hyphen, and so on, were shut out.[77] Even now, the hyphen key on your computer keyboard is not a hyphen at all but rather a hyphen-minus: Christopher Latham Sholes's cuckoo still lurks in the nest of the true dash.[78]

* * *

Finally, though, attitudes may be shifting against the stubby hyphen-minus and the havoc it has wreaked on grammar and typography for more than a century. Granted, the double hyphen is still acknowledged as an occasional necessity in *The Chicago Manual of Style*, but the *Oxford Style Manual* has turned away from such crude approximations for proper punctuation.[79] Finding the appropriate *real* dash is made easier now that Unicode, the modern successor to ASCII, has a robust set of no fewer than twenty-three dashes serving the Latin alphabet and other scripts, and most modern word-processing software will silently insert en and em dashes where once the hyphen-minus ran riot.[80] And fittingly for this online world where everyone is a publisher of sorts, William Wallace Cook's crusade against the double hyphen has been renewed by the authors of web design magazines and desktop-publishing books who inveigh against lazy, hyphen-minus–ridden type.[81]

Both plain dashes and Nicolson Baker's dashtards are currently undergoing a quiet literary revival, if largely in an arch fashion. In parodying the literary tropes of earlier works, postmodern writers such as Thomas Pynchon and John Barth have taken up dashes and dash hybrids as the perfect emblems of times past. Barth's "metafictional" story *Lost in the Funhouse*, which mixes narrative and explicatory asides in a single flow of text, deploys and explains the dash almost within the same breath:

> *En route* to Ocean City [Ambrose] sat in the back seat
> of the family car with his brother Peter, age fifteen, and
> Magda G —, age fourteen, a pretty girl and exquisite
> young lady, who lived not far from them on B — Street in
> the town of D —, Maryland. Initials, blanks, or both were
> often substituted for proper names in nineteenth-century
> fiction to enhance the illusion of reality.[82]

Thomas Pynchon's 1997 novel *Mason & Dixon*, on the other hand, a fantastical account of the eponymous survey, is a loving pastiche of nineteenth-century literature that positively brims with dash hybrids. If the quantity of dashes seen in the wild is any indication of its future survival, Pynchon may have singlehandedly removed it from the list of endangered marks of punctuation.[83]

Chapter 9 ❧ The Manicule

I n paleography, the study of ancient writing, the disembodied hand ☞
hanging proudly to the right of this sentence is called a manicule.
Though it jars a little here, blotting the pristine margin like a ketchup
stain on a white shirt, in ages past a page without a manicule would
have been thought a barren place indeed.

The key to the manicule—the thing that sets it apart from the letters, numbers, and punctuation that make up the contents of today's
average page—is its conspicuous anthropomorphism. It is difficult to
disguise a pointing hand as anything else, and that is precisely what
the manicule represented in the late medieval period. It depicted the
reader's hand on the page, a freeze-framed projection of the index
finger following the eye as it lingered on a passage of interest or flicked
back and forth between a marginal note and the text itself.

Weathering the transition to hot metal type with barely a break
in its stride, manicules continued to grace the margins of book for
hundreds of years afterward. Yet like so many other marks of punctuation, the arrival of printing heralded its ultimate downfall, and today
it is regarded as a typographic novelty to be trotted out for pieces
requiring a certain period flavor. In his 2005 essay "Towards a History
of the Manicule"—the publication of which earned him the mantle of
the manicule's sole historian—Professor William H. Sherman of York
University noted that "between at least the twelfth and eighteenth
centuries, [the manicule] may have been the most common symbol
produced both for and by readers in the margins of manuscripts and

printed books."[1] Only two centuries later the manicule is almost nowhere to be seen: its fall has been precipitous indeed.

* * *

Unlike most marks of punctuation, which circulate amongst a writer's words, the manicule's story is intimately bound to the reader's practice of annotating books. Scholars and critics have been annotating texts for thousands of years, though the papyrus scrolls on which ancient works were written left little room for substantial notes. More often than not, such *scholia* were collected into entirely separate works that required cumbersome cross-referencing between original texts and their commentaries. And it was all too easy to find oneself with mismatching editions.[2]

Then, around the fourth century, the growing popularity of a disruptive new vehicle for the written word made note-taking a more practical proposition. The *codex*, or book, made of robust pages of animal-hide parchment bound between protective wooden boards, was accessible and portable where the papyrus scroll was fragile and cumbersome.[3] The book's paginated format also allowed for the provision of generous margins, and after a faltering start in Roman law books of the fourth to sixth centuries, the addition of marginal notes grew more and more widespread until it was a rare-indeed book that was not embroidered by a reader's scrawl.[4] This historical penchant for note-taking peaked during the Renaissance, but to understand *why* it was so prevalent it is first necessary to understand how differently books were viewed in that era.

Book purchasing and book ownership in the twenty-first century—the stewardship, so to speak, of a copy of a written work—is almost effortless. Physical books are a mouse click away, borne to our doors by next-day delivery, and are so cheap they invite a lackadaisical approach to book care: dog-earing a page in lieu of a bookmark or lending a paperback to an unreliable friend are part and parcel of modern book ownership. E-books are even less demanding, available to read after the briefest of download intervals and impossible to mistreat; you may drop your iPad or sit on your Kindle, but your library will still be safe and pristine in the ethereal Internet "cloud."[*]

The situation in the Renaissance was somewhat different. Even compared with the twentieth-century ritual of visiting a bookshop, plucking a book from the shelf, and leafing through it, the purchasing process that confronted a typical book buyer of the fourteenth century was laborious and time consuming. Books were not so much bought as project-managed into existence.

Before a "book" could even be considered to exist as such, a buyer first had to choose the material it should hold. Manuscripts were often supplied unbound, and a single bound volume might contain two or more unrelated works.[6] Depending on the era, Shakespeare could be found alongside a religious work, or a calendar juxtaposed with an encyclopedia, and in one noteworthy example of "remixing," a sixteenth-century poet had another author's work bound into his notebook so that he could interweave original and cribbed lines.[7] Even the preparation of the manuscript itself might fall within the purview of the book buyer; in some cases, institutional customers such as universities and monasteries would procure the requisite supplies of parchment or paper and contract scribes to copy out the pages that were to be bound.[8] With the contents of a volume thus assembled, the purchaser might next have them embellished by a rubricator or illuminated by an illustrator. Only then, finally, would a binder be

---

[*] Safe, that is, until your e-book provider remotely deletes your copy of George Orwell's *Nineteen Eighty-Four* in an almost impossibly ironic act of copyright enforcement.[5]

contracted to finish the book according to the buyer's taste—adding a family crest to the cover, perhaps, or selecting a color scheme to match other volumes in his library.[9]

Books produced in this manner were eye-wateringly expensive. Even the rudely bound, cut-price editions of theological and philosophical tracts produced for universities were far beyond the reach of the average student.[10] In an echo of the earlier culture of the monastic scriptorium, such impoverished students would sometimes rent the original *exemplar* of a book and copy it out by hand.[11]

Having thus shepherded a book through its creation—selecting its contents, directing its illumination and binding; perhaps even having painstakingly copied it out in the first place—and having spent a princely sum in doing so, the Renaissance reader was invested in their book in a way quite unlike the modern consumer. It was second nature for a book's owner to brand it, to annotate and embellish it as they read; to underline pithy phrases and fill the margins with notes.[12] The imperative to take notes as one read moved the seventeenth-century Jesuit scholar Jeremias Drexel to write that "reading is useless, vain and silly when no writing is involved, unless you are reading [devotionally] Thomas a Kempis or some such. Although I would not want even that kind of reading to be devoid of all note-taking."[13]

With the note-taker's canvas in place, schemes emerged for how best to organize copious marginal annotations. One early attempt came courtesy of Robert Grosseteste, the renowned thirteenth-century bishop of Lincoln whose French nickname of "big head" came from "the greatness of his head, having large stowage to receive, and store of brains to fill it."[14] Sometime between 1235 and 1243 Grosseteste devised and documented a system of four hundred signs, consisting of the letters of the Greek and Roman alphabets and a battery of attendant symbols, which he used to index related subjects in the Bible.[15] Unfortunately, his capacious head was not quite big enough to

Figure 9.1   A thirteenth-century text annotated using some of
Robert Grosseteste's numerous symbols of reference.

make it work: he found his system too complex for sustained use, and
in later works went back to more traditional note-taking techniques.[16]

Later, Erasmus, the influential fifteenth-century Christian scholar
whose writings informed the Protestant Reformation, put forward a

more realistic suggestion.[17] He opined that the conscientious reader should "observe occurrences of striking words, archaic or novel diction, cleverly contrived or well adapted arguments, brilliant flashes of style, adages, example, and pithy remarks worth memorizing," and that "such passages should be marked by an appropriate little sign."[18] Erasmus left the choice of this "appropriate little sign" to his readers, and overwhelmingly, they chose the manicule.

* * *

U nlike the pilcrow, which wended its way from *K* for *kaput* to the more familiar ¶ over a millennium, or the octothorpe, which metamorphosed from "lb" to ℔ and then #, the manicule's bluntly representational form has remained nearly unchanged since its earliest reported instances. Once, there were no manicules; then, springing fully formed into existence, there they were.

The earliest attested manicules appeared in the *Domesday Book,* the exhaustive survey of England carried out for William I in 1086.[19] The "Winchester Roll" or "King's Roll," as it was called at first, was intended to be an authoritative record of land ownership—a "doomsday" judgment from which no deviation would be brooked, occasioning the book's later nickname.[20] Frustratingly, the only direct reference to the manicules used in this nine-hundred-year-old document is a brief aside in a rambling 1824 treatise on the art of *Typographia.* Its author, John Johnson, lists "☞" (no name is given) alongside other "marginal references" such as the Maltese cross (✠), the ancient Greek *asteriskos* (※), the dagger (†), and a bevy of apparently abstract geometric symbols, then dismissively writes that these inscrutable marks "in most instances explain themselves."[21] He says no more on the subject.

The manicule next surfaced in the twelfth century, though solid facts about its use in this period are thin. Geoffrey Ashall Glaister's comprehensive *Encyclopedia of the Book* describes the symbol as the "digit," and alleges that it was "found in early twelfth century (Spanish) manuscripts."[22] As with Johnson's dismissal of the *Domesday Book*'s "self-explanatory" reference marks, Glaister's factoid is dashed off with no corroboration (this author has come across at least one twelfth-century English book displaying a manicule, as seen in Figure 9.2), and detailed information about this early chapter of the manicule's life remains tantalizingly out of reach.[23]

Starting in the fourteenth century, life in Europe began to shift away from medieval norms. New trade routes to the Orient and

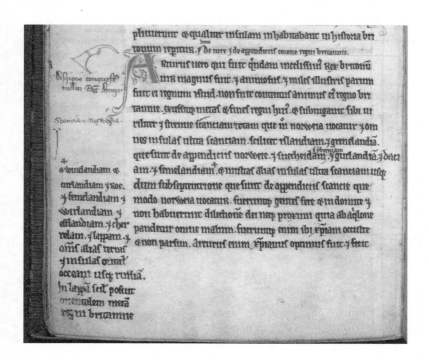

Figure 9.2　A twelfth-century English text, *Leges angliae* (Laws of England), decorated with a manicule. Also noteworthy here are two cross-shaped asterisks linking a marginal note with the main text, and the numerous Tironian *ets* scattered throughout.

the assimilation of Arabian trading practices broadened Western horizons, while the fusty ranks of monks and theologians who had dominated academic study for centuries gave way to a new breed of "humanists" emanating from Florence, Naples, and other wealthy Italian city-states, and who concerned themselves with matters of earthly rather than divine import.[24] In 1453, this flowering of intellectual life intersected with two seismic political events felt across the Continent: Constantinople fell to the ascendant Ottoman Turks, sending a stream of Greek scholars and ancient texts to the West, and the cessation of the Anglo-French Hundred Years' War brought peace—if only a temporary one—to northern Europe. The Renaissance was in full bloom, and by some definitions the modern world itself was at hand.[25]

Whatever its status had been in the murk of the eleventh and twelfth centuries, the manicule became a firm favorite of the Renaissance humanists. Commenting and building on classical works once derided as pagan frippery, for the next three hundred years, humanist scholars populated the margins of their Ciceros, law manuals, and notebooks with pointing hands drawn in a remarkable variety of styles.[26] The most basic were nothing more than fists with an index finger extended to indicate some word or line of interest, though the appearance of even these simple pointing hands varied according to the artistic gifts of their creators. The fourteenth-century Italian scholar Petrarch (often credited as the father of humanism) had the disconcerting habit of giving his manicules a thumb and *five* fingers, whereas a hundred years later, those of his countryman Bernardo Bembo* were the very model of anatomical accuracy.[29]

---

* Bernardo Bembo was the father of Cardinal Pietro Bembo, whose account of a journey to Mount Etna was published by the Venetian printer Aldus Manutius. Manutius commissioned his punchcutter, Francesco Griffo, to create a new type for the work; modern versions of the elegant, readable typeface Griffo designed for *De Aetna* are still in use today and are named Bembo after Manutius's eminent client.[27] Notably, Griffo also went on to cut the first italic letters, modeled on the handwriting of Niccolò Niccoli, an earlier Renaissance humanist.[28]

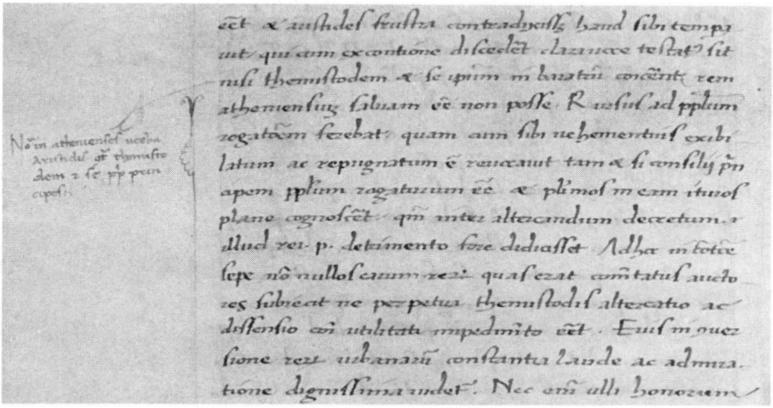

Figure 9.3   A manicule delicately links a marginal note to the main text in a fifteenth-century copy of Plutarch's *Six Lives*.

Some manicules terminated abruptly at the wrist, while others emerged from sleeves of varying sophistication to reveal, in turn, something of the fashions of their time.[30] Petrarch's flowing sleeves, for instance, gave way to delicate, lace-trimmed cuffs in later centuries, and continuing the trend, modern-day manicules often show the sober cuff of a suit-wearing businessman.[31] Cuffs and sleeves also provided convenient containers for notes on the pointed-to material, binding a note to its target text.[32]

If a reader's interest stretched to a few lines or a paragraph, a manicule's fingers could be elongated to bracket the required text; in some extreme cases, inky, snake-like fingers crawl and intertwine across entire pages to indicate and subdivide relevant text in a horror-film parody of the hand's physical form.[33] Very occasionally, manicules were not manicules at all; in one fourteenth-century Cicero (see Figure 9.4) a five-limbed octopus curls about a paragraph, and in a seventeenth-century treatise on the medicinal properties of plants, tiny penises point out discussions of the male genitalia.[34]

Figure 9.4   A reader takes a creative detour from the tradition of manicule as pointing hand. Taken from a copy of Cicero's *Paradoxa Stoicorum* from the fourteenth century.

Despite the familiarity and ease with which readers deployed manicules, the mark somehow contrived to go without a commonly accepted name for much of its life. In studying the symbol, William H. Sherman discovered no fewer than nine distinct terms by which it was known: in addition to Sherman's preferred "manicule," at one time or another the ☞ was called a "hand," "hand director," "pointing hand," "pointing finger," "pointer," "digit," "index," or "indicator."[35] "Indicule," "maniple," and "pilcrow" have also been bandied around as names for this severed mitt, though all three are incorrect: "indicule" is most likely a simple mishearing or conflation of "indicator" and "manicule," "maniple" denotes a handkerchief-like vestment sometimes worn by Catholic priests, and veteran punctuation-philes will no doubt perceive a simple case of mistaken identity behind the erroneous use of the word "pilcrow."[36]

This welter of competing aliases may stem from the intensely personal nature of the mark. Though the manicule was part of the furniture of the written page for centuries, it was not a mark of punctuation provided by the writer for the edification of the reader but a part of the apparatus of reading itself, a visual breadcrumb inked into the margin by and for one particular reader. The manicule placed to the right of this line may be of vital significance to me, for instance, ☜ but utterly unimportant to you; one reader's manicule is another's nuisance to be ignored, avoided, or removed. Indeed, some book collectors prefer to "restore" the cluttered margins of annotated books to their original, pristine cleanliness—or barren emptiness, according to your interpretation—and it may simply be that the manicule never warranted an agreed name.[37]

The term "manicule" itself, taken from the Latin *maniculum*, or "little hand," is only used of necessity; having granted the symbol a common name, paleographers can finally get on with investigating the many hands pointing the way through the margins of Renaissance life.[38]

* * *

Politically speaking, the world of the Renaissance was influenced in large part by events of the 1450s. The Hundred Years' War had barely ended before rival English royal houses plunged back into conflict in the War of the Roses; the Ottoman Empire conquered Constantinople and Athens, both former jewels of Western civilization, and at the heart of Europe the feuding Italian city-states whose artistic and intellectual endeavors defined the spirit of the age negotiated a peace that would last for forty years.[39] All this was as to nothing, however, when compared with the subtle earthquake emanating from Mainz in Germany, and Johannes Gutenberg's

Figure 9.5   One of Archbishop William Scheves's hand-drawn
manicules decorates a fifteenth-century printed book.

printing press would go on to shape the era more surely than any
battle, siege, or treaty.

The manicule weathered the movable-type revolution without
fuss: the orderly neatness of printed books failed to restrain readers
from jotting in their margins exactly as they had done in the past.
Readers such as William Scheves, a fifteenth-century archbishop of
St. Andrews, Scotland, were sufficiently unfazed by this innovative
technology to decorate margins with manicules as elaborate as they
had ever been, while works as lofty as the 1476 Bible published by the
prolific French printer Nicolas Jenson were not immune to similar
encroachments from the reader's pen.[40]

Significantly for a mark inextricably linked to readers rather than writers, the first printed manicules were not long to appear. In his 1942 book *Roman Numerals, Typographic Leaves and Pointing Hands* (one of the few studies, other than Sherman's *History of the Manicule*, to be at least partly dedicated to the symbol) Paul McPharlin describes a work printed in 1490 in which manicules placed in the text point to associated notes in the margin ☞.[41] This move from the wings to middle of the page is perhaps unsurprising—after all, were not countless other letters, numbers, and symbols now rendered in print?—but it proved to be the opening salvo in a battle for the soul of the manicule.

A tug-of-war between readers and writers ensued in the years after the manicule's first appearance in print. As discussed in chapter 6, "The Asterisk and Dagger (*, †)," the margin, once the reader's workspace and sketchbook, was gradually colonized by writers seeking to provide their own explanatory notes or commentaries.[43] Printed and hand-drawn manicules found themselves on opposite sides of the battle, each employed by a different camp to further its own agenda. Sherman points out one particular sixteenth-century work in which "the anonymous reader's manicules draw attention to a completely different set of passages than those marked by the printer's fists, and they sometimes face off across the gutter of a single opening."[44]

As if to emphasize the split with its traditional roots, the manicule gained new names specific to the printing industry. Though it retained its pointing index finger, the friendly "hand" became the sterner "fist" or "mutton fist"—old English slang for a "large coarse red fist."[45] (The evocative but elusive term "bishop's fist" may be apocryphal.)[46] And in contrast to the varied appearance of hand-drawn manicules, suffused as they were with the personality of their creators, printed manicules were sober, regular, and officious.

This is not to say that printed manicules were always indicative of intellectual rigor or professionalism on the part of a book's

In addition to his work on the history of books and printing, McPharlin was a well-regarded puppeteer. His contemporary and friend W. A. Dwiggins shared his love of both typography and puppetry, surely the first and last time in history where such a pairing of professions and personalities have coincided.[42]

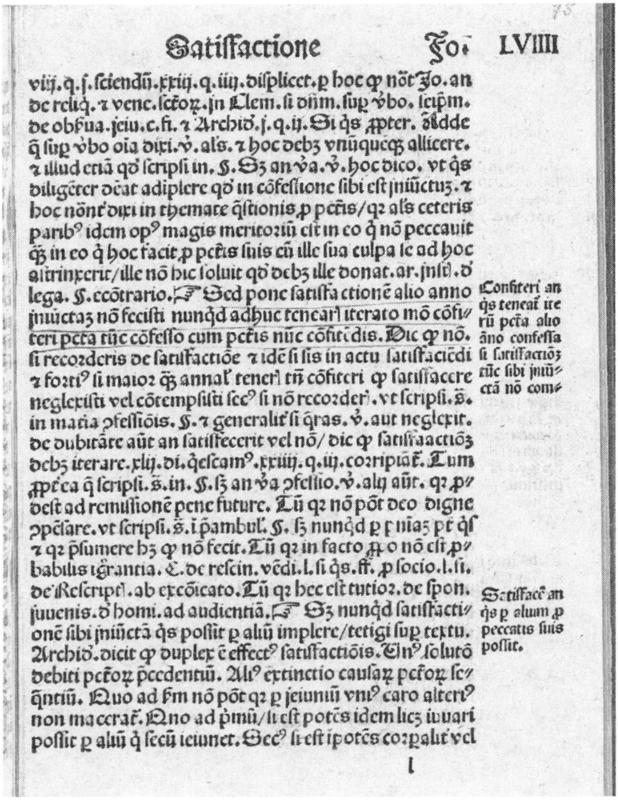

Figure 9.6   In-line printed manicules link marginal notes to words in the text. This is taken from a work printed by Albrecht Kunne in Memmingen in 1490 with the snappy title *Repetitio capituli "Omnis utriusque sexus" de poenitentiis et remissionibus*, or, roughly, "Lecture on the Canon 'Omnis utriusque sexus'; On [the Sacrament of] Penance and the Remission [of Sins]."

author or editor. In one farcical episode, the "Great Bible" commissioned by King Henry VIII of England—the Bible's first authorized English translation—had all the annotations struck from its second edition, leaving manicules stranded throughout the text ☞ without corresponding notes. A sheepish preface directed readers to seek pastoral help if they could not understand a passage thus marked.[47]

The printed manicule grew steadily more common as authors and publishers moved to protect the integrity of their work. In some cases the desire to guide readers to the "correct" interpretation of a work became an all-consuming passion: entire margins were sacrificed to notes that rammed home the official line, leaving little or no room for the reader's own critical judgments.[48] By the nineteenth century the hand-crafted manicule was out on its ear, pushed into irrelevance by its implacable printed counterpart.[49]

* * *

E ven as the spat between printed and hand-drawn manicules raged on in the margins, printers began to deploy their neatly cut fists outside their usual role as reference marks.

The so-called incunable period (from the Latin *incunabula*, for "cradle" or "swaddling clothes") that followed the arrival of printing saw a variety of experiments in book and page layout.[50] Perhaps the most jarring omission from early printed books was the lack of a proper title page: the closest analogous feature was the "colophon," a single leaf at the back of the book that described its provenance to a greater or lesser degree, including details such as its title, date and place of its printing—though curiously enough, almost never its author.[51] Over time the colophon was increasingly transposed to the front of the book to greet the reader as he or she opened it, and became in the process a playground for typographic experimentation. The haphazard contents of these early title pages could be surrounded by a decorative woodcut border or surmounted by an engraved illustration, but by the second half of the sixteenth century, printers had reached an unspoken accord that other than illustrations forming part of the work itself, the only characters to appear on their pages

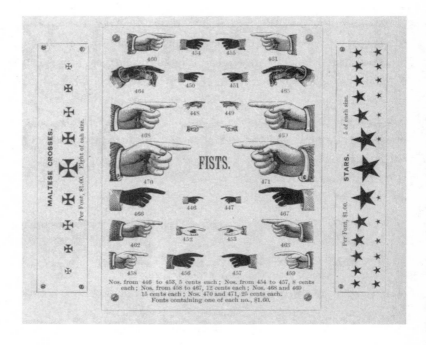

 Figure 9.7 A representative array of typographic fists and other ornaments, taken from an 1887 type specimen book.[53]

should be drawn straight from their type cases.[52] Thus it was that typographic ornaments, or "dingbats," as they are often now called, came into their own.

Leaflike "fleurons," from the Old French *floron*, or "flower," often embellished title pages or colophons, and indeed one of the oldest fleurons of all—the "hedera," or ivy leaf (❦), that appeared in some classical Greek texts—is still seen on occasion today.[54] Also popular were modular "arabesque" ornaments, derived from the abstract patterns of Islamic art and championed by the French type designer Robert Granjon, that could be placed together to form linear separators or repeating borders.[55] The fist proved a natural addition to the ranks of these typographic decorations, guiding the reader's eye to a work's title or an author's name:* the manicule had escaped its utilitarian roots and established itself as a versatile component of the printer's toolbox.[57]

Freed from the rigid responsibility of life as a reference mark, the manicule began turning up in an ever-wider variety of contexts. Thomas Bewick, a prominent engraver in the late eighteenth century, wrote in a letter about "the few sets I now have left on ☞," using the manicule to represent the word "hand" in the same way that modern writers might use @ for "at."[58] The historian C. W. Butterfield considered the symbol important enough for schoolchildren to be educated in its use, explaining in his 1858 textbook on *A Comprehensive System of Grammatical and Rhetorical Punctuation* that "The Index is inserted before a part which is very remarkable."[59] Manicules even appeared on nineteenth-century gravestones, pointing "electrically heavenward," as Paul McPharlin put it.[60]

The most prominent sign of the fist's mini-renaissance was its use as a staple of advertising typography, where it bracketed ☞ punch lines ☜ and pointed the way to concert venues, shops, and hotels.[61] In keeping with the voracious appetite of the new American consumer, as the nineteenth century progressed, the demands of advertising caused fists to grow larger and more elaborate. Where once a simple outline had sufficed, type foundries now supplied filled variants (☞) to match the increasingly heavy letterforms demanded of them, and the biggest manicules moved from hot metal to woodblock printing to avoid the uneven cooling and cracking that affected lead type at larger sizes.[62]

---

* Paul McPharlin was less than impressed with the manicule's admission into the ranks of typographic ornaments. He considered the fist to be "too provocative to serve in the background; no matter how it may be blended with fleurons, it still points, and worries one with its importunity."[56]

Ultimately, the manicule was the architect of its own demise. Familiarity breeds contempt, and the fist was everywhere in the advertisements, posters, direction signs, and newspapers of the time.[63] Just as nowadays the average Internet user subconsciously ignores sponsored hyperlinks—the so-called banner blindness dreaded by online advertisers—so the manicule's usefulness as an eye-catching device waned during the second half of the nineteenth century.[64] By the 1890s, the fist was used almost entirely in an ironic capacity; with consumers wise to the tricks of the trade, when printers reached into their type cases for a fist it was as a self-conscious revival of this once-ubiquitous symbol.[65]

* * *

The typographic manicule remains a rare beast in modern printed works, though its bid for freedom from the margins of books has seen it prosper in certain niches. The pointing fist as directional sign is a stock in trade for businesses wishing to affect a

Figure 9.8   A self-explanatory manicule directs patrons to a theater.

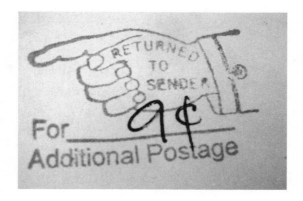

☞ *Figure 9.9* One of the USPS's many and varied "Return to Sender" stamps.

vintage air, whose signage and brochures are often littered with art-fully distressed manicules.*

Alternatively, the reader can catch sight of the manicule in another of its natural habitats by posting a letter carrying insufficient postage. In those parts of the USA that have not entirely automated the mail processing system, the United States Postal Service will brand the offending article with an accusatory red manicule before returning it to the sender.[66]

Passing out of the hands of the reader and into those of the writer, and subsequently leaping off the written page entirely, the manicule is one of the few marks to have risen above punctuation altogether: once synonymous with an existence in the margins, the manicule is in surprisingly good health.

---

* Such affectations are well documented at Flickr's engrossing Manicule group: http://www. flickr.com/groups/manicule/.

“”

Chapter 10 ❧ Quotation Marks

The quotation mark, or rather quotation marks (" "), since they never travel alone, is not the most glamorous of symbols. For the most part these acrobatic commas glide along serenely under the radar, marking out dialogue, signaling an ironic "scare quote," or signposting unfamiliar "terminology." They are paragons of unshowy functionality.

When the quotation mark *does* succeed in sparking debate, it attracts mild tut-tutting rather than genuine outrage. Though there is transatlantic disagreement over whether to enclose speech in 'single' or "double" quotes, for instance, it comes nowhere near the level of handwringing inspired by the semicolon, whose tricky usage has driven it almost to extinction.[1] Neither does the occasional unnecessary "use" of quotation marks induce the howling apoplexy provoked by a simple misplaced apostrophe: whereas one English council was driven to institute an apostrophe "swear box," café menu offers of "freshly baked 'bagels,'" "'fresh fish,'" and the like attract typically little more than a genteel ribbing.[2] Unlike the "Oxford," or serial, comma, quotation marks or "inverted commas" have never become a trending topic on Twitter, nor have they inspired a pop song in their name.[3]

Tellingly, even noted grammar stickler Lynne Truss cannot muster quite the same ire toward the quotation mark as she does for its companions the comma, semicolon, and so on. In addressing quotation marks, the grande dame of professional punctuational disparagement goes big in her opening, declaring that there is "a huge amount of ignorance concerning the use of quotation marks," but the few desultory pages that follow are as nothing compared with the entire chapters she devotes to the apostrophe and comma.[4] The quotation mark is quietly competent, thank you very much, and would like to be left alone to get on with things.

* * *

The germ of the modern quotation mark lies in a symbol that has lurked in the background throughout this book. Introduced at, yes, the Library of Alexandria, the *diple*, or "double" (>) was placed alongside a line to indicate some noteworthy text, while its dolled-up sibling, the *diple periestigmene* (≳), or "dotted diple," was used to mark passages where the scholar differed with the reading of other critics.[5]

Created by the proto-critic Aristarchus in the second century BC along with the asterisk and obelus,* and named for the two pen strokes used to form it, the *diple*'s pointed shape was at odds with its usage as a comparatively blunt instrument.[6] Used to indicate anything from an engaging turn of phrase to some notable historical incident, in some ways Aristarchus's angular mark was an ancient counterpart to the manicule, that other indicator of generic readerly interest.[7] But where a manicule often afforded insight into its creator's thoughts—a note on a billowing cuff, perhaps, or a few lines of text in the margin—the cryptic *diple* bore mute witness to whatever lay in the text.[8] There is something of interest here, the *diple* announced, but you must find it for yourself.

Even handicapped by this vague remit, the *diple* stuck, and though some ancient scribes overlooked it in favor of indenting or outdenting notable lines as they wrote, for centuries the *diple* remained the preeminent means of calling out important text.[9]

---

* See chapter 6, "The Asterisk and Dagger (*, †)," for more details on the asterisk and obelus and their creation at the Library of Alexandria.

Figure 10.1 A lone *diple* marks a line of interest in a papyrus scroll from the middle of the first century bearing a history of Sicily.

* * *

As valuable as Aristarchus's critical marks had been to the pagan Greeks, his tools of textual criticism were of even greater importance to the new Christian establishment. For it was no mere Homeric poetry that the "Fathers of the Church" sought to clarify

and disseminate but instead the words of God's Son and his greatest disciples, and thus it was that just as Origen had appropriated
the *asteriskos* and *obelos* for his exhaustive critical edition of the Old
Testament, so too the *diple* found renewed purpose in the service of
religion.[10] In the process, the *diple*'s once-expansive range of applications was honed to a fine point: under Christianity, the *diple* would
gain a meaning worthy of its form.

The volume of literature produced by and for Christians exploded,
along with the spread of the Church. Roughly one in fifty of all known
second-century Western manuscripts are of Christian origin, but by
the eighth century the ratio had risen to a staggering four out of every
five.[11] Authors praised, commented upon, and attacked one another's

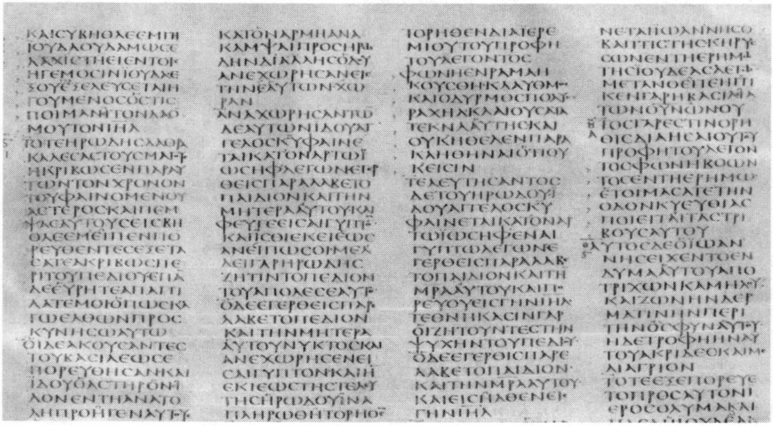

Figure 10.2   Diples in Matthew 2:6 of *Codex Sinaiticus*. Also visible
here are some of Aristophanes's points and accents. One of the most
important surviving early manuscripts, the fourth-century *Codex Sinaiticus*,
or "Sinai Book," is in essence the first complete Bible. Its constituent parts
are scattered among several of the world's major libraries.[12]

work, supporting their arguments by quoting the Bible—and what symbol could be more appropriate to the marking of this most noteworthy of texts, other than the familiar *diple*?[13] By the time Isidore of Seville came to write about punctuation in his seventh-century *Etymologies*, his description of the *diple* could be curt and unambiguous: "Our scribes place [the *diple*] in books of churchmen to separate or make clear the citations of Sacred Scriptures."[14] A very specific point indeed.

As in its earlier days, however, the *diple* was not the only method used to distinguish such scriptural quotations. Like the Bible itself, many theological works were passed down from generation to generation, and successive editions often displayed wildly different approaches to the same text. In about 590 AD, for instance, a grammarian named Dulcitius applied himself to editing a copy of Saint Augustine's *De Trinitate*, a Latin treatise on the triune nature of God.[15] Augustine's original fifth-century text had introduced quotations from the Bible with a verb of speaking (he wrote) but no punctuation; Dulcitius, on the other hand, employed *diples* to further distinguish quotations. Rendered in the unspaced capitals typical of the time, and terminated with a high point, Dulcitius presented the famous opening words of John 1:1 as follows:[16]

> \> HESAIDINTHEBEGINNINGTHERE
> WASTHEWORD·

The scribe of a different sixth-century copy of *De Trinitate*, meanwhile, challenged the unspaced tyranny of *scriptio continua* by quarantining quotations between letter-width gaps, with the *diple* nowhere to be seen:

> HESAYS IAMINTHEFATHERANDTHEFATHER
> INME[17]

Later, as *scriptio continua* finally yielded to spaces between words, a tenth-century edition of *De Trinitate* captured the transition in full flow. Written in a minuscule script and punctuated with a combination of embryonic word spacing and pointing, the same quotation was rendered:

> | hesays. iaminthefather &thefather inme˙[18]

A yet different approach to highlighting notable text can be seen in an eighth-century manuscript copied at the monastery of Wearmouth-Jarrow in the north of England. Quotations here were introduced not only by the traditional *diple* but were further distinguished by a different script: the main body of the text was composed in the lowercase, "insular" minuscules indigenous to the British Isles, whereas quotations were rendered in contrasting, uppercase uncial script.[19] The effect is to make quotations visually distinct from the original material; just as block quotations in modern books are set off by a different typographic treatment—indented, italicized, or smaller text, for example—so the scribes at Wearmouth-Jarrow were experimenting with analogous forms of information design more than a thousand years ago.[20]

Still other methods of marking quotations rose, prospered, and fell during the first millennium AD. The old Greek practice of insetting notable text was often used in early Latin manuscripts, for instance; some later scribes emphasized quotations by the simple expedient of underlining them, and still others wrote them in contrasting red ink.[21] On occasion the *diple* gave way to other signs fulfilling the same purpose: at various times and in different manuscripts, quotations could be indicated by a single or double dashlike mark in the margin (-, =), sometimes accessorized with dots like the ancient Greek lemniscus (÷) and hypolemniscus (∸).[22] These early Christian scholars may all

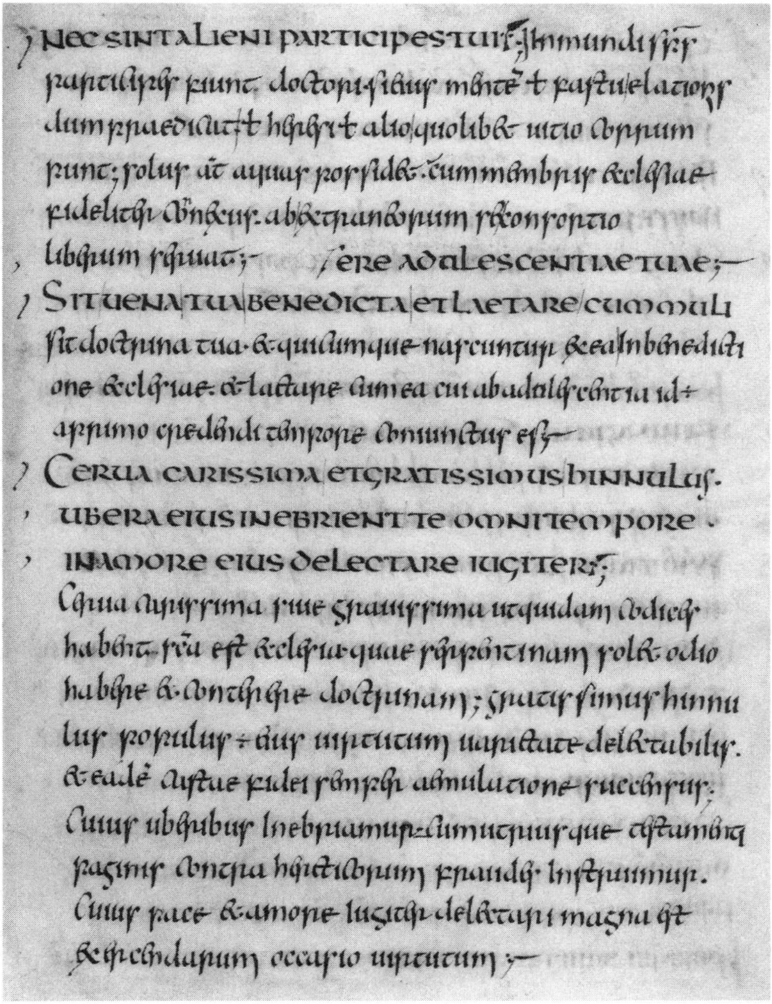

Figure 10.3 This manuscript, copied at Wearmouth-Jarrow in the first half of the eighth century, shows *diples* introducing new quotations. Quotations are in uppercase uncial, or "inch" script, and the original text is rendered in the "insular" minuscule script indigenous to the British Isles.

have been singing from the same hymn sheet, so to speak, but they could not agree on how to quote from it.

* * *

E ven within the swelling corpus of Christian writing, the *diple* occasionally took on roles beyond that of its traditional marker of Biblical quotations. In one fifth-century manuscript entitled *Apology Against Jerome*,* Rufinus of Aquileia berated his onetime friend and ally Saint Jerome for repudiating certain controversial beliefs earlier espoused by Origen (he of Hexapla fame), having previously supported them.²⁴ The precise details of this theological spat are beyond the scope of this book, but suffice it to say that then, as now, flip-flopping was not admired, and Rufinus was incensed by Jerome's self-serving changes of heart. Taking care to distinguish his own words from those of his craven opponent, Rufinus wrote in his introduction that

> in order that the insertions I am now making in this work
> from elsewhere may cause no confusion to the reader, they
> have single marks at the beginnings of the lines if they are
> mine and double ones if they are my opponent's.²⁵

The "mark" Rufinus spoke of was the *diple*, deployed singly or doubled up (>>) to distinguish between extracts from his own earlier works, and those of Jerome.²⁶ Though his was a Christian work, Rufinus's use of the *diple* was very much in the ancient, pagan Greek tradition,

---

* "Apologetics" usually referred to the intellectual defense of Christianity, but was also used in the titles of many works written to prosecute theological debates between rival Christian scholars and clerics.²³

even as he added a new layer of structure and meaning. In fact, those readers who recall the early days of the Internet may find Rufinus's doubled *diple* familiar; the "Usenet" system of online bulletin boards employed one or more right-pointing angle brackets (>, >>, >>>, and so on) at the start of quoted lines to indicate the level of the reply.[27] For instance:

```
>> Hello, how are you?
> I'm fine. How are you?
I'm also fine.
```

Though the *diple* kept its special place in Christian writing (and hence, in writing in general), it was buffeted over the centuries by successive quantum leaps in scribal practices. Latin succeeded Greek as the language of record in the West; papyrus scrolls gave way to parchment codices, and upstart minuscules muscled in on traditional majuscule scripts.[28] Against the background of this upheaval, the *diple* spawned an increasing variety of successors. In addition to the simple dashlike characters already occasionally used in its place, by degrees a series of "corrupt" or "debased" *diples* (to use the sniffy terminology of Patrick McGurk, a learned twentieth-century chronicler of early citation marks) began to appear in its stead. Some writers decorated the traditional > with a dot in the wedge between their pen strokes, while other manuscripts of French origin rotated this form to yield a V-shaped mark that cradled the dot in upraised arms. Similar to the gradual mutation of ℔ into #, or *et* into &, the arrowlike form of the *diple* itself gave rise to alternative symbols resembling the letters *s* and *r*, to curved marks suggesting the modern comma, and curiously, in Britain alone, to a distinctively Anglo-Saxon variant consisting of two dots and a commalike mark (..,).[29]

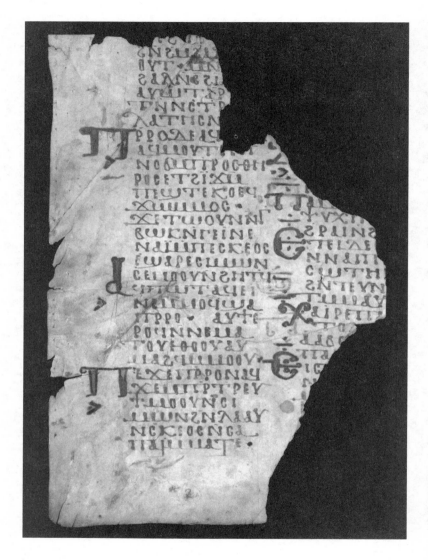

Figure 10.4　Dotted *diples* in an eighth-century psalter. Also visible in the margin of the right-hand column are a number of double dotted obeli, or lemnisci (÷).

By the close of the eighth century, the plain old > was nowhere to be seen, and for the next seven centuries manuscripts hosted a messy riot of imposters acting in its place. Only the arrival of printing could deliver the defibrillating jolt necessary to bring this ragtag army of "debased" *diples* into line.

* * *

Printing, as has been seen in previous chapters, fundamentally and permanently changed writing and punctuation. Time-consuming luxuries such as handpainted illustrations and rubricated marks of punctuation* fell victim to the economies of scale enabled by this new means of production.[30] The marking of quotations was affected too, and deeply so: Gutenberg's system of movable type made underlining and printing in colored ink time-consuming and imprac-tical; not to mention that early printers were curiously resistant to cutting punches for the *diple*'s divergent ranks of descendants.[31] Thus, the earliest printed books relied on a battery of temporary measures such as alternative typefaces and parentheses, along with nontypo-graphic methods such as verbs of speaking. Gutenberg's Bible itself did not graphically distinguish quotations at all.[32]

Then, at the start of the sixteenth century, the *diple* was effec-tively rebooted. The army of "corrupt" handwritten *diples* was replaced, en masse and essentially overnight, by simple double com-mas (,,).[33] Derived from the slanted virgule (/) and used to indicate a brief pause,† the comma was a relative newcomer to the manuscript tradition; its adoption by printers in lieu of the *diple* seems to be

---

* See chapter 1, "The Pilcrow (¶)," for more on the decline of the rubricated pilcrow in the face of the arrival of printing.
† See chapter 8, "The Dash (—)," for more on the virgule.

entirely without precedent, as if one day a printer reached into a
type case and pulled out the first mark that resembled a softened,
curved *diple*.[34]

Tentatively at first, but with increasing frequency and assertive-
ness, the double comma made itself indispensable to the new body of
printed work. Published in 1525, Bishop John Fisher's *Defensio Regie
Assertionis contra Babylonicam Capituitatem* (roughly, *Defense of the King's
Assertion Against the Babylonian Captivity*)—a short book with a long
title, and one written in the finest traditions of internecine theological squabbling—provides a snapshot of the comma's early appearance
and usage as a quotation mark.[35] Fisher's Luther-baiting screed hung
doubled commas in the margin to indicate lines that contained quoted
" text, though not precisely where that text began or ended. Unlike the
" inward-pointing *diple*, however, Fisher's commas were oriented so that
" they opened *toward* the text: commas in the outer margin of right-
" hand, or recto, pages were set as normal (,,), but those on left-hand,
" or verso, pages were rotated by 180 degrees (,,).[36] Though the name for
this practice would not be coined for another 250 years, the "inverted
comma" had been born.[37]

Despite the familiar appearance to modern readers of the quotation marks in *Defensio*, their usage was still in flux. Fisher used double
commas to indicate statements made by his opponent, Martin Luther,
but quotations from other sources—notably King Henry VIII, in
whose defense the book was written, not to mention scriptural and
other religious texts—received no special treatment other than a
parenthesized (*inquit*), or "he said."[38]

The precise vertical placement of these new quotation marks was
still to be sorted. Hung in the margin, Fisher's commas are not perfectly aligned with the main text and were probably added after it
had been set.[39]

Following *Defensio* by four years, the renowned French printer

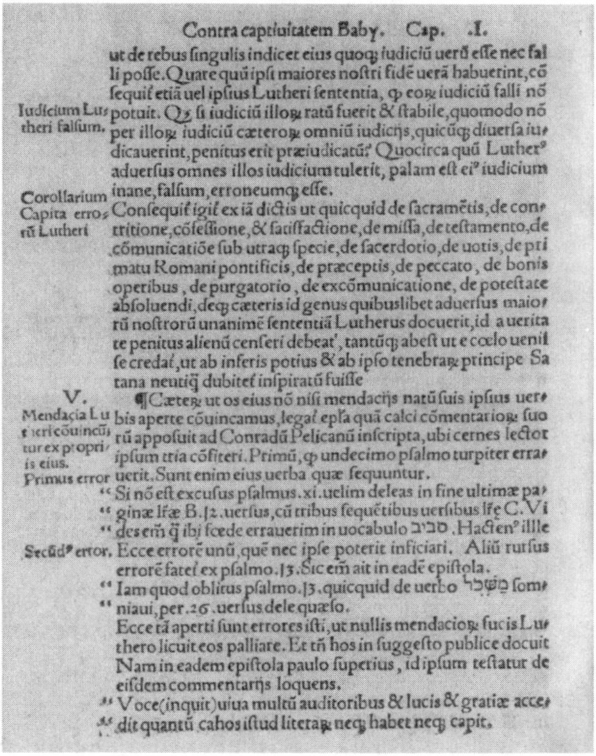
Contra captiuitatem Baby. Cap. .I.

ut de rebus singulis indicet eius quoq; iudiciū uerū esse nec fal li posse. Quare quū ipsi maiores nostri fidē uerā habuerint, cō sequit̄ etiā uel ipsius Lutheri sententia, q̄ eorū iudiciū falli nō potuit. Q̄ si iudiciū illorū ratū fuerit & stabile, quomodo nō per illorū iudiciū cæterorū omniū iudicijs, quicūq; diuersa iu dicauerint, penitus erit præiudicatū? Quocirca quū Luther⁹ aduersus omnes illos iudicium tulerit, palam est ei⁹ iudicium inane, falsum, erroneumq; esse.

Iudicium Lutheri falsum.

Corollarium

Capita errorū Lutheri

Consequit̄ igit̄ ex iā dictis ut quicquid de sacramētis, de con tritione, cōfessione, & satisfactione, de missa, de testamento, de cōmunicatiōe sub utraq; specie, de sacerdotio, de uotis, de pri matu Romani pontificis, de præceptis, de peccato, de bonis operibus, de purgatorio, de excōmunicatione, de potestate absoluendi, deq; cæteris id genus quibuslibet aduersus maio rū nostrorū unanimē sententiā Lutherus docuerit, id a uerita te penitus alienū censeri debeat, tantūq; abest ut e cœlo uenil se credat̄, ut ab inferis potius & ab ipso tenebrarū principe Sa tana neutiq̄ dubitet̄ inspiratū fuisse

V.

Mendacia Lutheri cōuincuntur ex proprijs eius.

¶ Cæterū ut os eius nō nisi mendacijs natū suis ipsius uer bis aperte cōuincamus, legat̄ ep̄la quā calci cōmentariorū suo rū apposuit ad Conradū Pelicanū inscripta, ubi cernes lector ipsum tria cōfiteri. Primū, q̄ undecimo psalmo turpiter erra uerit. Sunt enim eius uerba quæ sequuntur.

Primus error

“ Si nō est excusus psalmus .xi. uelim deleas in fine ultimæ pa
“ ginæ lr̄æ B.12. uersus, cū tribus sequētibus uersibus lr̄e C. Vi
“ des eīn q̄ ibi fœde errauerim in uocabulo סביב. Hactenꝰ illle

Secūdꝰ error.

Ecce errorē unū, quē nec ipse poterit inficiari. Aliū rursus errorē fatet̄ ex psalmo .13. Sic eīn ait in eadē epistola.
“ Iam quod oblitus psalmo .13. quicquid de uerbo מַשְׂכִּיל som
“ niaui, per .26. uersus dele quæso.
Ecce tā aperti sunt errores isti, ut nullis mendaciorū fucis Lu thero licuit eos palliare. Et tn̄ hos in suggesto publice docuit Nam in eadem epistola paulo superius, id ipsum testatur de eisdem commentarijs loquens.
“ Voce (inquit) uiua multū auditoribus & lucis & gratiæ acce
“ dit quantū cahos istud literarū neq; habet neq; capit.

☞ *Figure 10.5* A left-hand, or verso, page from John Fisher's 1525 *Defensio Regie Assertionis*, illustrating an early use of inverted commas as quotation marks. Commas placed in the outer margin of facing recto pages were not rotated. Note also the use of the pilcrow, which was used to open new sections.

Geoffroy Tory published a voluminous tract entitled *Champ Fleury* (literally "Field of Flowers," or, written as a single word, a French idiom for "Paradise") that illustrated some alternative solutions to the quotation quandaries facing early users of the mark.[40] *Champ Fleury* was both a typographic tour de force and an impassioned call for standards in language and writing, in which Tory held forth on the construction of letters in the newly revived roman style, on the use of accents as a guide to pronunciation, and on the apostrophe as a means of indicating omitted letters.[41] Like *Defensio*, quotations in *Champ Fleury* were marked with double commas, but the similarities ended there: unlike Fisher, Tory placed his quotation-commas in the inner margins to " avoid clashing with his frequent notes in the outer margins, and also " oriented them so that they opened *away* from the text as the *diple* had " done.[42] Not only that, but Tory quoted freely from classical authors; a sign of the new humanist world that was fast eroding the special status once enjoyed by scriptural and religious texts.[43]

* * *

The shifting of quotation marks from scriptural text to more general citations continued apace, and as the sixteenth century wore on, printers experimented with different methods of setting such material. The 1549 edition of *Champ Fleury*, for instance, rendered Latin quotations in italics, providing an opening for later texts to employ quotation marks *or* italics to indicate any text that their writers felt worthy of note.[44] The marking of "gnomic utterances or *sententiae*"*—weighty, proverbial, or otherwise notable aphorisms— was popular among readers and writers of the time; while writers could have *sententiae* rendered in italic type or called out by quotation marks, readers instead annotated them with symbols like the manicule or copied them into "commonplace books" for later refer-

---

* The Latin word *sententia* led to the English term "sententious," whose connotation of excessive self-importance comes from overuse of such "gnomic utterances."[45]

ence.[46] (The use of italics in particular has stuck, and nowadays a writer will italicize a word or words that are felt to be of particular importance.)[47]

At the same time, there was a growing awareness of the distinction between the different kinds of quotations a writer might employ. John Whitgift's deliriously titled 1574 book *The defense of the answere to the admonition against the reply by T*[homas] *C*[artwright] was stuffed with *sententiae*, general quotations, and points to be refuted, and gave each one a different typographic treatment—yet somehow, the book managed without quotation marks altogether. The author's words were set in blackletter and those of his opponents appeared in smaller blackletter script; Latin quotations were rendered in italic and their translations in roman, as were references to scripture.[48] Whitgift's pathological avoidance of the quotation mark was not unique: the first printed editions of Shakespeare's plays, published some years after *The defense against the answere*, also made do without quotation marks. Where one character repeated the words of another, either the Bard or his printers had seen fit to use a simple colon or comma to introduce the quotation.[49]

Then, near the end of the sixteenth century, quotation marks took two significant steps toward their modern form. First, inverted " commas moved from their splendid isolation in the margin into " the main body of the text itself, taking up positions at the leftmost " edge of each line in a quotation.[50] The second breakthrough came in 1574, when a book of cautionary poems called *The Mirour for Magistrates* first used quotation marks to indicate direct speech:

> " O queane (quoth shee) that cause of warres hast beene,
> " And deadly ate, the like was neuer seen.
> " Come on, for these my handes shall ridde thy life,
> " And take reuengement of our mortall strife[51]

Perhaps skeptical of the average reader's critical faculties, and unable to use the inverted comma in its *diple*-esque role of inviting especial attention to a line, the printers of the later 1587 edition took the precautionary measure of prefixing pithy nuggets of wisdom with five-pointed stars. On occasion, these typographic stars were in alignment with quotations of direct speech:

> " Bee faithfull all: as brethren ought agree :
> " For ★ concord keeps a Realme in stable stay:
> " But discord brings all kingdomes to decay.[52]

Unfortunately, the *Mirour*'s use of quotation marks in this way was a false dawn. The dizzying array of quotation marks, italics, and other typographic distinctions remained, with little sign of agreement on standard conventions of use.[53] Handwritten documents mirrored the indecision displayed by printed works: direct and reported speech might be signaled by any one of a number of competing techniques such as virgules, underlining, or verbs of speaking, with inverted commas largely reserved for sententious remarks.[54] The confused jungle of quotation methods had grown unruly once again.

* * *

When the inevitable pruning came, the impetus to standardize the use of quotation marks originated in the eighteenth century's newest form of literature, the novel. The same drive for realism that led Daniel Defoe, Henry Fielding, and Samuel Richardson to strike out identifying details with censorious em dashes* propelled

---

* See chapter 8, "The Dash (—)," for more on the use of the dash to enhance realism in early novels.

them away from the stilted, formal speeches that characterized earlier forms of fiction.[55] Eschewing paraphrased, reported speech filtered through a narrator, these new novelists presented readers with their characters' unvarnished words, and with this new directness came a need to separate speech from narration.[56]

Experimentation with new methods of setting dialogue accelerated. The 1765 edition of Defoe's *Moll Flanders*, for instance, indicated changes in speaker with paragraph breaks, though marginal inverted commas were retained for the occasional sententious quotation, which were also indented to further distinguish them from the body of the text.[57] The 1748 edition of Samuel Richardson's epistolary novel *Clarissa* also clung to traditional, per-line quotation marks when quoting from letters, though it made intermittent use of a new innovation: the opening quotation mark was sometimes placed at the exact point at which a quotation began, with a new "mark of silence," or closing quotation mark ("), accompanying it where the quotation ended.[58] For spoken dialogue, however, Richardson preferred to separate speakers with dashes or new lines.[59] The early part of the century also saw use of a technique that set the words of alternate speakers in roman and italic typefaces, while some works took the brute-force approach of simply presenting dialogue as stage play–like scripts, with each speaker's words introduced by their name.[60]

In all, the wayward scrum of previous centuries finally began to converge on a recognizably modern style. Richardson's practice of explicitly opening and closing quotations was gradually taken up in other works, and by the end of the eighteenth century, marginal quotation marks had largely been rendered obsolete.[61] Verbs of speaking retreated first to parentheses within the dialogue itself and were later ejected from quoted speech entirely to lie between two separate quotations, as demonstrated in *The History of Eliza Warwick,* an anonymous novel published in 1778:[62]

> 'Yes,' answered I, 'but I will soon follow you—your
> Huntley shall protect you in the unknown world you
> are launching into—he shall be your safeguard, your
> attendant, ever.' "No," cried she, with a firm voice, "no, I
> charge thee [...]"[63]

Eliza Warwick illustrates another decision that faced writers and printers—how best to employ single and double quotation marks. Double commas had become so prevalent that type foundries now habitually cast them on a single block of lead, halving the number of extra characters needed to set a quotation, but the manner in which these doubled commas related to their singular siblings was still up for grabs.[64] *Eliza Warwick*'s mysterious author—or perhaps its printers—used single and double quotes to differentiate between speakers in a dialogue, whereas *The Sorrows of the Heart*, another anonymously published work, used them instead to distinguish between direct and reported speech respectively.[65]

Finally, by the end of the eighteenth century, the growing pains of the double comma were largely past. Quotations were opened and closed by pairs of inverted commas, and the marginal marks that once "continued" quotations on to each new line were considered anachronistic.* A quotation spanning multiple paragraphs now opened each such paragraph with an additional pair of inverted commas, terminating with a single closing mark.[67] Single and double marks were used alternately to indicate direct and indirect speech (or vice versa, depending on national custom), and quotations in foreign languages

---

* This abandonment of per-line quotation marks may have led to the creation of the modern block quotation. Typography guru Robert Bringhurst suggests that some printers replaced marginal quotation marks with spaces to maintain a visual distinction with the main text, while the competing explanation is simply that indentation as an ancient means of quotation persisted into the modern era.[66] Little study has been done to support either viewpoint.

such as Latin were invariably set in italics.[68] The modern era of quotations was at hand—for English, at least.

* * *

P arallel to the rise of the English novel, Continental romances underwent the same transformation from ponderous formalism to dynamic realism; speechifying bombast became cut-and-thrust repartee, and French and German authors found themselves with the same need to improve the clarity of their dialogue.[69] French printers, though, did not settle for the expedient inverted comma: their *diple*-like guillemets (« ») echoed their ancient ancestry proudly.

Just as the reasons for the preeminence of the inverted comma remain elusive, the exact origin of the guillemet is equally uncertain. Some sources attribute the creation of the mark to one Guillaume Le Bé, a sixteenth-century punch cutter from Troyes, near Paris; as "guillemet" is the diminutive for "Guillaume," the character is said to have been named after its creator.[70] Unfortunately for this theory, Le Bé was born in 1525 and guillemets first appeared in 1527; it would have been a prodigious Little Willy indeed who had invented a new mark of punctuation at two years of age.[71] What *is* known for certain is that the mark, or at least something very like it, was described as early as 1540 by a French scholar and printer named Étienne Dolet, and that small, double parentheses of suspiciously guillemet-like appearance ((( ))) were cut by the renowned Claude Garamond sometime between 1530 and 1540.[72]

For the most part, European printers set quotations in the same range of methods as did their English counterparts, though some not without some gaudy detours en route. One modern scholar described a peculiar example of eighteenth century German typesetting " where „ opening, closing and marginal quotation marks are inverted commas, guillemets and gothic commas respectively. »⁷³ Despite the carnival of excess in this single work, on the whole German quotation practices were and remain relatively conservative. In modern texts, speech is enclosed with commas (though their placement and orientation differ from that of English works)—„thus"—or by spaced, inward pointing guillemets—» thus «.⁷⁴

Quoted speech in French texts, on the other hand, remains flamboyant, employing the dash as frequently as the guillemet and interspersing the two in a manner quite unfamiliar to Anglo-Saxon readers. Paradoxically, the early English novelist Samuel Richardson may be responsible for this state of affairs. His fondness for the dash as a means of separating alternate speakers was seized upon and promoted by a contemporary French literary theorist named Jean-François Marmontel.⁷⁵ Like German, basic speech in French is rendered using spaced guillemets, though they retain the outward-pointing orientation of English inverted commas, » thus «. This, though, is where the similarities stop: in running dialogue the *entire* conversation is surrounded by a single pair of guillemets, changes in speaker are conveyed with dashes, and verbs of speaking are permitted to remain within the text.⁷⁶ Using a passage from Alexandre Dumas's *The Count of Monte Cristo* as an example:

> « Hola! Edmond, do you not see your friends? Or are you too proud to speak to them?
> — No, my dear Caderousse, I am not proud—I am happy; and such happiness, I believe, is blinder than pride.
> — Bravo! There's an explanation, said Caderousse. »⁷⁷

Quotations spanning multiple paragraphs are set in yet another manner: having opened such a quotation with a quotation dash (rather than a guillemet) each subsequent paragraph is then opened with an *inward*-pointing guillemet.[78] These quirks and more still greet readers of today's French novels, and the guillemet and dash continue to dance around Gallic dialogue in a manner quite apart from the sober regularity of Anglo-Saxon text.

* * *

In the years since the anarchy and consolidation of the seventeenth and eighteenth centuries, usage of quotation marks in English has converged on a steady state largely unperturbed by changes of fashion in typography and grammar. And yet, in 1942 one rogue literary critic began a brave attempt to "reform" the quotation mark out of its hard-won roles.

A professor of English at Cambridge until 1939 and Harvard until 1974, the British literary critic Ivor A. Richards had a strong reformist bent.[79] Richards was an ardent supporter of "Basic English," an 850-word subset of the English language with a correspondingly simplified grammar invented by his Cambridge confederate, the philosopher C. K. Ogden.[80] Intended as an "international second language," Basic English presented a beguiling prospect to educators: Richards convinced the US Navy to use Basic English to help train Chinese sailors after World War II, for instance, and the language received mentions in *LIFE*, *Time*, and *Harper's*—even if, as in the latter case, it was not an entirely complimentary one.[81] Ogden's creation even made its way into fiction,* with the science-fiction authors H. G. Wells and Robert A. Heinlein both choosing Basic English as the lingua franca of their respective future worlds.[83]

---

* George Orwell was at first cautiously optimistic about the prospects of Basic English, though he later rebelled against the concept of constructed languages, satirizing them in *Nineteen Eighty-Four* with the Party's "Newspeak."[82]

Perhaps emboldened by the positive reception of Basic English, Richards permitted himself a brief digression in his 1942 manual of literary criticism, *How to Read a Page*, to propose a language reform of his own. In a note entitled "Specialized Quotation Marks," Richards listed the variety of competing meanings foisted on the symbol—to mark quotations themselves; as "scare quotes" implying irony or dubiety; to denote a word itself rather than the thing to which that word refers, and others—and bemoaned "how heavily we overwork this too serviceable device."[84]

Richards proposed to replace quotation marks with superscript letters in certain contexts *other* than dialogue and quotation. The letter w, for instance, indicated that the quoted term was being referred to as the word itself: ^{w}table^w in Richards's system was equivalent to writing "the word 'table.'" Upping the level of difficulty, r indicated that the quoted term referred back to a definition elsewhere, carrying roughly the meaning "as according to," as Richards illustrated with the example: "^{r}Nature^r for Whitehead is not Wordsworth's ^{r}Nature^r." Most straightforward was $!$, indicating a $^|$shriek$^|$ of surprise or derision, and perhaps most obscure was sw for "said with," used to compare two equivalent terms, as in Richards's highbrow statement: "^{sw}Art^{sw} is ^{sw}significant form^{sw}."[85]

Richards enthusiastically demonstrated his new system throughout the remainder of *How to Read a Page* and persisted with it in all of his professional writing until 1974, when only five years before his death he was finally persuaded to drop it from a collection of essays.[86] Given the steadfastly conventional quotation marks employed in this and almost every other modern book, it will come as no surprise that Richards's system did not catch on. Like Martin Speckter's interrobang, Richards's specialized quotation marks were up against a well-established orthodoxy, but even more than that, they inhabited a rarefied and exclusive academic world;

in the end, Richards was the sole inventor, user, and promoter of his system, and there could only be one outcome.[87] The quotation mark's two-millennia-long journey, from mute *diple* to pious scriptural bookmark to the pages of novels everywhere, was not about to be undone.

Chapter 11 ✎ Irony and Sarcasm

At its heart, irony is the presence of a second, contradictory meaning within a situation or expression. Dictionary definitions vary in the details, but all broadly agree on its main flavors.[1] "Socratic irony," for instance, is the use of feigned ignorance of the subject at hand—the way a teacher answers a student's question with another question, or a skilled debater gives his opponent enough rope to hang himself.* In "dramatic irony," the audience of a dramatic work is made aware of the true state of affairs while one or more of the characters are not; Romeo's despairing suicide in response to Juliet's apparent death, which the audience knows to be faked, is an oft-quoted example. "Situational irony" describes an occasion or event whose outcome is the opposite of but perversely appropriate to the expected outcome, and its sibling "cosmic irony" sees a guiding hand behind such occurrences. When someone mutters "Isn't that ironic?," he or she is almost certainly referring to a perceived situational irony.

In all these cases, the power to determine whether a given situation is ironic lies in the hands of its observers. Ironies such as these simply are, or are not; they neither benefit from nor require punctuation.

"Verbal irony," by contrast, the simple act of saying one thing while meaning something else, presents ample opportunity for both the ironist and audience to get it wrong. This form of irony in

---

* Proving that Socratic irony is not the sole preserve of classical Greek philosophers, Sacha Baron Cohen's comic characters Ali G, Borat, and Brüno use this very technique to skewer the attitudes, ignorance, or prejudices of those they meet.[2]

particular is a staple of modern communication: a study of conversations among American college students in 2000 found that verbal irony (along with its brattish stepchildren sarcasm, hyperbole, and understatement) accounted for fully 8 percent* of their conversational turns.[3] Despite lending itself well to the nuances and inflections of the spoken word, committing verbal irony to paper is fraught for both writer and reader, demanding a certain amount of skill on the part of the would-be ironist and an associated degree of perceptiveness of its audience. As such, it is the written presentation of verbal irony that has attracted the attention of a string of writers, academics, journalists, and typographers bent on "fixing" its shortcomings.

1. ੂ➤ Irony in History

The concept of irony got its name—though *not* yet an attendant mark of punctuation—in ancient Greece, where playwrights employed a cast of stock characters made recognizable by their physical characteristics, props, and personalities. One such staple of comic plays was the *eirôn*, a seeming buffoon who would best the *alazon*, his braggart opponent, by means of self-deprecation and feigned ignorance, and it was the cunning *eirôn* who gave his name first to the Greek *eirôneia* and then to the modern term "irony."[4] But though irony played a central role in the intellectual life of the ancient world, its writers were content to leave readers to figure it out for themselves: the written irony mark was born not at the ancient library of Alexandria or in the Senate of Rome, but instead at the heart of Restoration England.

The first documented mark created specifically to punctuate an ironic statement arrived in 1668, when the English vicar and natural

---

* The author's own experience suggests that this is a scandalous underestimate.

philosopher John Wilkins published his *Essay Towards a Real Charac-ter and a Philosophical Language*.[5] Brother-in-law of the royalists' bête noire Oliver Cromwell, after the Restoration, Wilkins was neverthe-less installed as the first secretary of the newly founded Royal Society; having already served as head of Wadham College, Oxford, and Trin-ity College, Cambridge, this mild-mannered clergyman was a minor Leonardo da Vinci of his day.[6] Among other enterprises, he posited the possibility of extraterrestrial life on the moon (and designed a flying machine to get there); speculated on the construction of submarine "Arks"; wrote the first book on cryptography in English; and fabricated transparent beehives that allowed honey to be extracted without kill-ing the bees inside.[7] *Essay*, though, was to be his crowning achievement.

Delayed by the partial destruction of his manuscript during the Great Fire of London of 1666, Wilkins pressed on to publish the book two years later.[8] *Essay* was a bold, bipartite endeavor: the "real charac-ter" of the title referred to a taxonomy of letters and symbols intended for "the distinct expression of all things and notions that fall under dis-course," while the corresponding "philosophical language" was a pho-netic guide to pronouncing the resultant terms.[9] Two centuries before the creation of Esperanto and three before C. K. Ogden put English under the knife,* Wilkins had created an entirely new language.[10]

Hubristic as this may seem now, *Essay* was merely the culmination of a peculiar seventeenth-century obsession with artificial language. The Renaissance had generated an explosion of information, with knowledge and ideas spreading like wildfire among an increasing liter-ate and scientific populace. Latin, however, once the go-to language for international scholarly discourse, was in decline. More seriously, a new breed of "natural philosophers" understood that the biases and limitations of natural language in general made it an imperfect tool for

---

* See chapter 10, "Quotation Marks (" ")," for more on C. K. Ogden's "Basic English."

communicating the new body of scientific knowledge: to Wilkins and his contemporaries, the notion of a purpose-built, universal language with which to analyze and transmit this information held a powerful fascination.[11] Thus it was that the mid-seventeenth century saw the invention of a succession of "philosophical languages" and "real characters," artificial taxonomies of things and concepts that were, crucially, free from the myriad complexities of linguistic evolution.[12]

Wilkins's entry into the arena was preceded by a host of other works. Between 1647 and 1652, for instance, a Dutch merchant named Francis Lodowyck published books proposing a "New Perfect Language and a Universal Common Writing," while the tongue-twisting novels *Ekskybalauron* (1651) and *Logopandecteision* (1652), written by the extravagantly dictioned Scottish author Sir Thomas Urquhart, boasted of (but did not fully deliver) Urquhart's own universal language.[13] Wilkins, meanwhile, had been collaborating with another Scot, the linguist George Dalgarno, but the two fell out over the structure of their "philosophical language"; Dalgarno beat Wilkins to print in 1661, rushing out his own treatise on *Ars Signorum*, or "The Art of Signs," though ultimately it was eclipsed by Wilkins's 1668 epic.[14] Wilkins' "real character" was the universal language to end all universal languages.

Wilkins's language was a sort of steroidal, all-encompassing Dewey Decimal System where concepts were organized into a rigid hierarchy. The notion of "a flame," for instance, was communicated by combining the "genus" *de*, meaning an element, the "difference" *b*, for fire, and the "species" *a*, meaning a part of that element, to yield the composite term *deba*.[15] In addition to this taxonomy, however, Wilkins strayed into punctuation and writing, and in doing so made a curious innovation: he declared that irony should be punctuated with an inverted exclamation mark (¡).[16]

It is not known what reason Wilkins had to coin this first irony mark. Sixty years earlier, the influential Dutch humanist Desiderius Erasmus had noted the lack of such punctuation, writing that "irony has no place, only different pronunciation," though whether Wilkins knew of or was inspired by Erasmus's musings on the subject is not recorded.[17] Regardless of his inspiration, however, Wilkins's choice of the ¡ seems most appropriate. The presence of an exclamation mark already modifies the tone of a statement, and inverting it to yield an *i*-like character both hints at the implied *i*-rony and simultaneously suggests the inversion of its meaning. Unfortunately, apt as his selection may have been, Wilkins's invention was not only the first of many proposed irony marks, but also the first of them to fail.

By the end of the seventeenth century the idea that a messy, chaotic universe could be brought to order with a manmade taxonomy had been proven quixotic, and the dream of a universal language with which to express that taxonomy had largely faded.[18] Wilkins' *Essay*, last best hope for the ill-fated universal-language movement, is nowadays regarded as a glorious failure; his little-remarked inverted exclamation point sank along with it, seemingly without trace.* A fateful precedent had been set.

* * *

Having lain dormant for close to two centuries, the irony mark next appeared—or rather, a *new* irony mark was created—on the other side of the English Channel. Born in France during the Revolution, after leaving school the surveyor Jean-Baptiste-Ambroise-Marcellin Jobard pinballed around the Low Countries of Europe for a decade, coming to rest in Brussels in 1819 as a naturalized Dutch citizen.[20] An early champion of lithography, a new and ingenious printing method that relied on the hydrophobic nature of oily inks,

---

* Linguaphiles may find some comfort in the fact that *Roget's Thesaurus* borrows heavily from Wilkins's classification scheme.[19]

as the years passed Jobard embraced an ever more diverse set of ventures: he used pipes hundreds of feet long to study the propagation of the human voice, advocated for the introduction of the railway to the newly independent state of Belgium, and lit his home with a self-designed system of gaslights.[21] By 1837, though, he had returned to his printing roots and become the proprietor of a pair of newspapers.

Thus it was that a reader perusing *Le Courrier Belge* [The Belgian mail] on the eleventh of October, 1841, might have been surprised to come across an article punctuated by a series of triangular, Christmas tree–like glyphs (◁).[22] The article began:

> *Qu'est-ce à dire? Quoi* ◁ *(1) lorsque la France piaffe et trépigne*
> *impatiente de se lancer sur les champs de bataille; lorsque*
> *l'Espagne, fatiguée d'une trève de quelque mois, recommence*
> *la guerre civile, la Belgique resterait tranquillement occupée*
> *d'industrie, de commerce, de chemins de fer et de colonisation!*
> *Mais c'est absurde.* [What to say? What ◁ (1) when France
> stamps and prances impatiently to get on the battlefield,
> when Spain, tired of a truce of some months, again
> engages in civil war, Belgium remains quietly occupied
> by industry, trade, railways and colonization! But this is
> absurd.]

Clearly exasperated with the turbulent politics of Europe's "long nineteenth century," Jobard had found it necessary to invent a mark to give his full voice to his ire. At the article's foot lay a crucial explanatory note: "(1) ◁ *Ceci un point d'ironie.*"—"(1) ◁ This," he said, "is an irony point." Jobard's Christmas tree appeared a handful times more in the article to open, close, and bookend paragraphs meant to be taken ironically.

Though his new mark went unused after this first outing, Jobard returned to the subject in a book published in 1842. Expanding his palette of nonstandard punctuation marks, he suggested that the same arrowlike symbol could be placed at different orientations to indicate "a point of irritation, an indignation point, a point of hesitation," and mused that other symbols, yet to be invented, might be used to convey sympathy or antipathy, affliction or satisfaction, and loud or quiet exclamations.[23]

A great intellectual of his time, Jobard's works are only dimly remembered within the Francophone world and have been almost wholly forgotten outside it. Fascinated by spiritualism in the latter part of his life, Jobard wrote a great deal on the subject. This obsession dominated and diminished his legacy to such an extent that it has all but disappeared.[24] Abandoned by its maker after a brief flirtation, his irony mark has suffered a similar fate.

The next writer to take up the baton was the Genevois philosopher Jean-Jacques Rousseau, who echoed Erasmus's complaint in his 1852 *Essai sur l'origine des langues* [Essay on the origin of language], asserting that the characteristic vocal inflections of an ironic statement are absent from its written representation.[25] Though Rousseau declined to solve the problem himself, it was clear that the irony candle burned brightly for Francophone writers.

Born a scant few years after Marcellin Jobard's death, the poet Marcel Bernhardt was next to throw his chapeau into the ring. Better known by his anagrammatic pseudonym Alcanter de Brahm, Bernhardt's 1899 book *L'ostensoir des ironies* [The monstrosity of irony] was a meandering philosophical tract in which he put forward a new mark of punctuation resembling a stylized, reversed question mark (⸮).[26] Alcanter's *point d'ironie* dripped with knowing humor: in a nod to the sentiment often conveyed by verbal irony, he described it as "taking the form of a whip," and, aware that irony loses its sting when it must be signposted in exactly the manner he was proposing, the French name for his new symbol was a pun with the additional meaning of "no irony."[27]

Wayne C. Booth, Professor Emeritus of English at the University of Chicago until his death in 2005, addressed Brahm's irony mark in

Figure 11.1 Alcanter de Brahm's "whiplike" *point d'ironie*, proposed in 1899 in *L'ostensoir des ironies.*

the dense 1974 tome *A Rhetoric of Irony.*[*] At first dismissing the *point d'ironie* as reducing the value of irony (Brahm himself would have been first to acknowledge the limitations of his creation), Booth goes on to suggest that any reader encountering such a mark would be faced with a dilemma: does the mark genuinely signal an ironic statement, or is the mark itself being used ironically?[28] Later, though, when discussing the variable degrees of success with which irony is deployed in literature, he drops in an ironic footnote of his own:

> If [Brahm] had ever developed his system he would surely have wanted a set of evaluative sub-symbols: * = average; † = superior; ‡ = not so good; § = marvelous; ‖ = perhaps expunge.[29]

Unsurprisingly, Booth's tongue-in-cheek "evaluative sub-symbols" never traveled beyond the pages of his book.

If Alcanter de Brahm's reversed question mark seems familiar, it may be because he was not the first to deploy such a mark—nor

---

[*] Booth's *Rhetoric* incorrectly presents Brahm's creation as a rotated question mark (¿).

even was he the first to use it in the service of irony. Henry Denham's sixteenth-century "percontation point" (encountered previously in relation to the interrobang) was a reversed question mark (⸮) used to terminate rhetorical questions, and was almost identical in form to Brahm's later symbol.[30] By taking it upon himself to highlight this sub-species of verbal irony with a dedicated mark of punctuation, Denham prefigured Alcanter's own irony mark by three centuries.

Both Denham's percontation point and Brahm's *point d'ironie* fared better than Wilkins's inverted exclamation mark and Jobard's Christmas tree, though neither one quite made the jump to common use. Benefiting, perhaps, from the malleable standards of sixteenth-century punctuation, Denham's percontation point puttered on for around fifty years, while Brahm's fin-de-siècle irony mark merited an entry in the *Nouveau Larousse Illustré* encyclopedia, preserved behind glass, as it were, until 1960.[31] In their respective times, neither amounted to anything more than a grammatical curiosity. The curse of the irony mark remained in force.

A few years after Alcanter de Brahm's whiplike *point d'ironie* appeared in the pages of the *Petit Larousse Illustré* for the last time, one of France's best-known authors revived the search for an irony mark with his own suggestion. And a mere suggestion it was, right from the very start: best known for novels of familial strife and youthful rebellion, Hervé Bazin adopted instead a distinctly playful tone for 1966's *Plumons l'oiseau: divertissement* or "Plucking the Bird: A Diversion." Born in Angers in 1911 to a strictly Catholic family, Jean Pierre Marie Hervé-Bazin railed against the strictures of bourgeois life from a young age, running away several times and generally doing his level best to infuriate his overbearing mother.[32] The feud spilled over into his breakthrough 1948 novel *Vipère au poing* [Viper in the fist] in which he fictionalized the struggles of his childhood—the novel features a domineering mother named Folcoche, from the French *folle* (crazy) and *cochonne* (pig)—to great critical acclaim and not a little scandal.[33]

By 1966 the firebrand writer had calmed somewhat, and *Plumons l'oiseau* was a gentle foray into spelling and grammar reform. Among discourses on the irrationality of modern French, descriptions of a proposed phonetic spelling system (*"l'orthographie lojike"*) and sundry grammatical changes, Bazin found time to pen a few pages on what he called *Les points d'intonation*, or "intonation points."[34] Like Rousseau, he contended that written language lacked the nuance and subtlety of the spoken word; unlike Rousseau, he addressed the problem by creating a whole range of new punctuation marks. In addition to the "love point," "conviction point," "authority point," "acclamation point," and "doubt point" was Bazin's own *point d'ironie*:

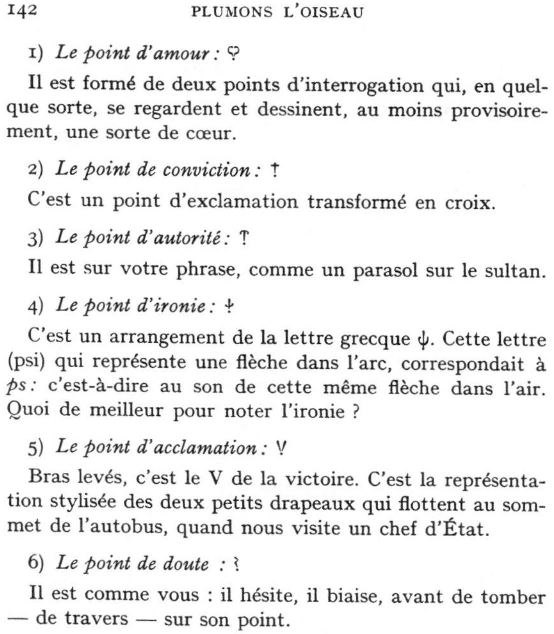

142   PLUMONS L'OISEAU

1) *Le point d'amour :* ♀

Il est formé de deux points d'interrogation qui, en quelque sorte, se regardent et dessinent, au moins provisoirement, une sorte de cœur.

2) *Le point de conviction :* ⸸

C'est un point d'exclamation transformé en croix.

3) *Le point d'autorité :* ⸑

Il est sur votre phrase, comme un parasol sur le sultan.

4) *Le point d'ironie :* ⸮

C'est un arrangement de la lettre grecque ψ. Cette lettre (psi) qui représente une flèche dans l'arc, correspondait à *ps :* c'est-à-dire au son de cette même flèche dans l'air. Quoi de meilleur pour noter l'ironie ?

5) *Le point d'acclamation :* ⱽ

Bras levés, c'est le V de la victoire. C'est la représentation stylisée des deux petits drapeaux qui flottent au sommet de l'autobus, quand nous visite un chef d'État.

6) *Le point de doute :* ⸘

Il est comme vous : il hésite, il biaise, avant de tomber — de travers — sur son point.

Figure 11.2 Hervé Bazin's menagerie of proposed punctuation marks, the psi-like *point d'ironie* among them.

Bazin explained his new mark thus:

> *Le point d'ironie:* ⸮
>
> This is an arrangement of the Greek letter ψ. This letter (psi) is an arrow in the bow, corresponding to *ps*: that is to say the sound of that same arrow in the air. What could be better to denote irony?[35]

Despite this picturesque explanation, his arrow-inspired *point d'ironie* found no targets beyond the pages of *Plumons l'oiseau,* and today it holds a status similar to those of Wilkins, Jobard, and Brahm before it—an intriguing but mostly forgotten footnote to the history of punctuation.

The irony mark's peculiarly self-defeating quality seemed unshakeable. Couched though it was in the esoteric language of textual criticism, Wayne C. Booth's arch dismissal of Brahm's earlier *point d'ironie* lit upon the problem: if the quality of irony in a statement is such that it must be telegraphed to the reader, is it still ironic? The problem that Wilkins, Bazin, and others had attempted to solve was the very thing that left each of their irony marks twisting in the wind.

* * *

In 2007, the centuries-long and stubbornly fruitless search for an irony mark gained a new postscript. With earlier marks largely forgotten and Wayne C. Booth's critique of the irony-mark concept now some decades past, a new pretender emerged to tilt at the windmill one more time.

Each year the Boekenbal, the gala opening of the Netherlands' annual book festival, has a particular theme. In March 2007, the theme was "In Praise of Folly—Jest, Irony and Satire," and that year saw the unveiling of the so-called *ironieteken*, a zigzag exclamation mark specially commissioned to mark the occasion.³⁶ Early signs were positive: designed by the award-winning, pan-European type foundry Underware, the *ironieteken* was rooted in traditional literary culture just as the *points d'ironie* of Alcanter de Brahm and Hervé Bazin had been before it, and, notionally at least, it could count on the support of some influential patrons.

Though the *ironieteken* had been commissioned solely to publicize the Boekenbal, Underware's Bas Jacobs nevertheless took his brief seriously. His simple adaptation of the exclamation mark was designed to be easily written by hand, and he considered that:

> A simple form is essential to give it a chance to be a success, in contradiction to the interrobang for example. And it has to look like it always existed, not too constructed or rational, but similar like existing punctuation marks.³⁷

Jacobs's understated *ironieteken* was launched in a blaze of publicity. Presented at the Boekenbal by the Minister of Culture to a packed house of prominent Dutch authors, the next day it featured in a full-page advertisement in the national newspaper *NRC Handelsblad*, with

Figure 11.3   Left to right: Underware's *ironieteken* as rendered in 72pt Dolly, Century Catalogue, Share, and Cardo typefaces.

Underware simultaneously making the mark available in a number of fonts for download through their website. The mark attracted a great deal of comment and might have gained even wider notice had not some commentators noted that two *ironieteken* placed in a row bore an unfortunate resemblance to the insignia of the infamous Nazi SS:[39] ⚡⚡

Whether or not this unhappy typographic coincidence was responsible for its demise, the ripples the *ironieteken* caused within the Dutch literary sphere did not persist. This graceful, considered symbol—for all intents and purposes the last "analog" irony mark—remains little more than a typographic curio. The ultimate resurrection of the idea would flow not from the typewriter of the traditional author or the pen of a type designer but instead the chat rooms and blogs of that mighty engine of ironic discourse, the Internet.

2. 〜 *Ironics*

Before the search for a written irony mark was revived in the twenty-first century, the hunt took an abrupt detour: if an irony *mark* could not be made to stick, perhaps an entire *script* was the answer. And whereas the pursuit of a serviceable irony mark had exerted a strange pull on a select few Continental writers, the idea of using a different typeface altogether was very much an Anglo-Saxon endeavor.

* * *

In 2005, the *Baltimore Sun*, newspaper of record in the state of Maryland, underwent a comprehensive facelift. Every aspect of its visual design was revisited: layout and masthead were changed, pictures were given pride of place, and a new typeface was commissioned from the French typographer Jean François Porchez.[39] It was named "Mencken" in honor of the iconoclastic H. L. Mencken, the *Sun*'s most famous writer. Porchez elaborated on the choice of name:

> According to the *London Daily Mail*, H. L. Mencken even ventured beyond the typewriter and into the world of typography. Because he felt Americans did not recognize irony when they read it, he proposed the creation of a special typeface to be called ironics, with the text slanting the opposite direction from italic type, to indicate that the writer was trying to be funny.[40]

Christened Henry Louis, the young Mencken took to using his initials "H. L." after his father broke the lowercase *r* letterpunches of a toy printing set one Christmas morning.[41] An editorialist for the *Sun* during the first half of the twentieth century, Mencken was "a humorist by instinct and a superb craftsman by temperament [with] a style flexible, fancy-free, ribald, and always beautifully lucid."[42] An avowed elitist who expressed amused contempt at the leveling tendencies of democracy, the so-called Sage of Baltimore did not think well of the common American. In 1926, for instance, he famously wrote:

> No one in this world, so far as I know—and I have researched the records for years, and employed agents to help me—has ever lost money by underestimating the intelligence of the great masses of the plain people. Nor has anyone ever lost public office thereby.[43]

Mencken's alleged suggestion of "ironics" seems entirely in keeping with his acid sense of humor.

The archives of the *Baltimore Sun*, however, are suspiciously void of references to Mencken's supposed invention.[44] Turning instead to Porchez's mention of the *Daily Mail* leads to a pair of articles written by that paper's columnist Keith Waterhouse, in each of which he makes a brief mention of Mencken's ironics. First, in 2003:

> Americans do not do irony.
> Their language guru H. L. Mencken once proposed a special typeface to be called ironics, facing the opposite way from italics, to indicate that the writer was trying to be funny.[45]

And later, in 2006:

> Irony has always been a headache for writers of wit who have to explain to readers of little wit that they were being ironic. The problem was solved by the great American journalist H. L. Mencken who invented a typeface sloping the opposite way to italics and called it Ironics.[46]

Waterhouse is certainly a credible authority on the English language, having penned the *Daily Mirror*'s in-house style guide—later published as *Waterhouse on Newspaper Style*—and also its purpose-written sequel *English Our English: And How to Sing It*.[47] Unfortunately, as with everything in journalism, attribution remains paramount, and in this case it is notably absent. Waterhouse's articles mark both the beginning and end of the trail, and if he was privy to some incontrovertible evidence that Mencken was the creator of the term "ironics," then he took it with him to the grave in September 2009.[48] Perhaps appropriately, given the circumstances, Jean François Porchez's font Mencken, named for this supposed creator of ironics, stuck most conservatively to roman, italic, and bold typefaces with nary an ironic character in sight.

* * *

Who, then, did create ironics? In Mencken's place a later twentieth-century newspaperman enters the frame, this time the English columnist and reviewer Bernard Levin. A 2008 article entitled "Ha Ha Hard," published in Levin's old paper *The Times* of London, began:

> Humour is a funny thing. Or sometimes it's not. It's certainly an easily misunderstood thing. The late, great Bernard Levin used to say that *The Times* should have a typeface called "ironics" to warn his more poker-faced readers when he wasn't being serious.[49]

Levin was similar to H. L. Mencken in many ways: prodigiously talented, prodigiously opinionated, and loyal to a single newspaper for much of his career.[50] Also like Mencken, Levin is an enticing candidate for originator of this script dedicated to irony, but again the truth fails to cooperate. Levin, by his own account, did not invent ironics, but was merely the first journalist to bring them to light. In a 1982 column for *The Times*,* Levin identified a certain Tom Driberg, a recently deceased Labour MP and Peer of the Realm, as their creator:

> As for trying to be funny—well, long ago the late Tom Driberg proposed that typographers should design a new face, which would slope the opposite way from italics, and would be called "ironics". In this type-face jokes would be

---

* Levin's column about ironics was also published by *Encounter,* a British literary and cultural journal that ran from 1953 to 1991, and that is worthy of a digression all of its own. *Encounter* had the bizarre distinction of having been set up and covertly funded by the US Central Intelligence Agency and the UK's Secret Intelligence Service, with the aim of making up for the lack of anti-Communist rhetoric emanating from the popular—and left-wing—*New Statesman.* Its CIA funding became public knowledge in 1967, prompting the resignation of its editor and cofounder Stephen Spender (coincidentally, an Oxford contemporary of Tom Driberg), who claimed to have known nothing about the identity of his backers.[51]

> set, and no-one would have any excuse for failing to see
> them. Until this happy development takes place, I am left
> with the only really useful thing journalism has taught
> me: that there is no joke so obvious that some bloody fool
> won't miss the point.[52]

While they may not have invented ironics, Levin and Mencken shared the same dim view of the relative wit of the common people.

That Tom Driberg—not H. L. Mencken, Keith Waterhouse, or indeed Bernard Levin—was the originator of ironics was seconded by Brooke Crutchley, onetime head of Cambridge University Press. In a 1994 letter to *The Independent*, Crutchley wrote:

> The late Tom Driberg had an idea for avoiding such
> misunderstandings, namely, the use of a typeface slanted
> the opposite way to italics. He suggested it should be
> known as 'ironics'.[53]

So much as is possible within a newspaper's letter pages and editorial columns, here was independent confirmation of Driberg as inventor of ironics.

Born in England in 1905, the son of a civil servant, Thomas Edward Neil Driberg gave every appearance of being a respectable politician, a successful journalist, and a devout churchman. A member of the Communist Party of Great Britain as a young man, in 1945, Driberg switched allegiance to the Labour Party and subsequently enjoyed a long career as a Labour MP. Serving as chairman of the Labour Party in 1957 and 1958, in 1965 he ascended to the heights of the Privy Council, a body that advises the queen in exercising her powers, and ultimately was named Baron Bradwell just a year before his death in 1976. Parallel to this were his journalistic endeavors: writing for the widely read broadsheet *Daily Express*, the young Tom Driberg landed notable scoops and later penned the paper's society gossip column under the alias "William Hickey." All the while, Tom was a staunch member of the Catholic-influenced Anglican High Church: his 1951 wedding to Ena Mary Binfield was described by one attendee as "outrageously ornate."[54]

Upon Driberg's death, though, fissures started to appear in his public image. First, his lifelong homosexuality, already an imperfectly kept secret, was revealed in his obituary in *The Times*.[55] It was the first posthumous outing of a public figure in the paper's history.[56] Further revelations emerged in 1979, when it was alleged that Driberg had been ejected from the Communist Party after the Russian mole Anthony Blunt discovered that Tom was spying on the Communists for MI5. Later still came details of Tom's ensnarement in a honey-trap operation during a 1956 visit to Moscow, after which he had *also* spied for the KGB under the code name "Lepage."[57] Most preposterous of all, in 1989 it was claimed that Aleister Crowley, Britain's most notorious practitioner of black magic and the self-proclaimed "Great Beast 666," had at one point anointed Driberg as his chosen successor.[58]

Tom Driberg's life was a mess of ironies: he was a married, gay churchman who lunched with occultists; a left-wing politician who reveled in frivolous society gossip; a patriot who spied both for his country and the dreaded KGB. It seems entirely apt for him to have proposed the creation of a typeface to invest text with a double meaning, which would be slanted the opposite way from italics, and that would be called "ironics."

Unfortunately, by the time Bernard Levin invoked Driberg's memory in 1982 not so much as a single word had been printed with the fabled ironic slant. Even as pioneering computer programs such as Donald Knuth's TEX* promised to slip the surly bonds of physical

---

* See chapter 7, "The Hyphen (-)," for details of the move to computerized printing.

type, as Martin K. Speckter had found to his cost, a novel typographic device with all the apparatus of writing and printing behind it would still get precisely nowhere without popular support.[59] And no one, it seemed, was willing to get behind ironics.

3. ❧ *Digital Sarcasm*

The latter part of the twentieth century was a fallow period for the irony mark. Ironics, only ever an apocryphal literary in-joke at best, were the sole flag-bearer for the punctuation of irony during this period, when even the tenacious French had given up on the problem. The merry-go-round of new irony points had ground to a halt.

Then came the Internet, plucking many a shady character from obscurity and thrusting them back into the light. The quotidian @ symbol became indispensable; the octothorpe was recast as the dashing hashtag, and the interrobang gained a new generation of admirers. The mythical ironics had their long-awaited debut, and the irony mark was revived too, though their new lease on life came with a caveat. The subtle shadings of verbal irony were bleached flat in the blinding glare of the new medium: what the Internet really wanted to communicate was not irony, but its laser-guided offspring, sarcasm.[60]

* * *

Runners-up in the Internet dash for an irony mark, ironics enjoyed a brief moment of notoriety in the summer of 2011. Nathan Hoang, June Kim, and Blake Gilmore launched Sartalics. com while interning at the NYC office of advertising agency Bartle Bogle Hegarty, and, appropriately for its new electronic milieu, they repurposed the resuscitated script to convey sarcasm rather than irony.[61]

In a case of independent innovation, Hoang, Kim, and Gilmore claim to have invented the concept of sartalics without prior knowledge of ironics, though the trio did their homework and name-checked H. L. Mencken on their home page as a possible progenitor of the form.[62] Sartalics.com was launched just a year shy of the interrobang's fiftieth anniversary, and as Martin K. Speckter had appeared in print, on television, and on radio to promote his symbol, so Hoang, Kim, and Gilmore used their twenty-first-century advertising nous to promote their project. Ironics were rebranded as sartalics for a snarky online world, and Twitter, YouTube, and the web were all put to work to spread the word.[63]

Cognizant of the headwinds that had greeted earlier irony marks, the aims of the Sartalics.com team were grander than the creation of a single mark of punctuation or a sarcastic typeface. What was needed, they said, was for sartalics to become a mere fact of computing and the web itself; they would have to become as prosaic, essential, and accessible as italics or bold type.[64] Serving as a salutary warning of the obstacles still to be overcome, their online examples of backward-skewed text did not display properly in Microsoft's Internet Explorer, rendering them nonsensical for more than a quarter of web users, and their method could be applied only to entire paragraphs at a time*—it was not yet possible to "sartalicize" individual words or phrases.[66]

The July 2011 launch of Sartalics.com generated a flurry of tweets and blog posts, though the novelty seemed to have worn off by the end of the following month.[67] Then, in December the same year, a separate, hitherto obscure attempt to create a similar sarcastic font was uncovered by the popular social news site Reddit.com; the post received more than five hundred comments within a matter of days,

---

* A later tweet from the team suggested using backslashes to surround \sarcastic\ terms as a stopgap measure.[65]

ABCDEFGHIJKLMNOPQRSTUVWXYZ&
abcdefghijklmnopqrstuvwxyz&
$¢£1234567890 .,—:;!?()[]* % ""''

☞ *Figure 11.4*   A specimen of Monotype Arial rendered using the "sartalics" method proposed by Nathan Hoang, June Kim, and Blake Gilmore at Sartalics.com. For the typographically inclined, each line is first set with roman letterforms and is subsequently skewed *in its entirety*, thus preserving letter spacing and allowing for convincing, "reverse italic"–style kerning.

and Sartalics.com basked in a renewed wave of attention from blogs and mainstream newspapers such as Canada's *Globe and Mail*.[68] Whether sartalics will survive in the long run is debatable, but their moment in the sun was far better reported than that of their analog antecedents.

* * *

In contrast to ironics' big-bang revival in the guise of sartalics, the irony mark's transformation into the sarcasm mark was slower burning. September 1999 saw the first halting steps toward this brave new world, when, at the fifteenth International Unicode Conference in San Jose, California, a group of academics presented a paper with the informative but turgid title "A Roadmap to the Extension of the Ethiopic Writing System Standard Under Unicode and ISO-10646."[69] Unicode is the de facto successor to ASCII, an exhaustive character set defining more than 109,000 symbols taken from more than ninety scripts, ancient and modern alike, including Latin, Arabic, Greek, Cyrillic, Japanese, Chinese, cuneiform, and others.[70] For a character to be included in Unicode is to have its mainstream use acknowledged, and so Asteraye Tsigie, Daniel Yacob, and their

coauthors lobbied for the inclusion of a number of Ethiopian collo-
qualisms. Documenting the use of one such character, they wrote:

> *Ethiopian Sarcasm Mark "Temherte Slaq"*
>
> Graphically indistinguishable from [the inverted
> exclamation point] (¡) Temherte Slaq differs in semantic
> use in Ethiopia. Temherte Slaq will come at the end of a
> sentence (vs at the beginning in Spanish use) and is used
> to indicate an unreal phrase, often sarcastical in editorial
> cartoons. Temherte Slaq is also important in children's
> literature and in poetic use.[71]

In a striking coincidence, this first electronic sarcasm mark
was identical in form to the first analog irony mark. John Wilkins's
inverted exclamation point lived again, if only in spirit. How Tsigie
and Yacob's fellow delegates received their proposal is unknown, but
its lasting effect is more easily gauged: thirteen years later, the *temherte
slaq* still forlornly awaits the Unicode Consortium's seal of approval.
However useful it might have been for ironists in its native Ethiopia,
and regardless of Tsigie and Yacob's considered appeal for its wider
adoption, their idea was dead on arrival. It was not an auspicious start
for the irony mark in the new Internet era.

In the wake of this luckless pioneer appeared a succession of electronic sarcasm marks that varied in form, scope, and gravity, with the
first new mark to follow the *temherte slaq* unveiled in 2001 by a blogger
named Tara Liloia. Observing that written sarcasm was chronically
misinterpreted as sincerity in online interactions, Liloia posted an
article venturing to solve the problem. In "The Sarcasm Mark," she
wrote:

> What I am proposing is a punctuation mark that clears
> up all confusion about sarcastic remarks for the reader.

> The closest thing to a sarcasm mark is the winking
> smiley—and he isn't really a professional tool. You can't
> write a missive to a business associate with little cutesy
> ASCII faces in it. It's just not done. [...] My solution is
> the tilde. ‿[72]

Tara Liloia's proposal of the tilde as a "professional" alternative to the cartoonish winking smiley was simple, easy to type, and conspicuously short-lived. Though the tilde did find limited use as a sarcasm mark in online forums (according, at least, to that beacon of scholarly rigor, *Urban Dictionary*‿), it failed to gain traction in the wider online community.[73] More significant than Liloia's tilde was her recognition of the need—seemingly peculiar to the Internet—to demarcate and regulate sarcasm: whereas literary authors and journalists had sought to clarify the use of irony, the rapid-fire, anonymous discourse of the Internet inevitably crystallized that irony into outright sarcasm.

As Liloia explained, the closest extant device to the sarcasm mark she sought was the "winking smiley" (; -) or ;))—an "emoticon," or combination of ASCII characters that suggests a particular facial expression when read on its side.* Though Liloia was content to dismiss them as unsuitable candidates for her high-minded pursuit of a sarcasm mark, emoticons have been part of Internet language since the days of the ARPANET and their history as a printed mark stretches back further still.†

When a joke about a fake mercury spill at Carnegie Mellon University was mistaken for a genuine safety warning, the denizens of the digital message board on which it had been posted cast about for

---

* ASCII, the American Standard Code for Information Interchange, is synonymous with the
fixed-width typefaces often used to compose emoticons and other "ASCII art."[74] See
chapter 3, "The Octothorpe (#)," and chapter 5, "The @ Symbol," for more on ASCII.
† See chapter 5, "The @ Symbol," for a brief history of the ARPANET.

a means to distinguish humorous posts from more serious content.[75] On September 19, 1982, faculty member Scott E. Fahlman entered the debate with the following message:

> I propose that [*sic*] the following character sequence for joke markers:
>
> :-)
>
> Read it sideways. Actually, it is probably more economical to mark things that are NOT jokes, given current trends. For this, use:
>
> :-([76]

The rest is Internet history: Fahlman's expressive, minimal icons became an integral part of online communication, if not always a welcome one.[77] These "smileys," as they came to be known, were effectively the first online irony marks, indicating that what has gone before should be read on a second, humorous level.[78] The smiley itself, however, is far older than its modern habitat. At the same time that Marcellin Jobard, Alcanter de Brahm, and Hervé Bazin were concocting new marks to convey irony, a series of Anglo-Saxon writers turned to the limited palette of the typewriter keyboard to create anthropomorphic indications of joy, sadness, and irony. Emoticons recur throughout modern history like defenestrations in Prague.

Though it is difficult to nail down the emoticon's first appearance in print, one likely contender appears in the *New York Times'* 1862 transcript of a speech made by President Abraham Lincoln.[79] The transcript records the audience's response to Lincoln's droll introduction as "(applause and laughter ;)"—containing an abbreviated form of the same winking smiley that Tara Liloia would later reject as a suitable tool for denoting sarcasm. Without corroborating evidence, however, it is impossible to decide whether this is a genuine emoticon. Counting in its favor, the transcript was typeset by hand, before mechanical typesetting brought with it the risk of gummed-up Linotypes accidentally transposing characters, and so it is plausible that ";)"—rather than the more grammatically sensible ");"—was intentional.[80] Moreover, later audience reactions to the same speech appear between square brackets rather than parentheses, reinforcing the likelihood that this particular interjection was deliberately typeset as such. On the negative side, this single ";)" was the only such "emoticon" in the entire speech, and the rest of the text suffers from enough typographic errors that it cannot be guaranteed to have been a calculated addition.[81] Though its form is undeniably familiar, the precise meaning of this first emoticon remains unknown.

The next appearance of the emoticon, on the other hand, was entirely deliberate—though it was also explicitly ironic in nature. Founded in 1871, the American satirical weekly *Puck* depended on cartoonists for much of its content, and in 1881 it carried a short article declaring that "the letterpress department of this paper is not going to be trampled on by any tyrannical crowd of artists in existence."[82] This mock war cry was accompanied by a series of typographic faces, constructed from points, parentheses, and dashes, which illustrated the supposed artistic credentials of the magazine's embattled compositors:[83]

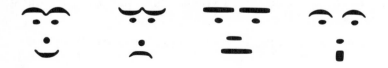

Figure 11.5   "Studies in Passions and Emotions": *left to right*, the emotions of joy, melancholy, indifference, and astonishment as depicted in *Puck* magazine, March 30, 1881.[84]

Sandwiched between a story satirizing the American judicial system, and one of the cartoons against which the "letterpress department" had directed its tirade, the article and its accompanying image have the feel of filler material. *Puck*'s right-way-up emoticons were clearly not expected to rock the typographic boat.

The meandering path toward the modern emoticon continued in 1887, when the celebrated (and feared) critic Ambrose Bierce penned a tongue-in-cheek essay on writing reform entitled "For Brevity and Clarity."[85] Alongside helpful contractions of phrases such as "join in the holy bonds of wedlock" (jedlock) and "much esteemed by all who knew him" (mestewed), Bierce presented a new mark of punctuation intended to help less fortunate writers convey humor or irony:

> While reforming language I crave leave to introduce an improvement in punctuation—the snigger point, or note of cachinnation. It is written thus ⌣ and represents, as nearly as may be, a smiling mouth. It is to be appended, with the full stop, to every jocular or ironical sentence; or, without the stop, to every jocular or ironical clause of a sentence otherwise serious—thus: "Mr. Edward Bok is the noblest work of God ⌣."[86]

Bierce's proposal of a "snigger point" or "note of cachinnation" (now almost extinct, "cachinnation" means "loud or immoderate laughter") was itself an ironic act rather, his mark a mere prop with which to poke fun at unduly serious writers.[87] Unsurprisingly, the ⌣ did not catch on.*

The last pre-Internet emoticons ambled casually into view at

---

* Somewhat improbably, Unicode defines a "smile" character, or ⌣, that appears suspiciously similar to Ambrose Bierce's "note of cachinnation."

the end of the 1960s. First, in 1967, a Baltimore *Sunday Sun* columnist named Ralph Reppert was quoted in the May edition of *Reader's
Digest*. Reppert, writing that his "Aunt Ev is the only person I know
who can write a facial expression," explained that:

> Aunt Ev's expression is a symbol that looks like this: —)
> It represents her tongue stuck in her cheek. Here's the
> way she used it in her last letter: "Your Cousin Vernie is
> a *natural* blonde again —)[.]"[88]

Like Bierce's snigger point, Aunt Ev's typographical creation was
clearly not a serious proposition, and its appearance was apparently
a one-off.

Two years later, and on a literary plane far removed from the *Reader's Digest*, the last known analog smiley sprung from the high mind of
the author Vladimir Nabokov. A famously controlling interviewee,
Nabokov insisted on being provided with questions in advance so that
he might formulate cogent replies.[89] Recounting a question asked by
Alden Whitman of the *New York Times* as to where Nabokov ranked
himself among writers of his era, the Russian émigré replied obliquely:
"I often think there should exist a special typographical sign for a
smile—some sort of concave mark, a supine round bracket, which I
would now like to trace in reply to your question."[90]

Nabokov had wittily, if unwittingly, re-created Ambrose Bierce's
grinning note of cachinnation. Though it is often mentioned in the
same breath as Fahlman's later emoticons, Nabokov's "supine round
bracket" was simply an unrelated typographic joke, and as with the
others that had gone before it, its life ended on the same page on which
it had begun.[91]

* * *

S o much for the winking smiley; despite its storied past, Tara
Liloia's unease with this playful mark drove her to create her own
sarcasm mark, and she was not alone. Fittingly, the next new mark
(though one that carried more than a hint of déjà vu about it) came
from a former contributor to the satirical newspaper and website the
Onion. In a 2004 article penned for the online magazine *Slate*, Josh
Greenman wrote:

> The English language must evolve. [...] We don't need
> more quotation marks that "hedge" or try to make the
> same "old" thing sound "fresh." What we need is an honest
> effort to incorporate the way we live today. My fellow
> Americans, we need to embrace a new punctuation mark—
> one that embraces the irony and edge of contemporary
> conversation and clarifies rather than condenses
> or confuses.
>
> It is time for the adoption of the sarcasm point.[92]

Through his work for the *Onion*, Greenman surely had greater experience than most of the "irony and edge of contemporary conversation."
His article was a polemic that echoed the fervor and enthusiasm of
Martin Speckter's interrobang manifesto of thirty-six years earlier—
albeit one shot through with the rich vein of irony required of any
truly *serious* irony or sarcasm mark proposal.[93] The title of his article,
boldly showing off his newly minted "sarcasm point," said it all: "A
Giant Step Forward for Punctuation¡"

Josh Greenman claims never to have encountered the *temherte
slaq* or John Wilkins's seventeenth-century irony mark, but the coincidence here is striking: three separate proposals to use ¡ as an irony
mark in two different languages and spanning four centuries. Though
Greenman's sarcasm mark was merely a prop for his satirical commentary rather than a genuine attempt to introduce a new mark of

punctuation, his selection of the inverted exclamation point remains a neat touch, a reversal of the polarity implied by its normally oriented counterpart.[94] Not that it mattered, of course; its job done, Greenman's ¡ lived and died within the context of a single opinion piece, passing into irrelevance as its author moved on to other things.

As if aware of the pitfalls inherent in suggesting a new mark of punctuation, the typographer Choz Cunningham hedged his bets when he put forward his own suggestion in 2006. His "snark" was composed of two easily typed, standard characters; it could be used to imply sarcasm *or* irony; and it appropriated an earlier sarcasm mark for good measure. Hosted at its very own website, TheSnark.org, Cunningham's proposal carried echoes of the revivification of the @ and # before it:

> The most eloquent solution was the tilde. Sitting there, dormant since the 1960s, it has lacked a popular or mainstream purpose despite being included on virtually all computer keyboards. Tara Liloia, an early blogger, proposed making sarcasm clearer by ending a sentence with it. [...] The classic [*point d'ironie*] and the sarcasm tilde were merged. Plain and stylized forms were explored. The Snark was born![95]

And giving an example, he wrote:

> A snark is very simple. At the end of the sentence where you want to finish with the mark, add a ~ (tilde) after the . (period).[96]

As well as the simple pairing of a period and a tilde (.~), Cunningham described an alternative form for the snark where the two characters were kerned more closely to yield a single glyph (⸮).[97]

The thoroughness of Cunningham's promotional efforts belied the difference between the snark and its predecessors: in place of the arch humor that had distinguished Liloia's and Greenman's short, sharp articles, TheSnark.org was comprehensive and deadpan. And though, after an initial flush of enthusiasm, TheSnark.org sank into that limbo specific to abandoned websites,* where the ever-receding date stamped on each page counts the months and years since its last update, Cunningham had nevertheless raised the bar. The quest for a workable irony or sarcasm mark was becoming an increasingly serious matter.

* * *

The irony mark's inconstant digital existence, begun with the abortive importation of the *temherte slaq* and sustained by a succession of futile pretenders, has most recently borne witness to one particularly determined project that almost—*almost*—cracked the problem. Outstripping the *ironieteken*, the *temherte slaq*, and their kin by far is the most remarked and reviled irony mark to date. The rise to infamy of the "SarcMark"® is unparalleled in the history of punctuation.

When a seasoned type foundry such as Underware can fall foul of unintended consequences of the kind engendered by a pair of juxtaposed *ironieteken*, it might be concluded that creating a new mark of punctuation is not for the typographically inexperienced. This did not deter the father-and-son team of Paul and Douglas J. Sak, of Shelby Township, Michigan—respectively an engineer and an accountant by trade—from not only designing a new sarcasm mark but also submitting a patent of its design and charging for its use.[98]

---

* At the time this chapter was first written, TheSnark.org was still available; some months later, during editing, it had been replaced by a generic placeholder page.

The Saks' plan for their "SarcMark" was a deadly serious, long-term endeavor. Working in secret, the Saks registered the domain name "SarcMark.net" in June 2008 and filed a patent application for a "font for a punctuation mark" the following month; having announced their invention publicly in January 2010, an application to register the term "SarcMark" as a trademark was lodged shortly thereafter.[99] The Saks were leaving nothing to chance.

As described on SarcMark.net, the case for the SarcMark was couched in much the same language as those of previous marks (ALL CAPS are from the original piece):

> With the spoken word, we use our tone, inflection and volume to question, exclaim and convey our feelings. The written word has question marks and exclamation points to document those thoughts, BUT sarcasm has NOTHING! In today's world with increasing commentary, debate and rhetoric, what better time could there be than NOW, to ensure that no sarcastic message, comment or opinion is left behind[.] Equal Rights for Sarcasm - Use the SarcMark[.][100]

Resembling an @ or a reversed 6 with a point in the middle, the SarcMark was intended to be of roughly the same size as existing glyphs, and included a point because of its presence in other

Figure 11.6   The SarcMark, as created by Doug and Paul Sak of Michigan.

terminal punctuation marks such as the question mark and exclamation point.[101] Like Underware's *ironieteken*, the SarcMark was available for download in a digital font; unlike the *ironieteken*, however, this font came at a price. The right to use the SarcMark for non-commercial purposes could be bought for the price of $1.99, with business users asked ominously to e-mail the Saks directly.

It is safe to say that the creators and supporters of other irony and sarcasm marks were not amused. Or perhaps they were.

Initial news reports of the character's creation were respectfully factual ("Sarcasm punctuation mark aims to put an end to email confusion" said *The Daily Telegraph*; "Hitting the mark with sarcasm" wrote *The Toronto Star*), but as news reports multiplied, the cynics weighed in.[102] Almost every aspect of the SarcMark succeeded in riling one commentator or another. Its visual design was flawed, as the gadget and electronics website *Gizmodo Australia* opined in an article that started as it meant to go on:

> *SarcMark: For When You're Not Smart*
> *Enough to Express Sarcasm Online*
>
> [...] for $US1.99 you get to download the symbol, which looks like an inverted foetus, and use it to illustrate your fantastic control over the English language every time you go online (insert Sarcmark).[103]

Others, echoing the hoary criticism that irony marks were unnecessary in the first place, argued that writers must convey sarcasm well or else avoid it entirely. Tom Meltzer of *The Guardian* covered the creation of the mark in a story written entirely in the sarcastic register, and concluded tartly:

> The real breakthrough of Sarcasm, Inc is the realisation that, despite having used sarcasm and irony in the

written word for hundreds of years, humans are simply
too stupid to consistently recognise when someone has
said the opposite of what they mean. The SarcMark
solves that problem, and you can download it as a font
for the reasonable price of $1.99 (£1.20). Our prayers are
answered.[104]

Neither was the backlash confined to opinion pieces. A scant
month after the Saks had sent out their first press releases, the mock-
revolutionary website of the "Open Sarcasm" movement appeared,
calling for the SarcMark to be blacklisted in favor of the tried and
tested inverted exclamation mark, or *temherte slaq*. Affecting a mili-
tant stance against the "greedy capitalists of Sarcasm, Inc.," the site
declared:

> A spectre is haunting the internet—the spectre of Open
> Sarcasm.
> Of late, certain capitalist forces have brought forth
> onto the internet the idea that sarcasmists everywhere
> must license and download their proprietary new
> "punctuation"—called the "SarcMark"®—in order to
> clarify sarcasm in their writing.
> A growing chorus of voices has joined together to decry
> this idea. It is high time that Open Sarcasmists should
> openly, in the face of the whole world, publish their views,
> their aims, their tendencies, and meet this nursery tale
> of the Spectre of Open Sarcasm with a manifesto of the
> punctuation itself. [...]
> SARCASMISTS OF THE WORLD, UNITE![105]

The rapid appearance of an entire website dedicated to the "forcible
overthrow" of the SarcMark was the very embodiment of Internet
activism: a deadly serious message inveighing against the rise of

capitalism over collectivism; proprietary designs over open standards; intellectual property over free speech; and all delivered with a healthy undercurrent of knowing humor.

All this, though, is perhaps to miss the point. Despite the righteous fury leveled at it from all quarters, the SarcMark had already broken into the rarefied atmosphere of the mainstream media, something that no other new punctuation mark since the interrobang had managed. Which other irony mark could claim to have received coverage in the *New York Daily News*, *The Guardian*, *The Daily Telegraph*, and at ABC News?[106] Unfortunately for the Saks, this media bonanza gave the lie to the old maxim that no news is bad news: it was difficult to find anything *but* bad news about the SarcMark, and needless to say, the legally unsinkable symbol was nevertheless holed below the waterline almost as soon as it was launched.

Even after these successive near misses, the irony mark (and, for that matter, the sarcasm mark) remains an elusive beast. Of the myriad ways in which irony and sarcasm have been represented over the centuries—Wilkins's and Greenman's ¡, Denham's and Brahm's ⸮, Bazin's ⸮, Mencken's and Driberg's ironics, Underware's ⸮, and all the rest—today the unasked-for burden rests squarely on the shoulders of the winking smiley. Easy to type, intuitive, and ubiquitous enough for an opportunistic Russian entrepreneur to claim to have trademarked it in 2008, this sly descendant of Scott E. Fahlman's original emoticons is surely the definitive irony mark.[107] Case closed ;)

Afterword

This book, as it turns out, is not just about unusual marks of punctuation, nor even punctuation in general. In following the warp and woof of individual shady characters throughout their lifetimes, it is the woven fabric of writing as a whole that emerges. And in today's writing, the printed and electroluminescent characters we read on a daily basis and the scrawled handwriting that occupies the diminishing gaps between computer monitors, tablet computers, and smartphone screens, this history stares right back at us.

The period, for instance, is a plain-speaking herald of the creative freedom once enjoyed at the library of Alexandria, while its younger siblings the asterisk and dagger are ominous reminders of the literary crusades prosecuted by early Christians. Roman letterforms take us to Trajan's Column in ancient Rome and to Charlemagne's medieval court; italics conjure up Aldus, Erasmus, and the new science of the Renaissance. The hurried swirl of the @ symbol is a relic of an era when time, paper, and ink were luxuries afforded only to a lucky few, while quotation marks, propelled to prominence by the mass-produced novel, remind us how much of those luxuries we now possess.

The bust and boom endured by punctuation with each new technological innovation is also on show: seen off by the arrival of printing, the delicately rubricated pilcrow no longer divides our books into chapters and paragraphs, though by way of recompense my computer now lets me type ‽, ☞, or ¶ at will. The squat hyphen-minus reminds us how efficiently the typewriter brutalized our ideas of civilized typography; that word processors now swiftly and automatically replace them with en and em dashes gives us hope that we might already have found our way back again.

Every character we write or type is a link to the past, and every shady character doubly so. I hope this book has inspired you to throw in a pilcrow, interrobang, or manicule the next time you sit down to write; after all they've been through, it's the least we can do in return.

Further Reading

❧ Parkes, M. B. *Pause and Effect: Punctuation in the West*. Berkeley: University of California Press, 1993. M. B. Parkes's comprehensive, magisterial, and infuriating masterpiece on the development of punctuation from ancient Greece onward. This heavyweight, scholarly tome dispenses with such niceties as readability, accessibility, and pleasing design, and yet is probably the single most useful work on the origins of modern punctuation.

❧ Bringhurst, Robert. *The Elements of Typographic Style: Version 3.2*. Vancouver, BC: Hartley and Marks, Publishers, 2008. The book that first got me hooked on typography: if you're remotely interested in printing, book design, or typographic characters, this is the book to get. A joy to read!

❧ Gill, Eric. *An Essay on Typography*. Jaffrey, NH: David R. Godine, January 1993. This most recent edition is oddly proportioned and does a poor job reproducing the pages of the original, but it is still an engaging book, and one that shows that not all typesetting need slavishly follow the same rules.

❧ The Digital Scriptorium. Available online at: http://www. digital-scriptorium.org/. This collaboration between the University of California–Berkeley and Columbia University hosts digitized images of an amazing set of manuscripts drawn from university libraries across the United States. Many a carefully inscribed shady character can be found here.

❧ Digitised Manuscripts at the British Library. Available online at: www.bl.uk/manuscripts/. Though less accessible than the Digital

Scriptorium, the British Library's collection of digitized manuscripts is second to none. Browsing, rather than searching, is rewarded.

☞ **Flickr: The ☞ Manicule Pool. Available online at: http://www. flickr.com/groups/manicule/pool/.** A collaboratively curated and absorbing collection of old and new pointing hands.

Acknowledgments

This book could not have been written without a huge amount of help from a great many people, and in trying to name them all I will almost certainly unintentionally omit some. For this I apologize.

I've been lucky enough to correspond with a number of people who have been deeply involved in creating, documenting, and using the characters in this book. In alphabetical order, Choz Cunningham, Bob Fleck, Vince Frost, Alan Giles, Josh Greenman, Allan Haley, Nathan Hoang, Bas Jacobs, Alex Jay, Doug Kerr, Dick Lyon, Harry McIntosh, Sumit Paul-Choudhury, Richard Polt, Jean Francois Porchez, Paul Saenger, Martin Schøyen, William H. Sherman, Kirsty Tough, and Peter Weil have kept me straight on many points. Last but not least, Penny Speckter has been amazing: she was the first person I dared e-mail out of the blue and her initial replies made me realize that this might all just be possible. Her continued support has been invaluable.

The photographs, scans, and illustrations in this book come from a variety of sources. Laura K. Balke, Martin Campbell-Kelly, Stan Carey, Todd Chatman, Dorothy Clayton, Bob Crotinger, Helen Cumming, Frank Davies, Consuelo W. Dutschke, Jean Gascou, David Gesswein, Daryl Green, Florian Hardwig, Jonathan Hoefler, Phillip Hughes, Ruth Ann Jones, David McKitterick, Richard Oram, Guy Pérard, Romeo Ruz, Rebecca Schalber, Julie Strawson, Cornelia Tschichold, Jim Vadeboncoeur Jr., James Voelkel, Debra White, and Bob Will have gone above and beyond the call of duty in helping me organize these images.

My friend Jeff Sanders edited my early drafts, encouraged me tirelessly, and provided an invaluable second opinion throughout the whole process. Alasdair Gillon and Dominic Crayford recommended that I read *An Essay on Typography* and *The Elements of Typographic Style* respectively, and had I not done so my interest in typography and punctuation might never have been kindled at all. Vanessa D'Andrea kindly translated some French material for chapter 11, while John Cowan and Alexander Brook wrangled a particularly tricky Latin book title into English for chapter 8. The newly minted Dr. Leigh A. Stork, PhD, who became first my girlfriend, then my fiancée, and finally my wife during the writing of this book, has put up with entirely too much talk of pilcrows and interrobangs over the past two years and yet inexplicably remains supportive of me and my work.

My agent, Laurie Abkemeier; my editor, Brendan Curry; and Melanie Tortoroli of W. W. Norton have been constant sources of help and support during the writing process. Rachelle Mandik's copyediting was instrumental in knocking the final manuscript into shape, and together, Judith Abbate's lively design and Brad Walrod's careful composition turned that manuscript into this book. They have all dealt with a first-time author's bombardment of questions with aplomb.

Last but not least, I must mention all the readers and commenters of ShadyCharacters.co.uk—there are too many of you to list, but without you none of this would have been possible.

Thank you all!

Notes

PREFACE

1. Eric Gill, *An Essay on Typography* (Jaffrey, NH: David R. Godine, 1993).

2. Theodore Rosendorf, "Pilcrow," in *The Typographic Desk Reference*, 1st edition (New Castle, DE: Knoll Press, 2009), 66.

I. THE PILCROW (¶)

1. Theodore Rosendorf, "Pilcrow," in *The Typographic Desk Reference*, 1st edition (New Castle, DE: Oak Knoll Press, 2009), 66; R. L. Trask, "The Other Marks on Your Keyboard," in *The Penguin Guide to Punctuation* (London: Penguin Reference Books, 1997) 132–35.

2. Robert Bringhurst, "Pilcrow," in *The Elements of Typographic Style: Version 3.2* (Vancouver, BC: Hartley & Marks, 2008), 315–16.

3. Ellen Lupton and Abbott Miller, "Period Styles: A Punctuated History," in *Design Writing Research* (London: Phaidon, 1999), 33; Amy Tikkanen, "Boustrophedon (writing style)," *Encyclopaedia Britannica*, http://www.britannica.com/EBchecked/topic/75943/boustrophedon [last accessed January 9, 2011].

4. James Fenton, "Read My Lips," *The Guardian*, July 29, 2006.

5. Paul Saenger, "Silent Reading: Its Impact on Late Medieval Script and Society," *Viator: Medieval and Renaissance Studies* 13 (1982): 367–414.

6. T. Julian Brown, John Higgins, Kathleen Kuiper, et al, "Punctuation," *Encyclopaedia Britannica*, http://www.britannica.com/EBchecked/topic/483473/punctuation [last accessed January 9, 2011].

7. Alexander Humez and Nicholas Humez, "Bang! The Dot Meets the Family," in *On the Dot: The Speck That Changed the World,* 1st edition (New York: Oxford University Press, 2008), 134; M. B. Parkes, "Introduction," in *Pause and Effect: Punctuation in the West* (Berkeley: University of California Press, 1993), 1–8.

8. J. Alan Kemp, "The Tekhne Grammatike of Dionysius Thrax: Translated into English," *Historiographia Linguistica* 13, no. 2 (1986): 343–63.

9. M. B. Parkes, "Influences of the Application of Punctuation," in *Pause and Effect: Punctuation in the West* (Berkeley: University of California Press, 1993), 65–96.

10. E. G. Turner and P. J. Parsons, "Introduction," in *Greek Manuscripts of the Ancient World* (London: University of London, Institute of Classical Studies, bulletin supplement, 1987), 1–23.

11. Brown et al, "Punctuation."

12. M. B. Parkes, "Antiquity: Aids for Inexperienced Readers and the Prehistory of Punctuation," in *Pause and Effect: Punctuation in the West* (Berkeley: University of California Press, 1993), 12.

13. Parkes, "Introduction," 1–8; G. A. Harrer, "Some Characteristics of Roman Lettering and Writing," *Studies in Philology* 28, no. 1 (1931).

14. Parkes, "Introduction," 10.

15. Brown et al, "Punctuation."

16. William A. Johnson, "The Function of the Paragraphus in Greek Literary Prose Texts," *Zeitschrift für Papyrologie und Epigraphik* 100 (1994): 65–68.

17. Roger Pearse, "More on the Paragraphos Mark," *Roger Pearse* (blog), November 10, 2010, http://www.roger-pearse.com/weblog/?p=5290.

18. F. Schironi, "Book-Ends and Book-Layout in Papyri with Hexametric Poetry," in *The Proceedings of the 25th International Congress of Papyrology* (Ann Arbor: MPublishing, University of Michigan Library, 2010).

19. Parkes, "Introduction," 10; M. B. Parkes, "Glossary of Technical Terms," in *Pause and Effect: Punctuation in the West* (Berkeley: University of California Press, 1993), 305.

20. Parkes, "Antiquity," 12.

21. Peter R. Brown, *The Rise of Western Christendom: Triumph and Diversity, A.D. 200–1000* (Cambridge, UK: Blackwell, 2006), 63.

22. Parkes, "Introduction," 13.

23. Michael Grant, "Constantine and the Christian God," in *The Emperor Constantine* (London: Weidenfeld & Nicolson, 1993), 139–40.

24. Paul Veyne, *When Our World Became Christian, 312–394* (Cambridge, UK: Polity, 2010), 54.

25. Grant, "Constantine and the Christian Church," 156–58.

26. Robert Browning, "The Chance of Power," in *The Emperor Julian,* first paperback edition (Berkeley: University of California Press, 1978), 78; Dorothy Watts, "The Pagan Revival of the Late Fourth Century AD 360–90," in *Religion in Late Roman Britain: Forces of Change* (New York: Routledge, 1998), 24.

27. Herbert Bloch, "A New Document of the Last Pagan Revival in the West, 393–394 A.D.," *The Harvard Theological Review* 38, no. 4 (1945): 240–41.

28. R. Malcolm Errington, *Roman Imperial Policy from Julian to Theodosius (Studies in the History of Greece and Rome)* (Asheville: University of North Carolina Press, 2006), 217.

29. Brown et al, "Punctuation."

30. Isidore and Stephen A. Barney, "Punctuated clauses [De posituris]," in *The Etymologies of Isidore of Seville* (Cambridge: Cambridge University Press, 2006), 50.

31. Ibid.; Parkes, "Glossary of Technical Terms," 306.

32. Bernhard Bischoff and University of Cambridge, "Uncial," in *Latin Paleography: Antiquity and the Middle Ages* (Cambridge: Cambridge University Press, 1995), 66–72; Lane Wilkinson, "The Humanistic Minuscule and the Advent of Roman Type," Paper (Chattanooga: University of Tennessee, n.d.), 12.

33. Saenger, "Silent Reading," 367–414.

34. Wilkinson, "The Humanistic Minuscule and the Advent of Roman Type," 12.

35. M. B. Parkes, "The Handwriting of St Boniface: A Reassessment of the Problems," *Beiträge zur Geschichte der deutschen Sprache und*

Literatur (PBB) 1976 (2009): 161; David Sacks, "K and its Kompeti-tors," in *The Alphabet: Unravelling the Mystery of the Alphabet from A to Z* (London: Hutchinson, 2003), 206.

36. W. Clarysse, J. Clarysse, B. Van Beek, et al, "Leuven Database of Ancient Books," *Trismegistos*, http://www.trismegistos.org/ldab/ [last accessed June 22, 2012]; M. B. Parkes, "The Development of the General Repertory of Punctuation," in *Pause and Effect: Punctuation in the West* (Berkeley: University of California Press, 1993), 43.

37. André Vauchez, Barrie Dobson, and Michael Lapidge, "Capitu-lum," in *Encyclopedia of the Middle Ages. 1, A–J* (Paris: Éditions du CERF [etc.], 2000), 278.

38. R. McKitterick, "Script and Book Production," in *Carolingian Cul-ture: Emulation and Innovation* (Cambridge: Cambridge University Press, 1994), 221–47.

39. M. A. Cassiodorus, *The Letters of Cassiodorus* (Teddington, UK: Echo Library, 2007), 60.

40. Geoffrey A. Glaister, "Rubricator," in *Glossary of the Book* (London: George Allen & Unwin, 1960), 361.

41. Parkes, "The Development of the General Repertory of Punctua-tion," 43.

42. Lupton and Miller, "Period Styles," 34.

43. Andrew Haslam, "Articulating Meaning: Paragraphs," in *Book Design* (London: Laurence King, 2006), 73–74.

44. Walter W. Skeat, *Notes on English Etymology; Chiefly Reprinted from the Transactions of the Philological Society* (Oxford, UK: The Clarendon Press, 1901), 215–16.

45. Haslam, "Articulating Meaning," 73–74; Jan Tschichold and Rob-ert Bringhurst, "Why the Beginnings of Paragraphs Must Be Indented," in *The Form of the Book* (London: Lund Humphries, 1991), 105–09.

46. Rosendorf, "Proofreaders' Marks," 68.

47. Eric Gill, *An Essay on Typography* (Jaffrey, NH: David R. Godine, 1993).

48. Fiona MacCarthy, "Ditchling Village, 1907–1913," in *Eric Gill* (Lon-don: Faber and Faber, 1989), 115.

49. Martin Hutner and Jerry Kelly, *A Century for the Century: Fine Printed Books from 1900 to 1999,* Grolier Club edition (Jaffrey, NH: David R. Godine, Publisher, 2004), xxxix.

50. Gill, *An Essay on Typography.*

51. Mark Thomson, "Visions of Joanna," *Eye Magazine* 62, 2006.

52. Fonts.com, "Joanna," http://www.fonts.com/FindFonts/Hidden Gems/Joanna.htm [last accessed March 20, 2011]; John Boardley, "A Brief History of Type—Part 5," *I Love Typography,* June 20, 2008, http://ilovetypography.com/2008/06/20/a-brief-history-of-type-part-5/.

53. Robert Bringhurst, "11.2 Serifed Text Faces," in *The Elements of Typographic Style: Version 3.2* (Vancouver, BC: Hartley & Marks, 2008), 234.

54. Patrick Rogers, "Stations of the Cross," *Oremus: Westminster Cathedral Magazine,* March 2005, http://www.westminstercathedral.org.uk/tour_stations.php [last accessed March 31, 2011].

55. Fiona MacCarthy, "Ditchling Common, 1913–1924," in *Eric Gill* (London: Faber and Faber, 1989), 125.

56. Fiona MacCarthy, "'Mad About Sex,'" *The Guardian,* October 16, 2009.

57. "*Ecstasy* by Eric Gill," *Art and Artists,* Tate Gallery, August 2004, http://www.tate.org.uk/art/artworks/gill-ecstasy-t03477 [last accessed March 21, 2011].

58. Douglas Cleverdon and Guy Brenton, "Portrait of Eric Gill," BBC Radio programme, 1961.

59. Fiona MacCarthy, *Eric Gill* (London: Faber and Faber, 1989).

60. Matthew Carter, "Big Caslon, 1994," *The Collection,* Museum of Modern Art, http://www.moma.org/collection/browse_results.php?object_id=139308 [last accessed August 18, 2012]; Adrian Frutiger, "Linotype Didot Font Family, 1991," *Linotype.com,* http://www.linotype.com/1012/linotypedidot-family.html [last accessed August 18, 2012]; Hermann Zapf, "Zapfino Font Family, 1998," *Linotype.com,* http://www.linotype.com/en/1175/zapfino-family.html [last accessed August 18, 2012]; D. Earls, "Jonathan Hoefler," in *Designing Typefaces* (Hove, UK: Rotovision, 2002) 12–23.

61. Matthew Carter and David Berlow, "Skia," *MyFonts,* January 2000, http://www.myfonts.com/fonts/apple/skia/ [last accessed August 18, 2012]; "Courier New," *Microsoft Typography,* http://www.microsoft.com/typography/fonts/family.aspx?FID=10 [last accessed August 22, 2012]; Jos Buivenga, "Museo Slab," exljbris Font Foundry, http://www.exljbris.com/museoslab.html [last accessed August 22, 2012].

62. Amy Guth, "Pilcrow Lit Fest 2009," http://pilcrowlitfest.com/ [last accessed March 17, 2011]; Jonathan Hoefler, "Pilcrow and Capitulum," *typography.com,* March 12, 2008, http://www.typography.com/ask/showBlog.php?blogID=84; Keith Miller, "The Clever Nostalgia of Adam Mars-Jones," *Times Literary Supplement,* March 26, 2008; Alice Rawsthorn, "Brand Obama, a Leader in the Image War," *New York Times,* April 4, 2008.

63. J. Morgan, "An Account of the Making of Common Worship: Services and Prayers for the Church of England," *Typography Papers 5* (2003): 33–64.

2.   THE INTERROBANG (‽)

1.   Laurence Chang, Peter Kornbluh, and US National Security Archive, *The Cuban Missile Crisis, 1962: A National Security Archive Documents Reader* (New York: The New Press, 1992); Erik Gregersen, "Telstar (communications satellite)," *Encyclopaedia Britannica,* http://www.britannica.com/EBchecked/topic/586427/Telstar [last accessed March 30, 2011]; Erik Gregersen, Shiveta Singh, and Amy Tikkanen, "Mercury (space project)," Britannica Online Encyclopedia. *Encyclopaedia Britannica,* http://www.britannica.com/EBchecked/topic/375884/Mercury [last accessed March 26, 2011].

2.   "Martin K. Speckter, 73, Creator of Interrobang," *New York Times,* February 16, 1988.

3.   Martin K. Speckter, "Making a New Point; Or, How About That . . . ," *Type Talks,* March–April, 1962.

4.   "The Missing Symbol," *Wall Street Journal,* April 6, 1962.

5.   "A Short History of the International Herald Tribune," *International Herald Tribune,* http://www.ihtinfo.com/media/59755/iht2064_short_history_2012-5.pdf [last accessed January 22, 2013].

6. Martin K. Speckter, "Toward the 2-Way Punctuation Mark," *Type Talks*, May–June, 1962.

7. Ibid.

8. Gideon O. Burton, "Interrogatio," *Silva Rhetoricae*, http:// humanities.byu.edu/rhetoric/figures/I/interrogatio.htm [last accessed March 27, 2011]; Theodore Rosendorf, "Exclamation Mark," in *The Typographic Desk Reference,* 1st edition (New Castle, DE: Oak Knoll Press, 2009), 46.

9. Ohmer Milton, *Will That Be on the Final!?* (Springfield, IL: C. C. Thomas, 1982).

10. Allan Haley, "The Interrobang Is Back," *x-height: FontHaus' Online Magazine*, web.archive.org/web/20080507055249/http://www. fonthaus.com/xheight/interrobang.cfm [last accessed January 23, 2013].

11. Mac McGrew, "Americana," in *American Metal Typefaces of the Twentieth Century* (New Castle, DE: Oak Knoll Press, 1993), 13.

12. American Type Founders, "ATF Americana (type specimen)," 1966.

13. "New Punctuation Mark," *Time,* July 21, 1967.

14. Ibid.; "Interrobang (!?) Expresses Modern Life's Incredibility," *Publishers' Auxiliary*, September 1968, 17; Penny Speckter, Personal correspondence, February 2009.

15. "New Punctuation Mark," *Time*; American Type Founders, "ATF Americana."

16. American Type Founders, "ATF Americana (advertisement)," *Art Direction,* July 1967, 51; Penny Speckter, Personal correspondence, April 2011.

17. "Business Bulletin," *Wall Street Journal*, September 5, 1968.

18. "Did You Say Interrobang!?" *Crosstalk* 1, no. 5 (November 1968): 2.

19. Martin K. Speckter, "Interrobang," *Type Talks*, November–December, 1968, 17.

20. "Interrobang Is Newest Mark of Punctuation," *Univac News*, September 1968, 3.

21. "What's Newest," *Newsweek*, September 16, 1968.

22. William Zinsser, "For Clear Expression: Try Words," *LIFE*, November 15, 1968, 24.

23. William Zinsser, "Clutter," in *On Writing Well* (New York: Harper & Row, 1988), 13.

24. "Handy 'Interrobang.'" *Joplin Globe*, September 8, 1968; Don Oakley, "Look, Girls, a New Key on Typewriter," *The Kansas City Kansan*, September 2, 1968.

25. Oakley, "Look, Girls, a New Key on Typewriter."

26. "Something New," *Richmond News Leader*, September 14, 1968.

27. Speckter, "Interrobang."

28. David Consuegra, *American Type: Design & Designers* (New York: Allworth Press, 2004), 172; Speckter, "Making a New Point."

29. *Newsweek*, "What's Newest"; Elmer Muffwinkle, "A Line o' Type or Two," *Chicago Tribune*, August 7, 1967.

30. E. Dickey, "Dionysius Thrax," in *Ancient Greek Scholarship: A Guide to Finding, Reading, and Understanding Scholia, Commentaries, Lexica, and Grammatical Treatises, from Their Beginnings to the Byzantine Period,* Classical Resources Series (New York: Oxford University Press, 2007), 77–80.

31. Geoffrey A. Glaister, "Matrix," in *Glossary of the Book* (London: George Allen & Unwin, 1960), 252.

32. Geoffrey A. Glaister, "Punch," in *Glossary of the Book* (London: George Allen & Unwin, 1960), 334.

33. Jack Belzer, Albert G. Holzman, and Allen Kent, *Encyclopedia of Computer Science and Technology* (New York: M. Dekker, 1975); Arthur H. Phillips, "Nonscanning Text Composition Photocomposers," in *Handbook of Computer-Aided Composition* (New York: M. Dekker, 1980), 299–360.

34. Speckter, "Interrobang."

35. Ibid.

36. Mac McGrew, "Americana," in *American Metal Typefaces of the Twentieth Century* (New Castle, DE: Oak Knoll Press, 1993), 13; Andrew Wolson, "American Type Founders 1892–1993," http://www.fontslate.info/foundry/atf.html [last accessed August 28, 2012].

37. McGrew, "Americana."

38. Haley, "The Interrobang Is Back."

39. "Americana Roman," *Fonts.com*, http://www.fonts.com/findfonts/ detail.htm?productid=86761 [last accessed April 13, 2011].

40. M. B. Parkes, *Pause and Effect: Punctuation in the West* (Berkeley: University of California Press, 1993).

41. M. B. Parkes, "Plates 34–35. The Percontativus Used by Two Sixteenth-Century London Printers: Henry Denham and Abell Jeffs," in *Pause and Effect: Punctuation in the West* (Berkeley: University of California Press, 1993), 218–19.

42. Ibid.

43. John Lennard, *The Poetry Handbook: A Guide to Reading Poetry for Pleasure and Practical Criticism* (Oxford, UK: Oxford University Press, 2005), 121.

44. Dumesnil, *Latin Synonyms* (London: Baldwin, Cradock & Joy, 1825), 326.

45. *Wall Street Journal*, "The Missing Symbol."

46. Michael W. Brenner, "!?: interrobang," *Typophile*, February 4, 2005, http://typophile.com/node/9086.

47. "Unicode Character 'INTERROBANG' (U+203D)," FileFormat. info, http://www.fileformat.info/info/unicode/char/203d/index. htm [last accessed April 15, 2011].

48. Michael J. Babcock, "Interrobang Letterpress," http://www. interrobangletterpress.com/ [last accessed April 15, 2011]; Adam Giles, Personal correspondence, December 2011.

49. Bomb Town, *?!INTERROBANG?!*, Stubborn Records, http://www. stubbornrecords.com/shop/customer/product.php?productid= 24427 [last accessed April 15, 2011]; *Interrobang?! Magazine*, http:// www.interrobangzine.com/ [last accessed April 15, 2011]; Fanshawe Student Union, *Interrobang*, http://www.fsu.ca/interrobang/index. asp [last accessed April 15, 2011].

50. Debra White, "Vintage Typewriter Key Cuff Links Interro- bang," Etsy.com, http://www.etsy.com/listing/65245062/vintage- typewriter-key-cuff-links [last accessed April 15, 2011].

51. Vince Frost, Personal correspondence, November 2011.

52. Kirsty Tough, Personal correspondence, August 2012.

53. Merriam-Webster Inc., *Merriam-Webster's Collegiate Dictionary* (Springfield, MA: Merriam-Webster, 1993); Penny Speckter, Personal correspondence, February 2009.

3. THE OCTOTHORPE (#)

1. Oxford English Dictionary, "Pound Sign, n.," *Oxford English Dictionary*, http://www.oed.com/view/Entry/263614 [last accessed August 27, 2012].

2. Reinhold Aman, ed, *Maledicta* 3, 1979.

3. Dumesnil, *Latin Synonyms* (Baldwin, Cradock & Joy, 1825), 414; F. P. Leverett, Jacobo Facciolati, Egidio Forcellini, et al, *A New and Copious Lexicon of the Latin Language* (Boston: J. H. Wilkins and R. B. Carter, 1837), 676.

4. Leverett et al, *A New and Copious Lexicon of the Latin Language,* 490.

5. A. Cappelli, D. Heimann, and R. Kay, *The Elements of Abbreviation in Medieval Latin Palaeography* (Lawrence: University of Kansas Libraries, 1982), 41.

6. Bernhard Bischoff and University of Cambridge, "Abbreviations," in *Latin Paleography: Antiquity and the Middle Ages* (Cambridge, UK: Cambridge University Press, 1995), 150; Oxford English Dictionary, "Tittle, n.," *Oxford English Dictionary*, http://www.oed.com/view/Entry/202640 [last accessed August 27, 2012].

7. Keith G. Irwin, *The Romance of Writing from Egyptian Hieroglyphics to Modern Letters, Numbers & Signs* (New York: Viking, 1961).

8. "Unicode Character 'L B BAR SYMBOL' (U+2114)," FileFormat. info, http://www.fileformat.info/info/unicode/char/2114/index.htm [last accessed May 7, 2011].

9. Oxford Dictionaries, "Pound," *Oxford Dictionaries Online*, http://oxforddictionaries.com/definition/pound [last accessed May 5, 2011].

10. E. Gibbon, "General Observations on the Fall of the Roman Empire in the West," in *The History of the Decline and Fall of the Roman Empire* (Paris: A. and W. Galignani, 1831), 641–45.

11. G. Halsall, *Barbarian Migrations and the Roman West, 376–568*, Cambridge Medieval Textbooks (Cambridge, UK: Cambridge University Press, 2007).

12. C. Lansing and E. D. English, "The Idea of a Middle Ages," *A Companion to the Medieval World,* Blackwell Companions to European History (Oxford, UK: Wiley-Blackwell, 2009), 3–6.

13. Brian Duignan, Gloria Lotha, Amy Tikkanen, et al, "Carolingian Dynasty (European dynasty)," *Encyclopaedia Britannica*, http://www.britannica.com/EBchecked/topic/96523/Carolingian-dynasty [last accessed May 28, 2012].

14. G. W. Trompf, "The Concept of the Carolingian Renaissance," *Journal of the History of Ideas* 34, no. 1 (1973): 3–26; André Vauchez, Barrie Dobson, and Michael Lapidge, "Carolingian Renaissance," in *Encyclopedia of the Middle Ages* (Paris: Éditions du CERF [etc.], 2000), 243.

15. C. U. Clark, "How Our Roman Type Came to Us," *The North American Review* 195, no. 677 (1912): 546–49; Lane Wilkinson, "The Humanistic Minuscule and the Advent of Roman Type," Paper (Chattanooga: University of Tennessee, n.d.), 12.

16. Angela Redish, "From Carolingian Penny to Classical Gold Standard," in *Bimetallism* (Cambridge, UK: Cambridge University Press, 2006), 1–12.

17. P. Spufford, "The Appearance of the Denier and the Revival of Trade," in *Money and Its Use in Medieval Europe*, Cambridge Paperback Library (Cambridge, UK: Cambridge University Press, 1993), 27–54.

18. D. Harper, "Soldier (n.)," *Online Etymology Dictionary*, http://www.etymonline.com/index.php?term=soldier [last accessed May 29, 2012].

19. Spufford, "The Appearance of the Denier and the Revival of Trade," 27–54.

20. Jeannette L. Nolen and Grace Young, "pound sterling (money)," *Encyclopaedia Britannica*, http://www.britannica.com/EBchecked/topic/473092/pound-sterling [last accessed April 23, 2011].

21. Oxford English Dictionary, "Pound Sign, n."

22. Daniel Defoe. *The fortunes and misfortunes of the famous Moll Flanders &c. who was born in Newgate, and during a life of continu'd variety for threescore years, besides her childhood, was twelve year a whore,*

*five times a wife (whereof once to her own brother) twelve year a thief,
eight year a transported felon in Virginia, at last grew rich, liv'd honest,
and died a penitent* (Printed for, and sold by W. Chetwood . . . and T.
Edling . . . MDDCXXI, 1722), 325; Merritt Moseley, "Pounds, Shillings, and Pence: Currency Values and Reading English Literature,
1750–1998," in Cindy Ho and Merritt Moseley, eds., *Philological Association of the Carolinas* volume XXV (Asheville: University of North
Carolina, 2008), 80–96.

23. Daniel Defoe, *The Fortunes & Misfortunes of the Famous Moll Flanders
     &C.* (Sioux Falls, SD: Nuvision Publications, 2007).

24. C. H. V. Sutherland, *English Coinage, 600–1900* (London: B. T. Batsford, 1973).

25. K. Menninger, "20-Group 'Man,'" in *Number Words and Number
     Symbols: A Cultural History of Numbers* (New York: Dover Publications, 1992), 49.

26. C. Sladen, "Holidays at Home in the Second World War," *Journal
     of Contemporary History* 37, no. 1 (2002): 67–89.

27. N. Spake, "The Shilling System," ScottishBrewing.com, 2005,
     http://www.scottishbrewing.com/history/shilling.php

28. Cato and Ernest Brehaut, *Cato the Censor on Farming*, volume 17 of
     Records of Civilisation (New York: Columbia University Press, 1933),
     xlvi.

29. Harry A. Miskimin, "Two Reforms of Charlemagne? Weights and
     Measures in the Middle Ages," *The Economic History Review* 20, no.
     1 (1967): 40–49; Nolen and Young, "Pound Sterling (money)."

30. Robert Friedberg, Arthur L. Friedberg, and Ira S. Friedberg, *Gold
     Coins of The World: Complete from 600 A.D. to the Present: An Illustrated
     Standard Catalogue with Valuations* (Williston, VT: Coin & Currency Institute, 1980), 760.

31. Lewis V. Judson, *Weights and Measures Standards of the United States:
     A Brief History* (Gaithersburg, MD: Department of Commerce,
     National Bureau of Standards, 1976), Appendix 8.

32. Drew Cullen, "Why Microsoft makes a complete hash out of C#,"
     The Register, July 4, 2002, http://www.theregister.co.uk/2002/07/04/
     why_microsoft_makes_a_complete/.

33. "2. Lexical analysis," *Python v2.7.1 documentation*, http://docs.python. org/reference/lexical_analysis.html#comments [last accessed May 5, 2011]; World Chess Federation, "E.I.01B," Appendices, *FIDE Handbook*, http://www.fide.com/fide/handbook?id=125& view=article [last accessed April 26, 2011].

34. Theodore Rosendorf, "Proofreaders' Marks," in *The Typographic Desk Reference*, 1st edition (New Castle, DE: Oak Knoll Press, 2009), 67.

35. David R. Yale and Andrew J. Carothers, *The Publicity Handbook: The Inside Scoop from More Than 100 Journalists and PR Pros on How to Get Great Publicity Coverage in Print, Online, and On the Air* (Lincolnwood, IL: NTC Business Books, 2001).

36. *Green Book*, 1973 (Geneva: International Telecommunication Union); Robert Fulford, "How Twitter Saved the Octothorpe," *National Post*, November 30, 2010, http://fullcomment. nationalpost.com/2010/11/30/robert-fulford-how-twitter-saved-the-octothorpe/.

37. John Baugh, Robert Hass, Maxine H. Kingston, et al, "Octothorpe," *The American Heritage Dictionary of the English Language* (Boston: Houghton Mifflin, 2000).

38. Joyce Blackburn, *James Edward Oglethorpe* (London: Lippincott, 1970).

39. Bringhurst, "Octothorpe."

40. Oxford Dictionaries, "Thorp." *Oxford Dictionaries Online*, http:// oxforddictionaries.com/definition/thorp [last accessed May 8, 2011].

41. Ralph Carlsen, "What the ####?" *Telecoms Heritage Journal* 28 (1996): 52–53.

42. Kay Dekker, "Letters: Internet Hash," *New Scientist*, March 1996.

43. Oxford English Dictionary, "Octothorp, n.," *Oxford English Dictionary*, http://www.oed.com/view/Entry/246467 [last accessed May 22, 2012].

44. E. Siever, S. Spainhour, and N. Patwardhan, *Perl in q Nutshell: A Desktop Quick Reference*, 2nd edition (Sebastopol, CA: O'Reilly, 2002), 33.

45. Erik Gregersen, "Bell Laboratories (American Company)," *Encyclopaedia Britannica*, http://www.britannica.com/EBchecked/topic/59675/Bell-Laboratories [last accessed May 10, 2011].

46. Douglas A. Kerr, "The ASCII Character 'Octatherp,'" (abstract), May 7, 2006, http://dougkerr.net/pumpkin/articles/Octatherp.pdf; T. Viswanathan, *Telecommunication Switching Systems and Networks* (Prentice-Hall of India Pvt. Ltd, 2004), 29.

47. Sheldon Hochheiser, "Pressing Matters: Touch-Tone Phones Spark Debate," *Encore*, first and second quarters, 1999, 13–14; T. Viswanathan, "Crossbar Switching," in *Telecommunication Switching Systems and Networks* (Prentice-Hall of India Pvt. Ltd, 2004), 67–68.

48. Regis J. Bates and Donald W. Gregory, *Voice & Data Communications Handbook (Standards & Protocols)*, 4th edition (San Francisco, CA: McGraw-Hill Osborne Media, 2001), 214.

49. Schenker, "Pushbutton Calling with a Two-Group Voice Frequency Code," 235–55.

50. Bates and Gregory, *Voice & Data Communications Handbook (Standards & Protocols)*, 214.

51. AT&T, "Milestones in AT&T History–1963," http://www.corp.att.com/history/milestone_1963.html [last accessed May 19, 2011].

52. Hochheiser, "Pressing Matters," 13–14.

53. K. Carlberg, J. Polk, and I. Brown, *MLPP in Context*, Kluwer International series in Engineering and Computer Science (Dordrecht, Netherlands: Kluwer Academic Publishers, 2003); A. A. Gokhale, "Voice Communications: Dual Tone Multiple Frequency (DTMF)," in *Introduction to Telecommunications* (Independence, KY: Thomson/Delmar Learning, 2004), 134–35.

54. Hochheiser, "Pressing Matters," 13–14.

55. Kerr, "The ASCII Character 'Octatherp.'"

56. American Standards Association Sectional Committee on Computers and Information Processing, X3 and Business Equipment Manufacturers Association (U.S.), *American standard code for information interchange: Sponsor: Business Equipment Manufacturers Association. Approved June 17, 1963* (Washington, DC: American Standards Association, 1963).

57. Douglas A. Kerr, Personal correspondence, May 2011.

58. Kerr, "The ASCII Character 'Octatherp.'"

59. Douglas A. Kerr, Personal correspondence, May 2011.

60. "You Asked Us: About the * and # on the New Phones," *The Calgary Herald*, September 9, 1972, 90.

61. Carlsen, "What the ####?" 52–53.

62. Shiveta Singh and Amy Tikkanen, "Jim Thorpe (American athlete)," *Encyclopaedia Britannica*, http://www.britannica.com/EBchecked/topic/593411/Jim-Thorpe [last accessed May 22, 2011].

63. Carlsen, "What the ####?" 52–53.

64. Dekker, "Letters: Internet Hash"; J. A. Simpson, E. S. C. Weiner, and Oxford University Press, *The Oxford English Dictionary* (Clarendon Press/Oxford University Press, 1989).

65. Susan Teltscher, Esperanza Magpantay, Ivan Vallejo, et al., "Introduction," in *Measuring the Information Society* (Geneva: International Telecommunication Union, 2012).

66. "What Are Hashtags ('#' Symbols)?" Help Center, http://support.twitter.com/articles/49309-what-are-hashtags-symbols [last accessed July 11, 2012].

67. Tim Dowling, "How the # Became the Sign of Our Times," *The Guardian*, December 8, 2010; Fulford, "How Twitter Saved the Octothorpe."

68. Lindy West, "2010's Symbol of the Year: #," *GQ*, December 2010.

4. THE AMPERSAND (&)

1. William Smith, "Patricii," in *Dictionary of Greek and Roman Antiquities* (London: Walton and Maberly, 1853), 875–77.

2. Anthony Everitt, "Always Be the Best, My Boy, the Bravest," in *Cicero: The Life and Times of Rome's Greatest Politician* (New York: Random House, 2001), 21–46.

3. Kathryn Tempest, "The Making of the Man (106–82 BC)," in *Cicero: Politics and Persuasion in Ancient Rome* (London: Continuum, 2011), 22.

4. Anthony Everitt, "The Forum and the Fray," in *Cicero: The Life and Times of Rome's Greatest Politician* (New York: Random House, 2001), 47–66.

5. Kathryn Tempest. *Cicero: Politics and Persuasion in Ancient Rome* (London: Continuum, 2011)

6. Anthony Everitt, "Against Catilina," in *Cicero: The Life and Times of Rome's Greatest Politician* (New York: Random House, 2001), 87–112.

7. Ibid.

8. "Letters," in *The Linguist: Journal of the Institute of Linguists, Volumes 38–41* (London: Institute of Linguists, 1999), 151.

9. Daniel B. Updike, "A Font and Its Case," in *Printing Types, Their History, Forms, and Use: A Study in Survivals, With Illustrations* (Cambridge, MA: Harvard University Press; Humphrey Milford; Oxford University Press, 1927), 15–26.

10. William J. Dominik and Jon Hall, "Cicero as Orator," in *A Companion to Roman Rhetoric* (Oxford, UK: Wiley-Blackwell, 2010), 275.

11. William Smith, "Catalina," in *Dictionary of Greek and Roman Biography and Mythology* (Boston: C.C. Little and J. Brown [etc., etc.], 1849), 631–32.

12. William Smith, "Cicero," in *Dictionary of Greek and Roman Biography and Mythology* (Boston: C.C. Little and J. Brown [etc., etc.], 1849), 713–14.

13. Marshall W. Fishwick, "Two Pivotal Essays," in *Cicero, Classicism, and Popular Culture* (Binghamton, NY: Haworth Press, 2007), 57.

14. Marcus T. Cicero, "Book VII," in E. O. Winstedt, ed., *Letters to Atticus*, volume 2 (Portsmouth, NH: Heinemann, 1913), 35.

15. A. Di Renzo, "His Master's Voice: Tiro and the Rise of the Roman Secretarial Class," *Journal of Technical Writing and Communication* 30, no. 2 (2000): 155–68.

16. Ibid.

17. Marcus T. Cicero, "Book XIII," in E. O. Winstedt, ed., *Letters to Atticus*, volume 3 (Portsmouth, NH: Heinemann, 1918), 161; Di Renzo, "His Master's Voice," 155–68.

18. Allien R. Russon, Kathleen Kuiper, Gloria Lotha, et al, "History and Development of Shorthand (shorthand)," *Encyclopaedia Britannica*, http://www.britannica.com/EBchecked/topic/541788/shorthand/53186/History-and-development-of-shorthand#ref 512802 [last accessed June 7, 2011).

19. David A. King, "On the Greek Origin of the Basingstoke Ciphers," in *The Ciphers of the Monks: A Forgotten Number-Notation of the Middle Ages* (Stuttgart: Franz Steiner Verlag, 2000), 62.

20. Russon et al, "History and Development of Shorthand (shorthand)."

21. Smith, "Cicero," 717.

22. Anthony Everitt, "Death at the Seaside," in *Cicero: The Life and Times of Rome's Greatest Politician* (New York: Random House, 2001), 307–19.

23. Di Renzo, "His Master's Voice," 155–68.

24. Robert Harris, "Senator," in *Imperium* (London: Arrow, 2009), 14.

25. Jan Tschichold and Frederick Plaat, *The Ampersand: Its Origin and Development* (London: Woudhuysen, 1957).

26. Maren Goldberg, Shiveta Singh, Amy Tikkanen, et al, "Vesuvius (volcano, Italy)," *Encyclopaedia Britannica*, http://www.britannica.com/EBchecked/topic/627039/Vesuvius [last accessed June 9, 2011].

27. Robert Bringhurst, "3.3 Ligatures," in *The Elements of Typographic Style: Version 3.2* (Vancouver, BC: Hartley & Marks, 2008), 50–53.

28. Robert Bringhurst, "Long S," in *The Elements of Typographic Style: Version 3.2* (Vancouver, BC: Hartley & Marks, 2008), 312.

29. W. Shakespeare, J. Bell, S. Johnson, et al, "Advertisement," in *The dramatick writings of Will. Shakspere with the notes of all the various commentators* (London: John Bell, 1788).

30. "Requiem: Features," typography.com, http://www.typography.com/fonts/font_features.php?featureID=44&productLineID=100020 [last accessed June 11, 2011].

31. Albrecht Heeffer, "On the Nature and Origin of Algebraic Symbolism," in Bart Van Kerkhove ed., *New Perspectives on Mathematical Practices. Essays in Philosophy and History of Mathematics* (Singapore: World Scientific, 2009), 1–27; S. Schwartzman, "Plus," in *The Words of Mathematics: An Etymological Dictionary of Mathematical Terms Used in English*, MAA Spectrum (Washington, DC: Mathematical Association of America, 1994), 167.

32. J. Tschichold and R. McLean, "Introduction to the English Language Version," in *The New Typography: A Handbook for Modern Designers* (Berkeley: University of California Press, 2006), xv.

33. Jan Tschichold, *Die neue Typographie: Ein Handbuch für zeitgemäss Schaffende* (Bildungsverband der Deutschen Buchdrucker, 1928).

34. "Jan Tschichold (German typographer and author)," *Encyclopaedia Britannica*, http://www.britannica.com/EBchecked/topic/607663/ Jan-Tschichold [last accessed June 18, 2011].

35. Otl Aicher, "Typographical Warfare," in Steven Heller and Philip B. Meggs, eds., *Texts on Type: Critical Writings on Typography* (New York: Allworth Press, 2001).

36. Jan Tschichold, *Formenwandlungen der &-Zeichen* (Frankfurt am Main: D. Stempel AG, 1953); Tschichold and Plaat, *The Ampersand*.

37. Frederic W. Goudy and Frederic W. Goudy Collection, Library of Congress, *Ands & Ampersands, From the First Century B.C. to the Twentieth A.D.* (New York: Typophiles, 1936); Paul Standard and Typophiles (New York, N.Y.), *The Ampersand: Sign of Continuity* (New York: George Grady Press, 1936).

38. Daniel B. Updike, "Type and Type-Forms of the Fifteenth Century in Italy," in *Printing Types, Their History, Forms, and Use: A Study in Survivals, With Illustrations* (Cambridge, MA: Harvard University Press; Humphrey Milford; Oxford University Press, 1927), 70–81.

39. Clark, "How Our Roman Type Came to Us," 546–49; Amy Tikkanen, "Roman Script (calligraphy)," *Encyclopaedia Britannica*, http://www.britannica.com/EBchecked/topic/508323/roman-script [last accessed August 16, 2012]; Wilkinson, "The Humanistic Minuscule and the Advent of Roman Type," 12.

40. Robert Bringhurst, "7.2.1 The Renaissance Roman Letter," in *The Elements of Typographic Style: Version 3.2* (Vancouver, BC: Hartley & Marks, 2008), 122–23.

41. B. L. Ullman, "A Rival System—Niccolò Niccoli," in *The Origin and Development of Humanistic Script*, Storia e Letteratura (Rome: Edizione di storia e letteratura, 1974), 59–77.

42. Daniel B. Updike, "The Aldine Italic," in *Printing Types, Their History, Forms, and Use: A Study In Survivals, With Illustrations* (Cambridge, MA: Harvard University Press; Humphrey Milford; Oxford University Press, 1927), 125–32.

43. Robert Bringhurst, "7.2.2 The Renaissance Italic Letter," in *The Elements of Typographic Style: Version 3.2* (Vancouver, BC: Hartley & Marks, 2008), 124–25.

44. Robert Bringhurst, "3.4 Tribal Alliances and Families," in *The Elements of Typographic Style: Version 3.2* (Vancouver, BC: Hartley & Marks, 2008), 57; Updike, "The Aldine Italic," 125–32.

45. Jonathan Hoefler, "Our Middle Name," typography.com, April 28, 2008, http://www.typography.com/ask/showBlog.phtp?blogID=98.

46. Bernhard Bischoff and University of Cambridge, "Latin Handwriting in the Middle Ages," in *Latin Paleography: Antiquity and the Middle Ages* (Cambridge, UK: Cambridge University Press, 1995), 127–36.

47. Wilkinson, "The Humanistic Minuscule and the Advent of Roman Type," 12.

48. Albert Kapr, *The Art of Lettering: The History, Anatomy, and Aesthetics of the Roman Letter Forms* (Munich: Saur, 1983).

49. "The Appearance of the Bible," *The Gutenberg Bible at the Ransom Center*, http://www.hrc.utexas.edu/exhibitions/permanent/gutenberg/html/6.html [last accessed June 24, 2011].

50. Tschichold and Plaat, *The Ampersand*.

51. Isidore and Stephen A. Barney, "Common Shorthand Signs [De notis vulgaribus], in *The Etymologies of Isidore of Seville* (Cambridge, UK: Cambridge University Press, 2006), 51.

52. Paul Saenger, "Tironian Notes," in *Space Between Words: The Origins of Silent Reading* (Palo Alto, CA: Stanford University Press, 1997), 115–19.

53. Russon, et al, "History and Development of Shorthand (shorthand)."

54. Bernhard Bischoff and University of Cambridge, "Latin Script in Antiquity," in *Latin Paleography: Antiquity and the Middle Ages* (Cambridge, UK: Cambridge University Press, 1995), 80–82.

55. Theodore Rosendorf, "Blackletter," in *The Typographic Desk Reference* (New Castle, DE: Oak Knoll Press, 2009), 100.

56. G. Reuveni, "From Reading Books to Consumption of Books and Back Again," in *Reading Germany: Literature and Consumer Culture*

in Germany Before 1933, Berghahn Series (Oxford, UK: Berghahn Books, 2006), 206.

57. "Ampersand," *Urban Dictionary*, http://www.urbandictionary.com/define.php?term=ampersand [last accessed July 3, 2011]; H. A. Long, "Birth Names," in *Personal and Family Names* (London: Hamilton, Adams & Co., 1883), 98.

58. "Ampersand," *Wikipedia*, http://en.wikipedia.org/wiki/Ampersand [last accessed July 23, 2012]; J. B. Shank, William L. Hosch, Marco Sampaolo, et al, "André-Marie Ampère (French physicist)," *Encyclopaedia Britannica*, http://www.britannica.com/EBchecked/topic/21416/Andre-Marie-Ampere [last accessed July 23, 2012].

59. E. S. Sheldon, "Studies and notes," in *Further Notes on the Names of the Letters*, volume II (Boston: Ginn & Company, 1893), 158.

60. J. S. Farmer and W. E. Henley, "Ampersand," in *A Dictionary of Slang and Colloquial English* (New York: G. Routledge & Sons, limited, 1905), 10.

61. A. Barrère and C. G. Leland, "Ampersand," in *A Dictionary of Slang, Jargon & Cant: Embracing English, American, and Anglo-Indian Slang, Pidgin English, Tinker's Jargon and Other Irregular Phraseology*, volume 1 (Edinburgh: The Ballantyne Press, 1889), 36–37.

62. "Ampersand," *Oxford Dictionaries Online*, http://oxforddictionaries.com/definition/ampersand [last accessed July 3, 2011].

5.   THE @ SYMBOL

1. Gina Smith, "Unsung Innovators: Ray Tomlinson, Who Put the @ Sign in Every E-mail Address," *Computerworld*, December 3, 2007, http://www.computerworld.com/s/article/9046658/.

2. Katie Hafner and Matthew Lyon, "The Third University," in *Where Wizards Stay Up Late: The Origins of the Internet* (New York: Pocket Books, 2003), 102; Ibid., 82.

3. Paul E. Ceruzzi, "Computing Comes of Age, 1956–1964," in *A History of Modern Computing* (Cambridge, MA: MIT Press, 2002), 74.

4. Paul E. Ceruzzi, "From Mainframe to Minicomputer, 1959–1969," in *A History of Modern Computing* (Cambridge, MA: MIT Press, 2002), 133.

5. Paul E. Ceruzzi, "The 'Go-Go' Years and the System/360, 1961–1975," in *A History of Modern Computing* (Cambridge, MA: MIT Press, 2002), 154.

6. J. Daintith and Oxford University Press, "Teletypewriter," in *Oxford Dictionary of Computing*, Oxford Paperback Reference (Oxford, UK: Oxford University Press, 2004), 529.

7. Ibid.

8. "Want to Take Your Teletype Around with You?" *Computerworld*, March 1968, 4.

9. John Markoff, "Outlook 2000: Technology & Media: Talking the Future With: Robert W. Taylor; An Internet Pioneer Ponders the Next Revolution," *New York Times*, December 20, 1999.

10. Ibid.

11. S. Segaller, "Something Seductive," in *Nerds 2.0.1: A Brief History of the Internet* (New York: TV Books, 1998), 69.

12. Sastri L. Kota, Kaveh Pahlavan, and Pentti A. Leppänen, "Overview of Broadband Satellite Networks," in *Broadband Satellite Communications for Internet Access,* 1st edition (New York: Springer, 2003).

13. Timothy Johnson, "Electronic Post for Switching Data," *New Scientist*, May 1976.

14. Katie Hafner and Matthew Lyon, "A Block Here, Some Stones There," in *Where Wizards Stay Up Late: The Origins of the Internet* (New York: Pocket Books, 2003), 80; Keenan Mayo and Peter Newcomb, "An Oral History of the Internet: How the Web Was Won," *Vanity Fair*, July 2008.

15. G. O'Regan, "The ARPANET," in *A Brief History of Computing* (New York: Springer, 2008), 182.

16. Ray Tomlinson, "The First Network Email," OpenMap, http://openmap.bbn.com/-tomlinso/ray/firstemailframe.html [last accessed July 10, 2011].

17. Ibid.

18. Ibid.

19. Bruno Giussani, *Storia di @: l'origine della "chiocciola" e altre poco note vicende dell'Internet* (Bellinzona, Switzerland: Messaggi Brevi, 2003).

20. Mark Ward, "H@ppy Birthday to You," BBC News, dot.life, October 8, 2001, http://news.bbc.co.uk/1/hi/in_depth/sci_tech/2000/dot_life/1586229.stm.

21. Katie Hafner, "Looking Back; In the Beginning, a Note to Himself," *New York Times*, December 6, 2001.

22. Ray Tomlinson, "Frequently Made Mistakes," OpenMap, http://openmap.bbn.com/-tomlinso/ray/mistakes.html {last accessed July 10, 2011].

23. Sasha Cavender, "ASAP Legends," *Forbes*, October 10, 1998, http://www.forbes.com/asap/1998/1005/126.html.

24. J. Abbate, "'The Most Neglected Element': Users Transform the ARPANET," in *Inventing the Internet* (Cambridge, MA: MIT Press, 2000), 107–08; N. Newman, "How the Government Created the Internet," in *Net Loss: Internet Prophets, Private Profits, and the Costs to Community* (University Park: Pennsylvania State University Press, 2002), 57.

25. I. Tuomi, "Combination and Specialization," in *Networks of Innovation: Change and Meaning in the Age of the Internet*, SITRA (Series) (Oxford, UK: Oxford University Press, 2006), 139.

26. Robert Bringhurst, "At," in *The Elements of Typographic Style: Version 3.2* (Vancouver, BC: Hartley & Marks, 2008), 303.

27. B. L. Ullman, "Abbreviations and Ligatures," in *Ancient Writing and Its Influence* (Lanham, MD: Cooper Square Publishers, 1963), 187.

28. Bernhard Bischoff and University of Cambridge, "Uncial," in *Latin Paleography: Antiquity and the Middle Ages* (Cambridge, UK: Cambridge University Press, 1995), 66–72; F. P. Leverett, Jacobo Facciolati, Egidio Forcellini, Imm Scheller, G. H. Lünemann, and H. W. Torrey, *A New and Copious Lexicon of the Latin Language* (Boston: J. H. Wilkins and R.B. Carter; C. C. Little and James Brown, 1837), 16.

29. Tony Long, "May 4, 1536: C U @ the Piazza," Wired.com, May 4, 2009, http://www.wired.com/thisdayintech/2009/05/dayintech_0504/.

30. Keith G. Irwin, *The Romance of Writing from Egyptian Hieroglyphics to Modern Letters, Numbers, & Signs* (New York: Viking, 1961).

31. Dario Olivero, "Quella chiocciola anticainventata dagli italiani [That old snail invented by Italians]," *La Repubblica*, July 28, 2000, http://www.repubblica.it/online/tecnologie_internet/chiocciola/chiocciola/chiocciola.html; Phillip Willan, "merchant@florence Wrote It First 500 Years Ago," *The Guardian*, July 31, 2000, http://www.guardian.co.uk/technology/2000/jul/31/internetnews.internationalnews.

32. Karen S. Chung, "Summary: The @ Symbol," *The Linguist List*, July 2, 1996, http://linguistlist.org/issues/7/7-968.html.

33. Giorgio Stabile, "L'icon@ dei mercanti [The icon of the merchants]," Trecanni.it, http://web.archive.org/web/20080609015621/http://www.treccani.it/iniziative/eventi_icona.htm [last accessed July 31, 2011].

34. Chelsey Parrott-Sheffer and Michael Ray, "Amphora (pottery)," *Encyclopaedia Britannica*, http://www.britannica.com/EBchecked/topic/21654/amphora [last accessed July 31, 2011].

35. William Smith, "Quadrantal," in *Dictionary of Greek and Roman Antiquities* (London: Walton and Maberly, 1853), 979–80.

36. "Arroba," *Merriam-Webster Online*, http://www.merriam-webster.com/dictionary/arroba [last accessed July 31, 2011].

37. "Quintal," *Merriam-Webster Online*, http://www.merriam-webster.com/dictionary/quintal [last accessed July 31, 2011].

38. "Arroba," *Merriam-Webster Online*, http://www.merriam-webster.com/dictionary/arroba [last accessed July 31, 2011].

39. Stabile, "L'icon@ dei mercanti."

40. S. G. Gaya, *Tesoro lexicográfico, 1492–1726* (Consejo Superior de Investigaciones Científicas, Patronato "Menéndez Pelayo," "Antonio de Nebrija," 1947).

41. Jorge Romance, "La arroba no es de Sevilla (ni de Italia)," *Purnas.com*, June 30, 2009, http://www.purnas.com/2009/06/30/la-arroba-no-es-de-sevilla-ni-de-italia/.

42. Oxford English Dictionary, "At Sign, n.," *Oxford English Dictionary*, http://www.oed.com/view/Entry/256344 [last accessed August 29, 2012]; Stabile, "L'icon@ dei mercanti."; A. A. Stewart, "Commercial

A," in *The Printer's Dictionary of Technical Terms: A Handbook of Definitions and Information About Processes of Printing; With a Brief Glossary of Terms Used in Book Binding* (Boston: School of Printing, North End Union, 1912), 35.

43. Stabile, "L'icon@ dei mercanti"; Stewart, "Commercial A," 35.

44. L. Day and I. McNeil, "Sholes, Christopher Latham," in *Biographical Dictionary of the History of Technology* (London: Taylor and Francis, 2003), 1104–05; John Pratt, "Type Writing Machine," *Scientific American*, July 1867, 3; C. Latham Sholes, Carlos Glidden, and Samuel W. Soulé, "Improvement in Type-Writing Machines," U.S. Patent 79,265, July 1868; C. E. Weller, "Home of First Typewriter," in *The Early History of the Typewriter* (Laponte, IN: Chase and Shepherd, 1921), 20–21; D. S. Wershler-Henry, "The Poet's Stave and Bar," in *The Iron Whim: A Fragmented History of Typewriting*, G - Reference, Information and Interdisciplinary Subjects Series (Ithaca, NY: Cornell University Press, 2005), 166–77.

45. Sholes, Glidden, and Soulé, "Improvement in Type-Writing Machines."

46. Weller, "Home of First Typewriter," 20–21.

47. The Editors of *Encyclopaedia Britannica,* Gloria Lotha, and Amy Tikkanen, "Christopher Latham Sholes," *Encyclopaedia Britannica*, http://www.britannica.com/EBchecked/topic/541481/Christopher-Latham-Sholes [last accessed July 25, 2012].

48. B. Bliven, *The Wonderful Writing Machine* (New York: Random House, 1954).

49. Guy Pérard, Personal correspondence, July 2012; Richard Polt, Personal correspondence, July 2011.

50. L. Heide, "The 1890 United States Census," in *Punched-Card Systems and the Early Information Explosion, 1880–1945*, Studies in Industry and Society (Baltimore: Johns Hopkins University Press, 2009), 24.

51. William R. Aul, "Herman Hollerith: Data Processing Pioneer," *Think*, November 1974, 22–24.

52. Heide, "The 1890 United States Census," 24.

53. Charles E. MacKenzie, "Early Codes: BCDIC," in *Coded Character Sets: History and Development* (Boston: Addison-Wesley, 1980), 66–67.

54. Ibid.

55. "Univac Fieldata Codes," National Space Science Data Center, http://nssdc.gsfc.nasa.gov/nssdc/formats/UnisysFieldata.htm [last accessed August 7, 2011]; Aul, "Herman Hollerith," 22–24; Charles E. MacKenzie, "Early Codes: FIELDATA," in *Coded Character Sets: History and Development* (Boston: Addison-Wesley, 1980), 64–66; Charles E. MacKenzie, "Early Codes: The Stretch Code," in *Coded Character Sets: History and Development* (Boston: Addison-Wesley, 1980), 67–75.

56. American Standards Association, Sectional Committee on Computers and Information Processing, X3 and Business Equipment Manufacturers Association (U.S.), *American Standard Code for Information Interchange: Sponsor: Business Equipment Manufacturers Association. Approved June 17, 1963* (Washington, DC: American Standards Association, 1963).

57. Shannon Cochran, "Morse Code Meets the Internet," in *Dr. Dobb's Journal: Software Tools for the Professional Programmer* 29 (Manhasset, NY: CMP Media, May 2004), 14.

58. Vint Cerf, "RFC 20: ASCII Format for Network Interchange," October 16, 1969, http://tools.ietf.org/html/rfc20; Oxford English Dictionary, "Commercial, adj. and n.," *Oxford English Dictionary*, http://www.oed.com/view/Entry/37081 [last accessed August 29, 2012].

59. Peter Marks, "Festival Review/Theater; Goethe's Password? A Classic Tale Retold," *New York Times*, July 24, 1998.

60. "El districte de la innovació" [Urban innovation], 22@Barcelona, http://www.22barcelona.com/content/blogcategory/50/281/lang,en/ [last accessed July 25, 2011].

61. Paola Antonelli, "@ at MoMA," *Inside Out*, March 22, 2010, http://www.moma.org/explore/inside_out/2010/03/22/at-moma/.

6. THE ASTERISK AND DAGGER (*, †)

1. Geoffrey A. Glaister, "Reference Marks," in *Encyclopedia of the Book* (New Castle, DE: Oak Knoll Press, 1996), 412; Jonathan Hoefler, "House of Flying Reference Marks, or Quillon & Choil,"

typography.com, June 4, 2009, http://www.typography.com/ask/
showBlog.php?blogID=190; K. Marie Stolba, "Psalm Tones," in *The
Development of Western Music: A History* (New York: McGraw-Hill,
1998), 33.

2. Robert Bringhurst, "Asterisk," in *The Elements of Typographic Style:
Version 3.2* (Vancouver, BC: Hartley & Marks, 2008), 303.

3. Samuel N. Kramer, "The Origin and Development of the Cuneiform System of Writing," in *The Sumerians: Their History, Culture,
and Character* (Chicago: University of Chicago Press, 1963), 302–04.

4. Oxford English Dictionary, "Museum, n.," *Oxford English Dictionary*, http://www.oed.com/viewdictionaryentry/Entry/124079 [last
accessed August 27, 2012].

5. T. W. Africa, "Copernicus' Relation to Aristarchus and Pythago-
ras," *Isis* 52, no. 3 (1961): 403–09.

6. Theodore Vrettos, "The Mind of the City," in *Alexandria: City of
the Western Mind* (New York: Free Press, 2001), 29–74.

7. Rudolf Pfeiffer, "Alexandrian Scholarship at Its Height: Aristophanes of Byzantium," in *History of Classical Scholarship. From the
Beginnings to the End of the Hellenistic Age* (Oxford, UK: Clarendon,
1968), 171–209.

8. William Smith, "Zenodotus," in *Dictionary of Greek and Roman Biography and Mythology* (Boston: C. C. Little and J. Brown; [etc., etc.],
1849), 951.

9. Gregory Nagy, "The Quest for a Definitive Text of Homer," in
Homer's Text and Language (Champaign, IL: University of Illinois
Press, 2004), 3–24.

10. Rudolf Pfeiffer, "Zenodotus and His Contemporaries," in *History
of Classical Scholarship. From the Beginnings to the End of the Hellenistic
Age* (Oxford, UK: Clarendon, 1968), 105–22.

11. Isidore and Stephen A. Barney, "Punctuated Clauses [De posi-
turis]," in *The Etymologies of Isidore of Seville* (Cambridge, UK:
Cambridge University Press, 2006), 50; Oxford English Dictionary, "Obelus, n.," *Oxford English Dictionary*, http://www.oed.com/
viewdictionaryentry/Entry/129571 [last accessed August 27, 2012].

12. Rudolf Pfeiffer, "Aristarchus: The Art of Interpretation," in *History of Classical Scholarship. From the Beginnings to the End of the Hellenistic Age* (Oxford, UK: Clarendon, 1968), 210–33.

13. Oxford English Dictionary, "Asterisk, n.," *Oxford English Dictionary*, http://www.oed.com/viewdictionaryentry/Entry/12121 [last accessed July 31, 2011].

14. Kathleen McNamee, "Sigla," in *Sigla and Select Marginalia in Greek Literary Papyri* (Brussels: Fondation Égyptologique Reine Élisabeth, 1992), 9.

15. Vrettos, *Alexandria*.

16. F. W. Farrar, "Glory of Origen," in *Mercy and Judgment: A Few Last Words on Christian Eschatology, with Reference to Dr. Pusey's 'What Is of Faith?'"* (London: Macmillan, 1881), 306.

17. Eusebius, Christian F. Crusé, and Isaac Boyle, "The Education of Origen, from His Earliest Youth," in *The Ecclesiastical History of Eusebius Pamphilus, Bishop of Caesarea, in Palestine,* volume 6 (London: Lippincott, 1865), 204–07;

18. Farrar, "Glory of Origen," 306; William Smith, "Origenes," in *Dictionary of Greek and Roman Biography and Mythology* (Boston: C. C. Little and J. Brown; [etc., etc.], 1849), 579–60.

19. Epiphanius and Frank Williams, "Against Origen, also called Adamantius, 44 but 64 of the series," in *The Panarion of Epiphanius of Salamis: Books II and III (Sects 47–80, De Fide)* (Leiden: E. J. Brill, 1994), 134; Eusebius et al, "The Resolute Act of Origen," 212; Theodore Vrettos, "The Soul of the City," in *Alexandria: City of the Western Mind* (New York: Free Press, 2001) 163–207.

20. Jennifer M. Dines and Michael A. Knibb, "Facts and Fictions," in *The Septuagint* (London: T&T Clark, 2005), 159–75; Jennifer M. Dines and Michael A. Knibb, "The Status of the Septuagint: From Philo to Jerome," in Ibid., 63–80.

21. Jennifer M. Dines and Michael A. Knibb, "Textual Developments to the Fifth Century CE," in Ibid., 81–104.

22. Henry B. Swete and Thackeray, "The Hexapla, and the Hexaplaric and Other Recensions of the Septuagint," in *An Introduction to the*

Old Testament in Greek (Cambridge, UK: Cambridge University Press, 1900), 59–86.

23. McNamee, "Sigla," 12.

24. Thomas H. Horne, "The Septuagint Greek Version," in *An Introduction to the Critical Study and Knowledge of the Holy Scriptures*, volume 2 (Printed for T. Cadell, 1821), 49.

25. J. E. Dean and the British Library, *Epiphanius' Treatise on Weights and Measures: The Syriac Version*, Studies in Ancient Oriental Civilization (Chicago: The University of Chicago Press, 1935).

26. Swete and Thackeray, "The Hexapla," 59–86.

27. Dines and Knibb, "Textual Developments to the Fifth Century CE," 81–104.

28. British Library, "Gutenberg's Texts—Indulgences," *Gutenberg Bible,* http://www.bl.uk/treasures/gutenberg/indulgences.html [last accessed March 13, 2012].

29. H. C. E. Midelfort, "Review: Printing, Propaganda, and Martin Luther," *Central European History* 28, no. 2 (1995).

30. Donald K. McKim, "Luther's Wittenberg," in *The Cambridge Companion to Martin Luther* (Cambridge, UK: Cambridge University Press, 2003), 20–38.

31. Kenneth G. Appold, "The Luther Phenomenon," in *The Reformation: A Brief History* (London: Wiley-Blackwell, 2011), 43–80.

32. McKim, "Luther's Wittenberg," 20–38.

33. Oxford English Dictionary, "Obelisk, n. and adj.," *Oxford English Dictionary,* http://www.oed.com/viewdictionaryentry/Entry/129568 [last accessed August 27, 2012].

34. McKim, "Luther's Wittenberg," 20–38.

35. Stolba, "Psalm Tones," 33.

36. C. H. Timperley, "On References, &c.," in *A Dictionary of Printers and Printing: With the Progress of Literature, Ancient and Modern, Bibliographical Illustrations*... (H. Johnson, 1839), 9–12; Daniel B. Updike, "Some Notes on Liturgical Printing," *Dolphin: A Journal of the Making of Books*, no. 2 (1935): 208–16.

37. "Unicode Character 'LATIN CROSS' (U+271D)," FileFormat.info, http://www.fileformat.info/info/unicode/char/271d/index.htm [last accessed May 30, 2012].

38. R. A. Sayce, "Compositorial Practices and the Localization of Printed Books, 1530–1800," *The Library*, s5-XXI (1966): 1–45.

39. M. B. Parkes, "The Technology of Printing and the Stabilization of the Symbols," in *Pause and Effect: Punctuation in the West* (Berkeley: University of California Press, 1993), 50–64; Sayce, "Compositorial Practices and the Localization of Printed Books, 1530–1800," 1–45.

40. George H. Clark, "Foreign Policy," in *Oliver Cromwell* (New York: Harper & Bros., 1895), 157–82.

41. N. Malcolm, C. Cavendish, J. Pell, et al, "The Life of John Pell," in *John Pell (1611–1685) and His Correspondence with Sir Charles Cavendish: The Mental World of an Early Modern Mathematician* (Oxford, UK: Oxford University Press, 2005), 150–54.

42. Ibid., 163–64.

43. F. Cajori, "Signs for Division and Ratio," in *A History of Mathematical Notations* (New York: Cosimo, 2011), 268–78.

44. Parkes, "The Technology of Printing and the Stabilization of the Symbols," 50–64.

45. W. W. E. Slights, "The Edifying Margins of Renaissance English Books," in *Managing Readers: Printed Marginalia in English Renaissance Books*, Editorial Theory and Literary Criticism (Ann Arbor: University of Michigan Press, 2001), 19–60.

46. H. J. Jackson, "History," in *Marginalia: Readers Writing in Books*, Nota Bene Series (New Haven: Yale University Press, 2002), 44–80; Slights, "The Edifying Margins of Renaissance English Books," 19–60.

47. Jenny Swanson, "The Glossa Ordinaria," in G. R. Evans ed., *The Medieval Theologians* (London: Blackwell Publishers, 2001), 156–67.

48. Parkes, "The Technology of Printing and the Stabilization of the Symbols," 50–64.

49. C. Zerby, "The Early Years," in *The Devil's Details: A History of Footnotes* (New York: Touchstone Books, 2003), 44.

50. Parkes, "The Technology of Printing and the Stabilization of the Symbols," 50–64; Zerby, "The Early Years," 44.

51. E. Partridge, "Oddments," in *You Have a Point There: A Guide to Punctuation and Its Allies* (n.p.: Hamilton, 1953), 226.

52. University of Chicago Press, "Footnotes," in *Manual of Style, Being a Compilation of the Typographical Rules in Force at the University of Chicago Press, To Which Are Appended Specimens of Types in Use* (Chicago: University of Chicago Press, 1906), 71–73; R. M. Ritter, "References and Notes," in *The Oxford Style Manual* (Oxford, UK: Oxford University Press, 2003), 557; University of Chicago Press, "Endnotes Plus Footnotes," in *The Chicago Manual of Style,* 16th edition (Chicago: University of Chicago Press, 2010), 677.

53. J. Hodgson, J. Hodgson-Hinde, J. Raine, and J. C. Bruce, *A History of Northumberland, Part II*, volume III of *A History of Northumberland, in Three Parts* (London: E. Walker, 1840), 157–322.

54. E. Gibbon, *The History of the Decline and Fall of the Roman Empire* (A. and W. Galignani, 1831), 284–85; Gibbon, Ibid., 11; Gibbon, Ibid., 191.

55. Fred Rodell, "Goodbye to Law Reviews," *Virginia Law Review* 23, no. 1 (1936).

56. A. J. Mikva, "Goodbye to Footnotes," *University of Colorado Law Review* 56 (1984): 647, 194.

57. Modern Language Association of America, "Content Notes," in *MLA Handbook for Writers of Research Papers* (New York: Modern Language Association of America, 2009), 230–31.

58. Betsy Hilbert, "Elegy for Excursus: The Descent of the Footnote," *College English* 51, no. 4 (1989).

59. Alexandra Horowitz, "Will the E-Book Kill the Footnote?" *New York Times*, October 7, 2011.

60. Zerby, *The Devil's Details.*

61. J. G. Ballard, *War Fever* (New York: Collins, 1990); Vladimir Nabokov, *Pale Fire: A Novel* (New York: Putnam, 1962).

62. Nicolas Wroe, "A Life in Writing," *The Guardian*, September 18, 2009, http://www.guardian.co.uk/culture/2009/sep/19/nicholson-baker-interview.

63. M. Richler, *Barney's Version: A Novel* (London: Chatto & Windus, 1997).

64. David Foster Wallace, *Infinite Jest: A Novel* (Boston: Little, Brown and Company, 1996).

65. Adam Augustyn, Gloria Lotha, and Amy Tikkanen, "Barry Bonds (American baseball player)," *Encyclopaedia Britannica*, http://www.britannica.com/EBchecked/topic/760211/Barry-Bonds [last accessed March 20, 2012].

66. Allen Barra, "Roger Maris's Misunderstood Quest to Break the Home Run Record," *The Atlantic*, July 27, 2011, http://www.theatlantic.com/entertainment/archive/2011/07/roger-mariss-misunderstood-quest-to-break-the-home-run-record/242586/.

67. Allen Barra, "An Asterisk Is Very Real, Even When It's Not," *New York Times*, May 27, 2007; Matt Slater, "From Balco to Bonds, Baseball's Asterisk Era," BBC News, April 14, 2011, http://www.bbc.co.uk/blogs/mattslater/2011/04/from_balco_to_bonds_baseballs.html; Michael Wilbon, "Tarnished Records Deserve an Asterisk," *Washington Post*, December 4, 2004.

68. "Future Eligibles," Baseball Hall of Fame, http://baseballhall.org/hall-famers/rules-election/future-eligibles [last accessed March 20, 2012]; Jack Curry, "Barry Bonds Ball Goes to the Hall, Asterisk and All," *New York Times*, July 2, 2008.

69. Michael Kranish and Susan Milligan, "Bush Wins Election*," *Boston Globe*, November 27, 2000; G. H. Stempel and J. N. Gifford, "'Dewey Defeats Truman,'" in *Historical Dictionary of Political Communication in the United States* (Westport, CT: Greenwood Press, 1999), 38.

70. Mary F. Berry, Cruz Reynoso, Christopher Edley, Yvonne Y. Lee, Elsie Meeks, and Victoria Wilson, "Voting Irregularities in Florida During the 2000 Presidential Election," *U.S Commision on Civil Rights*, June 2001, http://www.usccr.gov/pubs/vote2000/report/main.htm; State Elections Offices, "2000 Official Presidential General Election Results," December 2001, http://www.fec.gov/pubrec/2000presgeresults.htm.

71. Parul Jain and Michael Ray, "Bush v. Gore (law case)," *Encyclopaedia Britannica*, http://www.britannica.com/EBchecked/topic/934324/Bush-v-Gore [last accessed August 11, 2012].

72. Nedda Allbray, "As the President-Elect Takes Center Stage; With an Asterisk," *New York Times*, December 15, 2000.

73. E. Sweets and L. Dubose, "Meeting Multiple Mollies," in *Stirring It Up with Molly Ivins: A Memoir with Recipes* (Austin: University of Texas Press, 2011), 13–17.

74. Garry Wills, "Outstripping the News," *New York Review of Books*, November 25, 2010, http://www.nybooks.com/articles/archives/2010/nov/25/outstripping-news/.

75. G. Vecsey, "Armstrong, Best of His Time, Now with an Asterisk," *New York Times*, August 24, 2012.

76. Reginald Nievera, "What Barry Bonds and George W. Bush Have in Common," *ChicagoNow*, December 27, 2011, http://www.chicagonow.com/ignorance-is-bliss/2011/12/what-barry-bonds-and-george-w-bush-have-in-common/; Peter Smith, "George W. Bush and Barry Bonds: Asterisks All Around," *The Huffington Post*, June 11, 2007, http://www.huffingtonpost.com/peter-smith/george-w-bush-and-barry-b_b_51649.html.

77. "Unicode Character 'TWO ASTERISKS ALIGNED VERTICALLY' (U+2051)," FileFormat.info, http://www.fileformat.info/info/unicode/char/2051/index.htm [last accessed May 30, 2012]; C. W. Butterfield, "Of the Asterism," in *A Comprehensive System of Grammatical and Rhetorical Punctuation: Designed for the Use of Schools* (Cincinnati, OH: Longley, 1858), 37; Oxford English Dictionary, "Asterism, n.," *Oxford English Dictionary*, http://www.oed.com/viewdictionaryentry/Entry/12124 [last accessed August 27, 2012].

78. Oxford English Dictionary, "Diesis, n.," *Oxford English Dictionary*, http://www.oed.com/viewdictionaryentry/Entry/52420 [last accessed August 27, 2012].

7. THE HYPHEN (-)

1. J. D. Petit, "World War I and the Literacy Test," in *The Men and Women We Want: Gender, Race, and the Progressive Era Literacy Test*

Debate (Rochester, NY: University of Rochester Press, 2010), 103–27; Simon Rabinovitch, "Thousands of Hyphens Perish as English Marches On," *Reuters*, September 21, 2007.

2. V. D. Benedetto, "At the Origins of Greek Grammar," *Glotta* 68, no. 1–2 (1990): 19–39.

3. Rudolf Pfeiffer, "The Epigoni: From Aristarchus' Pupils to Didymus," in *History of Classical Scholarship. From the Beginnings to the End of the Hellenistic Age* (Oxford, UK: Clarendon, 1968), 252–79.

4. E. Dickey, "Dionysius Thrax," in *Ancient Greek Scholarship: A Guide to Finding, Reading, and Understanding Scholia, Commentaries, Lexica, and Grammatical Treatises, from Their Beginnings to the Byzantine Period*, Classical Resources Series (New York: Oxford University Press, 2007), 77–80; J. Alan Kemp, "The Tekhne Grammatike of Dionysius Thrax: Translated into English," *Historiographia Linguistica* 13, no. 2 (1986): 343–63.

5. Dickey, "Dionysius Thrax," 215.

6. D. J. Murphy, "Hyphens in Greek Manuscripts," *Greek, Roman, and Byzantine Studies* 36, no. 3 (1995): 296–99; E. G. Turner and P. J. Parsons, "Introduction," in *Greek Manuscripts of the Ancient World*, Bulletin Supplement, University of London Institute of Classical Studies (University of London, 1987), 1–23.

7. Paul Saenger, "The Hyphen," in *Space Between Words: The Origins of Silent Reading* (Palo Alto: Stanford University Press, 1997), 69–70.

8. Paul Saenger, "Silent Reading: Its Impact on Late Medieval Script and Society," *Viator: Medieval and Renaissance Studies* 13 (1982): 367–414.

9. Bernhard Bischoff and University of Cambridge, "Palimpsests," in *Latin Paleography: Antiquity and the Middle Ages* (Cambridge, UK: Cambridge University Press, 1995), 11–12; Bernhard Bischoff and University of Cambridge, "Writing Instruments," in Ibid., 18–29; Saenger, "The Hyphen," 69–70.

10. D. Christian, S. Jacobsen, Associated Press, and D. Minthorn, "Editing Marks," in *Associated Press Stylebook and Briefing on Media Law* (New York: Basic Books, 2009), 407.

11. Paul Saenger, "The Circle of Sedulius Scottus," in *Space Between Words: The Origins of Silent Reading* (Palo Alto: Stanford University Press, 1997), 109–15.

12. Murphy, "Hyphens in Greek Manuscripts," 296–99.

13. Ibid.

14. Saenger, "Silent Reading," 367–414.

15. N. R. Ker, "Introduction," in *Catalogue of Manuscripts Containing Anglo-Saxon*, volume 1 (Oxford, UK: Clarendon Press, 1957), xxxv–xxxvi; Paul Saenger, "Traits d'Union," in *Space Between Words: The Origins of Silent Reading* (Palo Alto: Stanford University Press, 1997), 65–67.

16. E. A. Lowe, "Punctuation," in *The Beneventan Script: A History of the South Italian Minuscule* (Oxford, UK: Clarendon Press, 1914), 277–79; Saenger, "Traits d'Union," 65–67.

17. Paul Saenger, Telephone interview, April 2012.

18. Rabinovitch, "Thousands of Hyphens Perish as English Marches On."

19. Morimichi Watanabe, "An Appreciation," in C. M. Bellitto, T. M. Izbicki, and G. Christianson, eds., *Introducing Nicholas of Cusa: A Guide to a Renaissance Man* (Mahwah, NJ: Paulist Press, 2004), 24.

20. Brian A. Pavlac, "Reform," in Ibid., 112.

21. John Man, "A Hercules Labouring for Unity," in *The Gutenberg Revolution: How Printing Changed the Course of History* (London: Transworld Publishers, May 2010), 84–104.

22. John Man, "In Search of a Bestseller," in Ibid., 141–62.

23. British Library, "The Three Phases in the Printing Process," *Gutenberg Bible*, http://www.bl.uk/treasures/gutenberg/threephases.html [last accessed May 30, 2012].

24. John Boardley, "The Origins of ABC," *I Love Typography*, August 7, 2010, http://ilovetypography.com/2010/08/07/where-does-the-alphabet-come-from/; S. Füssel, "The 'Work of the Books': The 42-Line Bible," in *Gutenberg and the Impact of Printing* (Farnham, UK: Ashgate Pub., 2005), 18–22.

25. British Library, "The Copy on Vellum—The Decoration," *Gutenberg Bible*, http://www.bl.uk/treasures/gutenberg/vellumdecoration.html [last accessed March 13, 2012].

26. H. Zapf, "About Micro-Typography and the Hz-Program," *Electronic Publishing* 6, no. 3 (1993): 283–88.

27. Ibid.

28. B. L. Ullman, "The Gothic Script of the Late Middle Ages," in *Ancient Writing and its Influence* (Lanham, MD: Cooper Square Publishers, 1963), 118–30.

29. "The Appearance of the Bible," *The Gutenberg Bible at the Ransom Center,* http://www.hrc.utexas.edu/exhibitions/permanent/gutenberg/html/6.html [last accessed June 24, 2011].

30. R. G. C. Proctor and F. S. Isaac, *An Index to the Early Printed Books in the British Museum with Notes of Those in the Bodleian Library* (n.p.: BiblioBazaar, 2010).

31. S. Füssel, "Bringing the Technical Inventions Together," in *Gutenberg and the Impact of Printing* (Farnham, UK: Ashgate Pub., 2005), 15–18.

32. Johannes Gutenberg, "Latin Bible (the 'Gutenberg Bible')," *Special Collections and Archives,* http://smu.edu/bridwell_tools/specialcollections/Highlights2010/06117-Gutenberg-Bible-Leave.jpg [last accessed August 27, 2012]; University of Chicago Press, "Word Division," in *The Chicago Manual of Style,* 16th edition (Chicago: University of Chicago Press, 2010), 358–61.

33. Gutenberg, "Latin Bible (the 'Gutenberg Bible')"; R. M. Ritter, "Punctuation," in *The Oxford Style Manual* (Oxford: Oxford University Press, 2003), 133–40.

34. John Man, "The Bible," in *The Gutenberg Revolution: How Printing Changed the Course of History* (London: Transworld Publishers, May 2010), 169–70.

35. Geoffrey A. Glaister, "Hand Composition," in *Encyclopedia of the Book* (New Castle, DE: Oak Knoll Press, 1996), 216–18.

36. Harry McIntosh, Personal interview, April 2012.

37. T. L. De Vinne, "Notes and Illustrations," in *The Practice of Typography: Modern Methods of Book Composition* (New York: Century, 1904), 276–88; A. Hutt, "The Birth of the Newspaper," in *The Changing Newspaper: Typographic Trends in Britain and America 1622–1972* (London: Gordon Fraser, 1973), 15–42; R. Wendorf, "Unnoticed:

Secret Life of Type Faces," Lecture, Boston Athenaeum, April 28, 2005, http://forum-network.org/lecture/unnoticed-secret-life-type-faces.

38. University of Chicago Press, "Divisions," in *Manual of Style, Being a Compilation of the Typographical Rules in Force at the University of Chicago Press, to which Are Appended Specimens of Types in Use* (Chicago: University of Chicago Press, 1906), 68–70.

39. L. Null and J. Lobur, "Introduction," in *The Essentials of Computer Organization and Architecture* (Burlington, MA: Jones & Bartlett Learning, 2010), 1–46; W. Reyburn, *Flushed with Pride: The Story of Thomas Crapper* (Clifton-upon-Terne: Polperro Heritage Press, 2010).

40. M. Twain, F. Anderson, and R. P. Browning, "April–August 1885," in *Mark Twain's Notebooks & Journals*, volume 3 of *Mark Twain Papers* (Berkeley: University of California Press, 1980), 147.

41. C. H. Gold, "Occam's Razor: The Simplest Explanation," in *"Hatching Ruin," or, Mark Twain's Road to Bankruptcy*, Mark Twain and His Circle Series (Columbia: University of Missouri Press, 2003), 1–12.

42. "The Press: Linotype at 50," *Time*, July 13, 1936; Geoffrey A. Glaister, "Lanston, Tolbert," in *Encyclopedia of the Book* (New Castle, DE: Oak Knoll Press, 1996), 273–74; Geoffrey A. Glaister, "Mergenthaler, Ottmar," in Ibid., 320; Lawrence W. Wallis, "The Monotype Chronicles (1896–1906)," Monotype Imaging, http://www.monotypeimaging.com/aboutus/mt1896_1906.aspx [last accessed August 27, 2012].

43. K. Hillstrom and L. C. Hillstrom, "Telephones, Typewriters and Linotype Machines," in *Communications, Agriculture and Meatpacking, Overview/Comparison* (Santa Barbara, CA: ABC-CLIO, 2007), 43–49.

44. Geoffrey A. Glaister, "Linotype," in *Encyclopedia of the Book* (New Castle, DE: Oak Knoll Press, 1996), 295–96.

45. J. R. Rogers and Mergenthaler Linotype Company, "The Keyboard," in *Linotype Instruction Book: A Detailed Description of the Mechanism and Operation of the Linotype with Instructions for Its*

Erection, Maintenance, and Care (New York: Mergenthaler Linotype Company, 1925), 3–18.

46. Mergenthaler Linotype Company, "The Linotype Self-Quadder," in *Linotype Machine Principles* (New York: Mergenthaler Linotype Co., 1940), 391–409.

47. Geoffrey A. Glaister, "Monotype," in *Encyclopedia of the Book* (New Castle, DE: Oak Knoll Press, 1996), 329–31.

48. Geoff Barlow and Simon Eccles, "Single-character Composition—Monotype," in *Typesetting and Composition* (London: Blueprint, 1992), 38–40.

49. S. Loxley, "Detour: Meltdown," in *Type: The Secret History of Letters* (London: I. B. Tauris, 2004), 55–62.

50. Mergenthaler Linotype Company, "Gas and Electric Metal Pot," in *Linotype Machine Principles* (New York: Mergenthaler Linotype Co., 1940), 152–212.

51. Illinois Department of Factory Inspection, *Annual Report Volume 22 (1914–1915)* (Springfield, IL: Philips Bros., State Printers, 1915).

52. Geoff Barlow and Simon Eccles, "Electronic Output Machines," in *Typesetting and Composition* (London: Blueprint, 1992), 49–69.

53. Geoffrey A. Glaister, "Intertype Fotosetter," in *Encyclopedia of the Book* (New Castle, DE: Oak Knoll Press, 1996), 253.

54. Barlow and Eccles, "Electronic Output Machines," 49–69.

55. D. E. Knuth, "Digital Typography," in *Digital Typography*, CSLI Lecture Notes (CSLI Publications, 1999), 1–18.

56. Ibid.

57. D. E. Knuth, "Computers and Typesetting," in Ibid., 555–62; D. E. Knuth, "The New Versions of TeX and METAFONT," in Ibid., 563–70.

58. University of Chicago Press, "Word Division," 358–61.

59. *The New Merriam-Webster Pocket Dictionary* (New York: Pocket Books, 1974); Donald E. Knuth, "The Plain TeX Hyphenation Tables," Comprehensive TeX Archive Network, http://www.ctan. org/tex-archive/systems/knuth/dist/lib/hyphen.tex [last accessed April 5, 2012].

60. D. E. Knuth, "Digital Typography," in *Digital Typography*, CSLI Lecture Notes (CSLI Publications, 1999), 67–155.

61. T. L. De Vinne, "Signatures," in *The Practice of Typography: Modern Methods of Book Composition* (New York: Century, 1904), 269–76.

62. Knuth, "Breaking Paragraphs into Lines," in *Digital Typography*, CSLI Lecture Notes (CSLI Publications, 1999), 67–155.

63. Zapf, "About Micro-Typography and the *hz*-Program," 283–88.

64. Robert Bringhurst, "2.4 Etiquette of Hyphenation & Pagination," in *The Elements of Typographic Style: Version 3.2* (Vancouver, BC: Hartley & Marks, 2008), 42–44.

65. Bringhurst, "2.1 Horizontal Motion," 25–36.

66. S. Garfield, "American Scottish," in *Just My Type: A Book About Fonts* (London: Profile, 2010), 197–204.

67. Ibid.

68. Toby Thain, Robert Koritnik, Hrant H. Papazian, Simon Daniels, Charles Ellertson, John Hudson, and Thomas Phinney, "Origins of InDesign's New Paragraph Layout Engine?" *Typophile*, June 20, 2007, http://www.typophile.com/node/34620; Hàn T. Thành, *Micro-Typographic Extensions to the Tex Typesetting System*, PhD thesis, Masaryk University Brno, October 2000.

69. Eric Gill, *An Essay on Typography* (Jaffrey, NH: David R. Godine, 1993).

70. James Hartley and Richard L. Mills, "Unjustified Experiments in Typographical Research and Instructional Design," *British Journal of Educational Technology* 4, no. 2 (1973): 120–31; S. J. Muncer, B. S. Gorman, S. Gorman, and D. Bibel, "Right Is Wrong: An Examination of the Effect of Right Justification on Reading," *British Journal of Educational Technology* 17, no. 1 (1986): 5–10.

71. A. Rafaeli, "The School of Close Spacing," in *Book Typography* (New Castle, DE: Oak Knoll Press, 2005), 9–30.

8. THE DASH (—)

1. Eric S. Raymond, "-," in *The New Hacker's Dictionary* (Cambridge, MA: MIT Press, 1996), 45.

2. R. M. Ritter, "En Rule," in *The Oxford Style Manual* (Oxford: Oxford University Press, 2003), 140–41; University of Chicago Press, "En Dashes," in *The Chicago Manual of Style,* 16th edition (Chicago: University of Chicago Press, 2010), 331–33.

3. Oxford English Dictionary, "Aposiopesis, n." *Oxford English Dictionary*, http://www.oed.com/view/Entry/9392 [last accessed August 27, 2012]; University of Chicago Press, "Em Dashes," in *The Chicago Manual of Style,* 16th edition (Chicago: University of Chicago Press, 2010), 333–35.

4. Will Hill, "Page Layout," in *The Complete Typographer: A Foundation Course for Graphic Designers Working with Type* (London: Thames & Hudson, 2010), 130–35; University of Chicago Press, "Em Dashes," 333–35.

5. Robert Bringhurst, "5.2 Dashes, Slashes & Dots," in *The Elements of Typographic Style: Version 3.2* (Vancouver, BC: Hartley & Marks, 2008), 80–84.

6. J. Joyce and D. Kiberd, *Ulysses,* Penguin Classics (New York: Penguin Books, 2000), 1.

7. Theodore Rosendorf, "Dash," in *The Typographic Desk Reference* (New Castle, DE: Oak Knoll Press, 2009), 40.

8. Bas Jacobs, Personal correspondence, April 2012.

9. J. Alan Kemp, "The Tekhne Grammatike of Dionysius Thrax: Translated into English," *Historiographia Linguistica* 13, no 2. (1986): 343–63.

10. M. B. Parkes, "The Development of the General Repertory of Punctuation," in *Pause and Effect: Punctuation in the West* (Berkeley: University of California Press, 1993), 41–49.

11. C. Kleinhenz, "Buoncompagno da Signa," in *Medieval Italy: An Encyclopedia*, volume 1 of *The Routledge Encyclopedias of the Middle Ages* (New York: Routledge, 2004), 163–64.

12. J. N. Adams, *The Latin Sexual Vocabulary* (Baltimore: Johns Hopkins University Press, 1982), 14; F. P. Leverett, Jacobo Facciolati, Egidio Forcellini, Imm Scheller, G. H. Lünemann, and H. W. Torrey, "Virgula," in *A New and Copious Lexicon of the Latin Language*

(Boston: J. H. Wilkins and R. B. Carter; C. C. Little and James Brown, 1837), 967.

13. M. B. Parkes, "Virgula," in *Pause and Effect: Punctuation in the West* (Berkeley: University of California Press, 1993), 307.

14. Parkes, "The Development of the General Repertory of Punctuation," 41–49.

15. M. H. Corréard, V. Grundy, J. B. Ormal-Grenon, and N. Rollin, "Virgule," in *The Oxford-Hachette French Dictionary: French-English, English-French* (Oxford: Oxford University Press, 2007), 896.

16. Parkes, "The Development of the General Repertory of Punctuation," 41–49.

17. Francisco Alonso Almeida, "Punctuation Practice in a Late Medieval English Medical Remedybook," *Folia Linguistica Historica* 22, no. 1 (2001): 207–32; T. C. Davis, "Repertoire," in *The Broadview Anthology of Nineteenth-Century British Performance* (Peterborough, ON: Broadview Press, 2011), 13–26.

18. G. Ambrose and P. Harris, "Virgule," in *The Visual Dictionary of Typography* (London: AVA Publishing, 2010), 266; J. Lennard, "Dash," in *The Poetry Handbook: A Guide to Reading Poetry for Pleasure and Practical Criticism* (Oxford, UK: Oxford University Press, 2005), 136–37.

19. Oxford English Dictionary, "Dash, n.1," *Oxford English Dictionary*, http://www.oed.com/viewdictionaryentry/Entry/47366 [last accessed August 27, 2012].

20. Robert Bringhurst, "2.1 Horizontal Motion," in *The Elements of Typographic Style: Version 3.2* (Vancouver, BC: Hartley & Marks, 2008), 25–36; Ephraim Chambers, "Quadrat," in *Cyclopædia, or, An universal dictionary of arts and sciences containing the definitions of the terms, and accounts of the things signify'd thereby, in the several arts, both liberal and mechanical, and the several sciences, human and divine : the figures, kinds, properties, productions, preparations, and uses, of things natural and artificial : the rise, progress, and state of things ecclesiastical, civil, military, and commercial : with the several systems, sects, opinions, &c. among philosophers, divines, mathematicians, physicians, antiquaries, criticks, & c :*

the whole intended as a course of antient and modern learning, volume 2 (Printed for J. and J. Knapton [and 18 others], 1728), 926.

21. Theodore Rosendorf, "Didot Point," in *The Typographic Desk Reference* (New Castle, DE: Oak Knoll Press, 2009), 11; Theodore Rosendorf, "Point," in Ibid., 22.

22. Bringhurst, "5.2 Dashes, Slashes & Dots," 80–84.

23. A. A. Stewart, "Mutton Quad," in *The Printer's Dictionary of Technical Terms: A Handbook of Definitions and Information about Processes of Printing; with a Brief Glossary of Terms Used in Book Binding* (Boston, MA: School of Printing, North End Union, 1912), 160.

24. J. Southward, *Practical Printing: A Handbook of the Art of Typography* (London: J. M. Powell & Son, 1884), 11.

25. Bringhurst, "2.1 Horizontal Motion," 25–36; Chambers, "Quadrat," 926.

26. T. Julian Brown, John Higgins, Kathleen Kuiper, et al, "Punctuation," *Encyclopaedia Britannica,* http://www.britannica.com/EBchecked/topic/483473/punctuation [last accessed January 9, 2011].

27. Nicholson Baker, "Survival of the Fittest," *New York Review of Books,* November 4, 1993.

28. W. Shakespeare and S. McMillin, "Compositorial Prudence," in *The First Quarto of Othello,* New Cambridge Shakespeare: Early Quartos (Cambridge, UK: Cambridge University Press, 2001), 21–25.

29. W. Shakespeare and S. McMillin, "3.3.5," in Ibid., 96; W. Shakespeare and S. McMillin, "2.3.283–84," in Ibid., 91; W. Shakespeare and S. McMillin, "5.2.92," in Ibid., 140.

30. J. Henley, "The End of the Line?," *The Guardian,* April 4, 2008, http://www.guardian.co.uk/world/2008/apr/04/france.britishidentity

31. Jane Austen, *Pride and Prejudice: A Novel* (Printed for T. Egerton, 1813); Baker, "Survival of the Fittest."; Charles Dickens, *Oliver Twist* (London: Richard Bentley, 1839); Herman Melville, *Moby-Dick, or, the Whale* (New York: Harper & Bros.; Richard Bentley, 1851).

32. J. Johnson, "Points," In *Typographia,* volume 2 (London: Hurst, Rees, Orme, Brown & Green, 1824), 54–63.

33. University of Chicago Press, "Capitalization," in *Manual of Style, Being a Compilation of the Typographical Rules in Force at the University of Chicago Press, to which Are Appended Specimens of Types in Use* (Chicago: University of Chicago Press, 1906), 19; University of Chicago Press, "Dashes," in Ibid., 53–56; University of Chicago Press, *A Manual of Style: For Authors, Editors and Copywriters* (Chicago: University of Chicago Press, 1969).

34. E. Partridge, "Compound Points," in *You Have a Point There: A Guide to Punctuation and Its Allies* (n.p.: Hamilton, 1953), 86–88.

35. H. L. Mencken and A. Cooke, "The Baltimore of the Eighties," in *The Vintage Mencken* (New York: Vintage Books, 1955), 4–18.

36. Baker, "Survival of the Fittest."

37. Oxford English Dictionary, "Eclipsis, n.," *Oxford English Dictionary*, http://www.oed.com/view/Entry/59368 [last accessed August 27, 2012]; Oxford University Press, "Ellipsis," *The Concise Oxford Dictionary of English Etymology*, 1996, http://www.oxfordreference.com/views/ENTRY.html?entry=t27.e4910 [last accessed April 19, 2012].

38. Robert Bringhurst, "Ellipsis," in *The Elements of Typographic Style: Version 3.2* (Vancouver, BC: Hartley & Marks, 2008), 308; J. Wilson, "Marks of Ellipsis," in *The Elements of Punctuation: With Rules on the Use of Capital Letters: Being An Abridgement of the "Treatise On English Punctuation.": Prepared for Schools* (Boston: Crosby, Nichols and Company, 1856), 136.

39. S. W. Maugham, *The Constant Wife: A Comedy in Three Acts* (New York: George H. Doran Company, 1926).

40. Alvin D. Coox, "The Dutch Invasion of England: 1667," *Military Affairs* 13, no. 4 (1949), 223–33; M. E. Novak, "After the Revolution," in *Daniel Defoe: Master of Fictions: His Life and Ideas* (Oxford, UK: Oxford University Press, 2001), 11–31.

41. M. E. Novak, "Marriage and Rebellion," in *Daniel Defoe: Master of Fictions: His Life and Ideas* (Oxford, UK: Oxford University Press, 2001), 71–100; Pat Rogers, "Defoe in the Fleet Prison," *The Review of English Studies* 22, no. 88 (1971): 451–55.

42. M. E. Novak, "A 'True Spy' in Scotland," in *Daniel Defoe: Master of Fictions: His Life and Ideas* (Oxford, UK: Oxford University Press, 2001), 289–312.

43. I. Watt, "Realism and the Novel Form," in *The Rise of the Novel: Studies in Defoe, Richardson, and Fielding* (London: Chatto & Windus, 1960), 34.

44. Daniel Defoe, *The fortunes and misfortunes of the famous Moll Flanders &c. who was born in Newgate, and during a life of continu'd variety for threescore years, besides her childhood, was twelve year a whore, five times a wife (whereof once to her own brother) twelve year a thief, eight year a transported felon in Virginia, at last grew rich, liv'd honest, and died a penitent* (Printed for, and sold by W. Chetwood . . . and T. Edling . . . MDDCXXI, 1722).

45. Ibid.; Maximillian E. Novak, "Defoe's 'Indifferent Monitor': The Complexity of Moll Flanders," *Eighteenth-Century Studies* 3, no. 3 (1970), 352.

46. Watt, "Realism and the Novel Form," 34.

47. Defoe, *Moll Flanders*.

48. K. Olsen, "Law and Order," in *Daily Life in 18th-Century England*, The Greenwood Press "Daily Life Through History" Series (Westport, CT: Greenwood Press, 1999), 205–20.

49. Defoe, *Moll Flanders*.

50. J. E. Luebering, "Epistolary Novel (literature)," *Encyclopaedia Britannica*, http://www.britannica.com/EBchecked/topic/190331/epistolary-novel [last accessed April 24, 2012].

51. Samuel Richardson, *Pamela: or, Virtue Rewarded* (Printed for C. Rivington; and J. Osborn, 1740).

52. Austen, *Pride and Prejudice*; Robert L. Stevenson, *Treasure Island* (London: Cassell, 1883).

53. T. Smollett, *The Adventures of Peregrine Pickle: In Which Are Included, Memoirs of a Lady of Quality* (Printed for the author, and sold by D. Wilson . . . , 1751).

54. J. Sutherland, "The Way We Live Now," in *The Stanford Companion to Victorian Fiction* (Palo Alto: Stanford University Press, 1990),

663–64; A. Trollope, *The Way We Live Now: A Novel* (New York: Harper & Brothers, 1875).

55. G. Hughes, "Damn," in *An Encyclopedia of Swearing: The Social History of Oaths, Profanity, Foul Language, and Ethnic Slurs in the English-Speaking World* (Armonk, NY: M. E. Sharpe, 2006), 116–18.

56. "Lord Ronald S. Gower Dies," *New York Times*, March 10, 1916; R. S. Gower, "Impressions of the Americans, and a Visit to Long-fellow," in *My Reminiscences*, volume 2 (London: K. Paul, Trench & Company, 1883), 257–69.

57. N. Hessell, "Samuel Johnson: Beyond Lilliput," in *Literary Authors, Parliamentary Reporters: Johnson, Coleridge, Hazlitt, Dickens* (Cambridge, UK: Cambridge University Press, 2011), 17–60.

58. Jonathan Swift, *Travels into Several Remote Nations of the World, In Four Parts* (Printed for B. Motte, 1726).

59. B. Clarke, "The Mature Eighteenth-Century Newspaper, 1750–1800," in *From Grub Street to Fleet Street: An Illustrated History of English Newspapers to 1899* (Farnham, UK: Ashgate, 2004), 77–104.

60. Hessell, "Samuel Johnson," 17–60.

61. Anonymous, "To Mr. Urban, on His Vol. XI," *Gentleman's Magazine* December 1741, 11.

62. James Boswell, "A Chronological Catalogue of the Prose Works of Samuel Johnson LL DNB," in *The Life of Samuel Johnson, L.L.D. Comprehending An Account of His Studies and Numerous Works* (London: C. Dilly, 1791), xv–xxi.

63. A. H. Reddick, "'The Plan of My Undertaking': The Composition and Purpose of the Plan of a Dictionary," in *The Making of Johnson's Dictionary, 1746–1773*, Cambridge Studies in Publishing and Printing History (Cambridge, UK: Cambridge University Press, 1996), 12–25.

64. Parliament (UK), "Living Heritage," Official Report, http://www.parliament.uk/about/living-heritage/evolutionofparliament/parliamentwork/communicating/overview/officialreport/ [last accessed April 24, 2012].

65. C. Emden, "Language in the Age of the Typewriter," in *Nietzsche on Language, Consciousness, and the Body*, International Nietzsche Studies (Champaign: University of Illinois Press, 2005), 27–31; Mark

Twain, Oliver Wendell Holmes Collection (Library of Congress), and Roy J. Friedman, Mark Twain Collection (Library of Congress), "The First Writing-Machines," in *The $30,000 Bequest and Other Stories* (New York: Harper & Bros., 1906), 224–28; C. E. Weller, "Home of First Typewriter," in *The Early History of the Typewriter* (Laponte, IN: Chase and Shepherd, 1921), 20–21.

66. J. L. Bell, "Dash It All!" *Oz and Ends*, May 14, 2008, http://ozandends. blogspot.co.uk/2008/05/dash-it-all.html; Frederic Heath, "The Typewriter in Wisconsin," *The Wisconsin Magazine of History* 27, no. 3 (1944).

67. Weller, "Home of First Typewriter," 20–21.

68. C. Latham Sholes, "Improvement in Type-Writing Machines," U.S. Patent 207,559, August 1878, http://www.google.com/patents/US207559.

69. D. H. Whalen, "Typing Other Than Letters," in *The Secretary's Handbook* (San Diego, CA: Harcourt Brace Jovanovich, 1973), 27–36.

70. Sholes, "Improvement in Type-Writing Machines."

71. I. Pitman, "Dash," in *Pitman's Typewriter Manual: A Practical Guide to Commercial, Literary, Legal, Dramatic and All Classes of Typewriting Work* (London: Sir Isaac Pitman & Sons, Ltd., 1893), 82; T. A. Reed, *A Biography of Isaac Pitman (Inventor of Phonography)* (London: Sydney, Griffith, Farran, Okeden and Welsh, 1890).

72. William W. Cook, "Our Friend, the T.W.," in *The Fiction Factory* (Ridgewood, NJ: The Editor Company, 1912), 88–93.

73. T. L. De Vinne, "Cases," in *The Practice of Typography: Modern Methods of Book Composition* (New York: Century, 1904), 10–36; I. Saltz, "Thinking Like a Typesetter," in *Typography Essentials: 100 Design Principles for Working with Type* (Beverly, MA: Rockport Publishers, 2009), 48–49.

74. Nate Piekos, "Comic Fonts and Lettering," *Blambot*, http://www.blambot.com/grammar.shtml [last accessed April 4, 2012].

75. Todd Klein, "Punctuating Comics: Dots and Dashes," *Todd's Blog*, September 23, 2008, http://kleinletters.com/Blog/?p=1946.

76. American Standards Association, Sectional Committee on Computers and Information Processing, X3 and Business Equipment

Manufacturers Association (U.S.), *American Standard Code for Information Interchange: Sponsor: Business Equipment Manufacturers Association. Approved June 17, 1963* (Washington, DC: American Standards Association, 1963).

77.   J. K. Korpela, "Hyphens and Dashes," in *Unicode Explained* (Sebastopol, CA: O'Reilly, 2006), 418–21.

78.   Microsoft, "Windows Keyboard Layouts," *Go Global Developer Center*, http://msdn.microsoft.com/en-us/goglobal/bb964651.aspx [last accessed July 26, 2012].

79.   University of Chicago Press, "Formatting," in *The Chicago Manual of Style,* 16th edition (Chicago: University of Chicago Press, 2010), 59–63.

80.   "Unicode Character Category 'Punctuation, Dash,'" FileFormat. info, http://www.fileformat.info/info/unicode/category/Pd/index. htm [last accessed April 30, 2012]; C. Grover, "Autocorrecting Math, Formatting, and Smart Tags," in *Word 2007: The Missing Manual* (Sebastopol, CA: O'Reilly Media, 2007), 154–56.

81.   N. French, "Small (but Important) Details," in *InDesign Type: Professional Typography with Adobe InDesign* (Upper Saddle River, NJ: Pearson Education, Limited, 2010), 93–94; David Kadavy, "Mind Your En and Em Dashes: Typographic Etiquette," *Smashing Magazine*, August 15, 2011, http://www.smashingmagazine.com/2011/08/15/mind-your-en-and-em-dashes-typographic-etiquette/.

82.   John Barth, *Lost in the Funhouse: Fiction for Print, Tape, Live Voice*, Universal Library (New York: Doubleday, 1968), 69.

83.   Thomas Pynchon, *Mason & Dixon* (New York: Henry Holt, 1997).

9.   THE MANICULE (☞)

1.   W. H. Sherman, "Towards a History of the Manicule," in *Used Books: Marking Readers in Renaissance England* (Philadelphia: University of Pennsylvania Press, 2009), 28–52.

2.   E. Dickey, "Introduction to Ancient Scholarship," in *Ancient Greek Scholarship: A Guide to Finding, Reading, and Understanding Scholia, Commentaries, Lexica, and Grammatical Treatises, from Their*

Beginnings to the Byzantine Period, Classical Resources Series (New York: Oxford University Press, 2007), 3–17.

3. L. Avrin, "Parchment," in *Scribes, Script, and Books*, ALA Classics (Chicago: American Library Association, 2010), 156–57; Edwin Yamauchi, "Review: The Birth of the Codex by Colin H. Roberts; T. C. Skeat," *The Journal of Library History (1974–1987)* 20, no. 2 (1985): 202–04.

4. Kathleen McNamee, "Another Chapter in the History of Scholia," *The Classical Quarterly* 48, no. 1 (1998): 269–88.

5. B. Stone, "Amazon Erases Orwell Books from Kindle," *New York Times*, July 17, 2009.

6. H. E. Bell, "The Price of Books in Medieval England," *The Library*, s4-XVII, no. 3 (1936): 312–32.

7. "Renaissance Books Reexamined," *Perspectives Newsletter*, January 2012.

8. Bell, "The Price of Books in Medieval England," 312–32.

9. Steven Orgel, "Margins of Truth," in A. Murphy, ed., *The Renaissance Text: Theory, Editing, Textuality* (Manchester, UK: Manchester University Press, 2000), 91–107.

10. Bell, "The Price of Books in Medieval England," 312–32.

11. R. W. Clement, "Medieval and Renaissance Book Production," *Library Faculty & Staff Publications*, Utah State University, 1997, 10.

12. Orgel, "Margins of Truth," 91–107.

13. Ann Blair, "Reading Strategies for Coping with Information Overload ca. 1550–1700," *Journal of the History of Ideas* 64, no. 1 (2003): 19.

14. F. S. Stevenson, "Origin and Name," in *Robert Grosseteste* (London: Macmillan and Co., 1899), 10–23.

15. S. Harrison Thomson, "Grosseteste's Topical Concordance of the Bible and the Fathers," *Speculum* 9, no. 2 (1934): 139–44.

16. R. W. Southern, "Grosseteste's Theological Index," in *Robert Grosseteste: The Growth of an English Mind in Medieval Europe*, Clarendon Paperbacks Series (Oxford, UK: Clarendon Press, 1992), 190–93.

17. Charles Nauert, "Desiderius Erasmus," in Edward N. Zalta, ed., *The Stanford Encyclopedia of Philosophy*, Center for the Study of Language

and Information, Winter 2009 Edition, http://plato.stanford.edu/
entries/erasmus/.

18. A. Moss, "The Commonplace-Book at Birth," in *Printed Commonplace-Books and the Structuring of Renaissance Thought* (Oxford, UK: Clarendon Press, 1996), 101–33.

19. Gloria Lotha, Shiveta Singh, and Amy Tikkanen, "Domesday Book (English history)," *Encyclopaedia Britannica*, http://www.britannica.com/EBchecked/topic/168528/Domesday-Book [last accessed May 9, 2012].

20. The National Archives, "Discover Domesday," http://www.national archives.gov.uk/domesday/discover-domesday/ [last accessed March 10, 2012].

21. J. Johnson, "Marks and Characters used in Domesday Book and other Ancient Records," in *Typographia*, volume 2 (London: Hurst, Rees, Orme, Brown & Green, 1824), 248–59.

22. Geoffrey A. Glaister, "Digit," in *Encyclopedia of the Book* (New Castle, DE: Oak Knoll Press, 1996), 141.

23. "Leges Angliae," (Rylands Medieval Collection Latin MS 155), John Rylands University Library Image Collections, page 20v, http://enriqueta.man.ac.uk/luna/servlet/detail/Man4MedievalVC-4-4-593783-121998:Leges-Angliae [last accessed July 26, 2012].

24. J. Brotton, "A Global Renaissance," in *The Renaissance: A Very Short Introduction* (Oxford, UK: Oxford University Press, 2006), 19–37; J. Kraye, "The Origins of Humanism," in *The Cambridge Companion to Renaissance Humanism*, Cambridge Companions to Literature (Cambridge, UK: Cambridge University Press, 1996), 1–19.

25. Brotton, "A Global Renaissance," 19–37.

26. Sherman, "Towards a History of the Manicule," 28–52.

27. "Aldus Manutius, Scholar-Pinter (c.1445–1515)," nls.uk, http://www.nls.uk/collections/rare-books/collections/aldus-manutius [last accessed May 14, 2012].

28. B. L. Ullman, "A Rival System—Niccolò Niccoli," in *The Origin and Development of Humanistic Script*, Storia e Letteratura (Rome: Edizione di storia e letteratura, 1974), 59–77.

29. A. C. de la Mare, *The Handwriting of Italian Humanists,* Number v. 1, pt. 1 (Brussels: Association Internationale de Bibliographie, 1973); N. Giannetto, "Schede per la Biblioteca de Bernardo," in *Bernardo Bembo: Umanista e politico veneziano,* Civiltà Veneziana: Saggi (Florence: L. S. Olschki, 1985), 267; Hostiensis (Henricus de Segusia), *Commentaria super decretalibus,* 14th century, f. 26v; Roderick C. Morris, "Petrarch, the First Humanist," *New York Times,* May 29, 2004.

30. Paul McPharlin, Bruce Rogers, Lessing J. Rosenwald Collection (Library of Congress), and Pforzheimer Bruce Rogers Collection (Library of Congress), "The Pointing Hand," in *Roman Numerals, Typographic Leaves and Pointing Hands: Some Notes on Their Origin, History, and Contemporary Use* (New York: Typophiles, 1942), 47–65.

31. Charles Hasler, "A Show of Hands," *Typographica* 8 (1953): 4–11; Joannes Canonicus, fl. 1329, *Quaestiones super Physica Aristotelis* [Questions on Aristole's physics], April 1475.

32. Albertus de Saxonia (Albert of Halberstadt), *Tractatus de logica,* 15th century, f. 5v.

33. Cicero (Quintus Tullius Cicero), *Paradoxa stoicorum,* 14th century, f. 5v.

34. Ibid., f. 1v; Dodoens, Rembert, 1517–1585, *Rams little Dodeon* (London: Simon Stafford, 1606); Sherman, "Towards a History of the Manicule," 28–52.

35. Sherman, "Towards a History of the Manicule," 28–52.

36. Oxford English Dictionary, "Maniple, n.," *Oxford English Dictionary,* http://www.oed.com/view/Entry/113518 [last accessed May 7, 2012]; Sherman, "Towards a History of the Manicule," 28–52.

37. Orgel, "Margins of Truth," 91–107.

38. Sherman, "Towards a History of the Manicule," 28–52.

39. Yamini Chauhan, Gloria Lotha, Shiveta Singh, et al, "Wars of the Roses," *Encyclopaedia Britannica,* http://www.britannica.com/EBchecked/topic/509963/Wars-of-the-Roses [last accessed May 16, 2012]; S. J. Shaw, "The Apogee of Ottoman Power, 1451–1566," in *History of the Ottoman Empire and Modern Turkey,* volume 1

(Cambridge, UK: Cambridge University Press, 1976), 53–68; Stanford J. Shaw, Malcolm E. Yapp, Fredric Williams, et al, "Ottoman Empire," *Encyclopaedia Britannica*, http://www.britannica.com/EBchecked/topic/434996/Ottoman-Empire [last accessed May 16, 2012].

40. Daryl Green, "Look at This Lovely 15th Century Manicula!" *Echoes from the Vault*, December 21, 2011, http://standrewsrarebooks.wordpress.com/2011/12/21/look-at-this-lovely-15th-century-manicula/; McPharlin, et al, "The Pointing Hand," 47–65.

41. McPharlin, et al, "The Pointing Hand," 47–65.

42. R. Howard, *Paul McPharlin and the Puppet Theater* (Jefferson, NC: McFarland, 2006).

43. H. J. Jackson, "History. In *Marginalia: Readers Writing in Books*," Nota Bene Series (New Haven: Yale University Press, 2002), 44–80; W. W. E. Slights, "The Edifying Margins of Renaissance English Books," in *Managing Readers: Printed Marginalia in English Renaissance Books*, Editorial Theory and Literary Criticism (Ann Arbor: University of Michigan Press, 2001), 19–60.

44. Sherman, "Towards a History of the Manicule," 28–52.

45. Oxford English Dictionary, "† mutton-fist, n.," *Oxford English Dictionary*, http://www.oed.com/view/Entry/253818 [last accessed August 27, 2012].

46. Sherman, "Towards a History of the Manicule," 28–52; William H. Sherman, Personal correspondence, May 2012.

47. T. Cranmer, "A Prologue or Preface Made by the Most Reverend Father in God, Thomas, Archbishop of Canterbury, Metropolitan and Primate of England," in *Miscellaneous Writings and Letters of Thomas Cranmer* (Vancouver, BC: Regent College Publishing, 2001), 118–25.

48. Jenny Swanson, "The Glossa Ordinaria," in G. R. Evans ed., *The Medieval Theologians* (London: Blackwell Publishers, 2001), 156–67.

49. Sherman, "Towards a History of the Manicule," 28–52.

50. David Spadafora, Tim Macy, Darshana Das, et al, "Incunabula," *Encyclopaedia Britannica*, http://www.britannica.com/EBchecked/topic/284960/incunabula [last accessed May 17, 2012].

51. Geoffrey A. Glaister, "Colophon," in *Encyclopedia of the Book* (New Castle, DE: Oak Knoll Press, 1996), 103.

52. S. H. Steinberg and Beatrice Warde, "The Title-Page," in *Five Hundred Years of Printing* (Vancouver, BC: Criterion Books, 1959), 105–14.

53. Palmer & Rey, *Palmer & Rey's Type Specimen Book*, 3rd edition (San Francisco: Palmer & Rey, 1887).

54. Robert Bringhurst, "Hedera," in *The Elements of Typographic Style: Version 3.2* (Vancouver, BC: Hartley & Marks, 2008), 311; Oxford English Dictionary, "Fleuron, n.," *Oxford English Dictionary*, http://www.oed.com/view/Entry/71509 [last accessed August 27, 2012].

55. Geoffrey A. Glaister, "Arabesque," in *Encyclopedia of the Book* (New Castle, DE: Oak Knoll Press, 1996), 14; Steinberg and Warde, "The Title-Page," 105–14.

56. McPharlin, et al, "The Pointing Hand," 47–65.

57. Hasler, "A Show of Hands," 4–11; Sherman, "Towards a History of the Manicule," 28–52.

58. June Holmes, "Thomas Bewick (1753–1828)," The Bewick Society, http://www.bewicksociety.org/life_and_work/tb_bio.html [last accessed May 17, 2012]; McPharlin, et al, "The Pointing Hand," 47–65.

59. C. W. Butterfield, "Of the Index," in *A Comprehensive System of Grammatical and Rhetorical Punctuation: Designed for the Use of Schools* (Cincinnati, OH: Longley, 1858), 37.

60. McPharlin, et al, "The Pointing Hand," 47–65.

61. J. L. Ringwalt, "Index or Fist," in *American Encyclopaedia of Printing*, Library of American Civilization (Philadelphia: Menamin & Ringwalt, 1871), 217.

62. Hasler, "A Show of Hands," 4–11; David Shields, "What Is Wood Type?" Hamilton Wood Type & Printing Museum, http://woodtype.org/about/whatis [last accessed May 17, 2012].

63. Ringwalt, "Index or Fist," 217.

64. J. P. Benway, *Banner Blindness: What Searching Users Notice and Do Not Notice on the World Wide Web*, PhD Thesis, Rice University, 1999.

65. McPharlin, et al, "The Pointing Hand," 47–65.

66. Michael M. Ludeman, "A New Type of 'Return to Sender' Endorsement Created by Ink Jet Printer Technology Part I: Texas P&DCs," *Machine Cancel Forum* 216 (April 2006), http://www.machinecancel. org/forum/ludeman/ludeman.html; The Auxiliary Markings Club, "Brief Auxiliary Markings Record," http://www.postal-markings. org/listing.html [last accessed March 19, 2012].

10. QUOTATION MARKS (" ")

1. Jon Henley, "The End of the Line?," *The Guardian*, April 3, 2008, http://www.guardian.co.uk/world/2008/apr/04/france. britishidentity.

2. "'Apostrophe-Box' for Spelling Errors," BBC News, January 31, 2002, http://news.bbc.co.uk/1/hi/england/1793450.stm; Victoria Moore, "Apostrophe Catastrophe! The Rogue Apostrophe Is Spreading Like Measles. It's Time to Fight Back . . . ," *Daily Mail*, November 18, 2008; Bethany Keeley, "Fresh Baked 'Bagels,'" *The "Blog" of "Unnecessary" Quotation Marks*, May 17, 2012, http:// www.unnecessaryquotes.com/2012/05/fresh-baked-bagels.html; Bethany Keeley, "Ask for 'Fresh Fish,'" *The "Blog" of "Unnecessary" Quotation Marks*, March 25, 2012, http://www.unnecessaryquotes. com/2012/03/ask-for-fresh-fish.html.

3. Robert Barr, "Twitter Oxford Comma Commotion Punctuated by Fact," *The Guardian*, June 30, 2011, http://www.guardian.co.uk/ world/feedarticle/9721001.

4. Lynne Truss, "Airs and Graces," in *Eats, Shoots and Leaves* (New York: Gotham, 2006), 148–55.

5. Kathleen McNamee, "Sigla," in *Sigla and Select Marginalia in Greek Literary Papyri* (Brussels: Fondation Égyptologique Reine Élisabeth, 1992), 9.

6. Rudolf Pfeiffer, "Aristarchus: The Art of Interpretation," in *History of Classical Scholarship. From the Beginnings to the End of the Hellenistic Age* (Oxford, UK: Clarendon, 1968), 210–33.

7. McNamee, "Sigla," 8.

8. Albertus de Saxonia (Albert of Halberstadt), *Tractatus de logica*, 15th century, f. 5v; Cicero (Quintus Tullius Cicero), *Paradoxa stoicorum*, fourteenth century, f. 5v; McNamee, "Sigla," 11.

9. British Museum Department of Manuscripts, and H. J. M. Milne, "British Museum Papyrus 178, inv no. 1184 verso, BMP 180 no. 815," in *Catalogue of the Literary Papyri in the British Museum* (London: The Trustees, 1927), 147; P. McGurk, "Citation Marks in Early Latin Manuscripts," *Scriptorium: revue internationale des études relatives aux manuscrits* 15, no. 1 (1961): 3–13.

10. C. G. Herbermann, "Fathers of the Church," in *The Catholic Encyclopedia: An International Work of Reference on the Constitution, Doctrine, Discipline, and History of the Catholic Church*, volume 6 (New York: Appleton, 1912), 1–18; McNamee, "Sigla," 12.

11. W. Clarysse, J. Clarysse, B. Van Beek, et al, "Leuven Database of Ancient Books," *Trismegistos*, http://www.trismegistos.org/ldab/ [last accessed June 22, 2012].

12. Zeki M. Dogan and Alfred Scharsky, *Virtual Unification of the Earliest Christian Bible: Digitisation, Transcription, Translation and Physical Description of the Codex Sinaiticus* (Berlin: Springer Berlin Heidelberg, 2008), 221–26.

13. R. H. Finnegan, "What Are Quote Marks and Where Did They Come From?" in *Why Do We Quote?: The Culture and History of Quotation* (Cambridge, UK: Open Book Publishers, 2011), 79–95.

14. Isidore and Stephen A. Barney, "Critical Signs [*De notis sententiarum*]," in *The Etymologies of Isidore of Seville* (Cambridge, UK: Cambridge University Press, 2006), 51.

15. James O'Donnell, Darshana Das, Brian Duignan, et al, "Saint Augustine," *Encyclopaedia Britannica*, http://www.britannica.com/EBchecked/topic/42902/Saint-Augustine/24817/Christian-Doctrine [last accessed June 25, 2012].

16. M. B. Parkes, "Antiquity: Aids for Inexperienced Readers and the Prehistory of Punctuation," in *Pause and Effect: Punctuation in the West* (Berkeley: University of California Press, 1993), 9–19; M. B. Parkes, "Plate 5. Vienna, Nationalbibliothek, MS lat. 2160*, fol. 3v," in Ibid., 168–169.

17. M. B. Parkes, "Plate 49. Paris, Bibliothèque nationale, MS Lat. 2630, fol 37," in *Pause and Effect: Punctuation in the West* (Berkeley: University of California Press, 1993), 246–47.

18. M. B. Parkes, "Plate 50. Paris, Bibliothèque nationale, MS Lat. 12132, fol 20v," in Ibid., 248–49.

19. "Insular Script," *Encyclopaedia Britannica*, http://www.britannica. com/EBchecked/topic/289453/Insular-script [last accessed June 25, 2012]; M. B. Parkes, "Changing Attitudes to the Written Word: Components in a 'Grammar of Legibility,'" in *Pause and Effect: Punctuation in the West* (Berkeley: University of California Press, 1993), 20–29.

20. R. Pettersson, "Quotations," in *Information Design: An Introduction*, Studies in Discourse and Grammar (Amsterdam: John Benjamins Publishing Company, 2002), 194.

21. Finnegan, "What Are Quote Marks and Where Did They Come From?" 79–95; McGurk, "Citation Marks in Early Latin Manuscripts," 3–13; C. J. Mitchell, "Quotation Marks, National Compositorial Habits and False Imprints," *The Library*, s6–5, no. 4 (1983): 359–84.

22. McGurk, "Citation Marks in Early Latin Manuscripts," 3–13.

23. Brian Duignan, "Apologetics," *Encyclopaedia Britannica*, http://www. britannica.com/EBchecked/topic/30078/apologetics [last accessed June 26, 2012].

24. S. Rebenich, "The Origenist Controversy," in *Jerome*, The Early Church Fathers (New York: Routledge, 2002), 41–51.

25. C. P. H. Bammel, "Products of Fifth-Century Scriptoria Preserving Conventions Used by Rufinus of Aquileia," *The Journal of Theological Studies* 35, no. 2 (1984): 347–93.

26. Ibid.

27. R. Gellens, "RFC 2646: The Text/Plain Format Parameter," The Internet Society, August 1999, http://www.ietf.org/rfc/rfc2646.txt.

28. L. Avrin, "Parchment," in *Scribes, Script, and Books*, ALA Classics (Chicago: American Library Association, 2010), 156–57; Lane Wilkinson, "The Humanistic Minuscule and the Advent of Roman Type," Paper (Chattanooga: University of Tennessee, n.d.), 12.

29. McGurk, "Citation Marks in Early Latin Manuscripts," 3–13.

30. J. A. Calosse, *Illuminated Manuscripts* (New York: Parkstone International, 2011).

31. Mitchell, "Quotation Marks, National Compositorial Habits and False Imprints," 359–84.

32. Finnegan, "What Are Quote Marks and Where Did They Come From?" 79–95.

33. M. B. Parkes, "The Technology of Printing and the Stabilization of the Symbols," in *Pause and Effect: Punctuation in the West* (Berkeley: University of California Press, 1993), 50–64.

34. Mitchell, "Quotation Marks, National Compositorial Habits and False Imprints," 359–84.

35. Edward Surtz, "John Fisher and the Scholastics," *Studies in Philology* 55, no. 2 (1958).

36. Mitchell, "Quotation Marks, National Compositorial Habits and False Imprints," 359–84.

37. N. Baker, "The History of Punctuation," in *The Size of Thoughts: Essays and Other Lumber* (New York: Random House, 1996); Oxford English Dictionary, "Inverted, adj.," *Oxford Dictionaries Online*, http://www.oed.com/view/Entry/99019 [last accessed August 27, 2012].

38. M. B. Parkes, "Plate 36. J. Fisher, Defensio regie assertionis contra Babylonicam capituitatem (Cologne, P. Quentel, July 1525), fols 57v–58r," in *Pause and Effect: Punctuation in the West* (Berkeley: University of California Press, 1993), 220–21; Parkes, "The Technology of Printing and the Stabilization of the Symbols," in Ibid., 50–64.

39. Mitchell, "Quotation Marks, National Compositorial Habits and False Imprints," 359–84.

40. "Geoffroy Tory," *Encyclopaedia Britannica*, http://www.britannica.com/EBchecked/topic/600302/Geoffroy-Tory [last accessed June 28, 2012]; Octavo Editions, "Geofroy Tory, *Champ Fleury*," http://www.octavo.com/editions/trychf/index.html [last accessed August 28, 2012].

41. "Geoffroy Tory," *Encyclopaedia Britannica*; Barbara C. Bowen, "Geofroy Tory's 'Champ Fleury' and Its Major Sources,'" *Studies*

in Philology 76, no. 1 (1979): 13–27; Parkes, "The Technology of Printing and the Stabilization of the Symbols," 50–64.

42. Mitchell, "Quotation Marks, National Compositorial Habits and False Imprints," 359–84.

43. Octavo Editions, "Geofroy Tory, Champ Fleury."

44. Parkes, "The Technology of Printing and the Stabilization of the Symbols," 50–64.

45. Margreta de Grazia, "Shakespeare in Quotation Marks," in J. I. Marsden, ed., *The Appropriation of Shakespeare: Post-Renaissance Reconstructions of the Works and the Myth* (Harlow, UK: Harvester Wheatsheaf, 1991), 57–71.

46. A. Moss, "The Commonplace-Book at Birth," in *Printed Commonplace-Books and the Structuring of Renaissance Thought* (Oxford, UK: Clarendon Press, 1996), 101–33; Oxford English Dictionary, "Sententious, adj.," *Oxford English Dictionary*, http://www. oed.com/view/Entry/176047 [last accessed August 27, 2012].

47. Parkes, "The Technology of Printing and the Stabilization of the Symbols," 50–64.

48. M. B. Parkes, "Plate 37, John Whitgift, The defense of the answere to the admonition against the reply by T[homas] C[artwright] (London, H. Bynneman for H. Toye, 1574), STC, 25430, p 150," in *Pause and Effect: Punctuation in the West* (Berkeley: University of California Press, 1993), 222–23.

49. De Grazia, "Shakespeare in Quotation Marks," 57–71.

50. Parkes, "The Technology of Printing and the Stabilization of the Symbols," 50–64.

51. J. Higgins, T. Blenerhasset, and L. B. Campbell, "Introduction," in *Parts Added to the Mirror for Magistrates*, Huntington Library Publications (Cambridge, UK: Cambridge University Press, 1946), 18–19.

52. Ibid.

53. Parkes, "The Technology of Printing and the Stabilization of the Symbols," 50–64.

54. A. G. Petti, "Punctuation," in *English Literary Hands from Chaucer to Dryden* (Cambridge, MA: Harvard University Press, 1977), 25–28.

55. R. H. Finnegan, "What Do They Mean?" in *Why Do We Quote?: The Culture and History of Quotation* (Cambridge, UK: Open Book Publishers, 2011), 95–108.

56. P. M. Logan, O. George, S. Hegeman, et al, "Dialogue," in *The Encyclopedia of the Novel*, volume 1 of *Wiley-Blackwell Encyclopedia of Literature* (Hoboken, NJ: John Wiley & Sons, 2011), 250–51.

57. Daniel Defoe, *The Life and Adventures of the Famous Moll Flanders, who was Born in Newgate…: Written from Her Own Memorandums* (J. Cooke, 1765); Ibid.

58. John Smith, "The Comma," in *The printer's grammar containing a concise history of the origin of printing; also, an examination of the Superficies, Gradation, and Properties of the different sizes of types cast by Letter Founders; Various Tables of Calculation; Models of Letter Cases; Schemes for casting off Copy, and Imposing; and Many Other Requisites for attaining a perfect Knowledge both in the Theory and Practice of the Art of Printing. With directions to authors, compilers, &c. How to prepare copy, and to correct their own proofs. Chiefly collected from Smith's edition. To which are added directions for pressmen, &c. The whole calculated for the Service of All who have any Concern in the Letter Press.* (London: Printed by L. Wayland; and sold by T. Evans, Pater-Noster-Row, 1787), 95–97.

59. Parkes, "The Technology of Printing and the Stabilization of the Symbols," 50–64; Samuel Richardson, *Clarissa, or, The history of a young lady comprehending the most important concerns of private life, and particularly shewing, the distresses that may attend the misconduct both of parents and children, in relation to marriage*, volume 8 (Bath, UK: Printed by S. Richardson and sold by A. Millar, J. and Ja. Rivington, John Osborn and by J. Leake, 1748).

60. Vivienne Mylne, "The Punctuation of Dialogue in Eighteenth-Century French and English Fiction," *The Library*, s6-I, no. 1 (1979): 43–61.

61. Mitchell, "Quotation Marks, National Compositorial Habits and False Imprints," 359–84.

62. Mylne, "The Punctuation of Dialogue in Eighteenth-Century French and English Fiction," 43–61.

63. Anonymous, *The History of Eliza Warwick* (London: Printed for J. Bew, 1778).

64. Mitchell, "Quotation Marks, National Compositorial Habits and False Imprints," 359–84.

65. J. Heriot, *The Sorrows of the Heart a Novel, In Two Volumes* (Printed for J. Murray, 1787); Parkes, "The Technology of Printing and the Stabilization of the Symbols," 50–64.

66. Robert Bringhurst, "5.4 Quotation Marks & Other Intrusions," in *The Elements of Typographic Style: Version 3.2* (Vancouver, BC: Hartley & Marks, 2008), 86–89.

67. Mitchell, "Quotation Marks, National Compositorial Habits and False Imprints," 359–84.

68. Parkes, "The Technology of Printing and the Stabilization of the Symbols," 50–64; R. M. Ritter, "Quotation Marks," in *The Oxford Style Manual* (Oxford, UK: Oxford University Press, 2003), 148–53; John Smith, "Of Composing," in *The printer's grammar containing a concise history of the origin of printing; also, an examination of the Superficies, Gradation, and Properties of the different sizes of types cast by Letter Founders; Various Tables of Calculation; Models of Letter Cases; Schemes for casting off Copy, and Imposing; and Many Other Requisites for attaining a perfect Knowledge both in the Theory and Practice of the Art of Printing. With directions to authors, compilers, &c. How to prepare copy, and to correct their own proofs. Chiefly collected from Smith's edition. To which are added directions for pressmen, &c. The whole calculated for the Service of All who have any Concern in the Letter Press* (London: Printed by L. Wayland; and sold by T. Evans, Pater-Noster-Row, 1787), 160–83; University of Chicago Press, "Quotation Marks: Double or Single," in *The Chicago Manual of Style,* 16th edition (Chicago: University of Chicago Press, 2010), 630–31.

69. Mylne, "The Punctuation of Dialogue in Eighteenth-Century French and English Fiction," 43–61.

70. Oxford Dictionaries, "Guillemet," *Oxford Dictionaries Online*, http://oxforddictionaries.com/definition/guillemet [last accessed

August 27, 2012]; A. Yardeni, "Printed Hebrew Script," in *The Book of Hebrew Script: History, Palaeography, Script Styles, Calligraphy & Design* (London: The British Library, 2002), 101–18.

71. A. Rey, *Dictionnaire Historique de la Langue Française: Mille Ans de Langue Française* (New York: French & European Publications, Incorporated, 1992).

72. N. Catach, *La ponctuation: (Histoire et système),* Que Sais-Je? (Paris: Presses Universitaires de France, 1994); Swati Chopra and J. E. Luebering, "Etienne Dolet," *Encyclopaedia Britannica,* http://www.britannica.com/EBchecked/topic/168169/Etienne-Dolet [last accessed July 2, 2012].; P. Faucheux, L. Martinez, J. Rivière, et al, *Les Caractères de l'Imprimerie nationale* (Paris: Impr. nationale éditions, 1990).

73. Mitchell, "Quotation Marks, National Compositorial Habits and False Imprints," 359–84.

74. Ibid.

75. Mylne, "The Punctuation of Dialogue in Eighteenth-Century French and English Fiction," 43–61.

76. Ibid.

77. A. Dumas, "The Catalan Village," in *The Count of Monte Cristo* (Parlour libr., 1848), 25.

78. Mylne, "The Punctuation of Dialogue in Eighteenth-Century French and English Fiction," 43–61.

79. Richard Storer, "Richards, Ivor Armstrong (1893–1979)," *Oxford Dictionary of National Biography,* October 2008, http://www.oxforddnb.com/view/article/31603.

80. C. K. Ogden, *Basic English: International Second Language* (San Diego, CA: Harcourt, Brace & World, 1968).

81. "Globalingo," *Time,* December 31, 1945; Rudolf F. Flesch, How Basic Is Basic English? *Harper's Magazine,* March 1944, 339–43; Ivy Low, "Madame Litvinoff," *LIFE,* October 1942, 115–24; Raven I. McDavid, Swati Chopra, and Amy Tikkanen, "Noah Webster," *Encyclopaedia Britannica,* http://www.britannica.com/EBchecked/topic/638653/Noah-Webster [last accessed July 4, 2012].

82. A. Rai, "The Roads to Airstrip One," in *Orwell and the Politics of Despair: A Critical Study of the Writings of George Orwell* (Cambridge, UK: Cambridge University Press, 1990), 113–49.

83. R. A. Heinlein, *Assignment in Eternity* (London: New English Library, 1971); H. G. Wells, P. Parrinder, and J. Clute, "Language and Mental Growth," in *The Shape of Things to Come: The Ultimate Revolution,* Penguin Classics (New York: Penguin, 2005).

84. I. A. Richards, "Specialized Quotation Marks," in *How to Read a Page: A Course in Effective Reading, With an Introduction to a Hundred Great Words* (New York: W. W. Norton & Company, 1942), 66–70.

85. Ibid.

86. J. P. Russo, "Experiment in America," in *I. A. Richards: His Life and Work* (New York: Routledge, 1989), 430–71.

87. Ann E. Berthoff, "I. A. Richards and the Philosophy of Rhetoric," *Rhetoric Society Quarterly* 10, no. 4 (1980): 195–210.

11. IRONY AND SARCASM

1. "Irony," *Oxford Dictionaries Online*, http://oxforddictionaries.com/definition/irony [last accessed August 22, 2011]; R. W. Gibbs and H. L. Colston, "Irony as Relevant Inappropriateness," in *Irony in Language and Thought: A Cognitive Science Reader* (London: Lawrence Erlbaum Associates, 2007), 136.

2. Jon Winokur, "You Call That Irony?" *Los Angeles Times*, February 11, 2007.

3. R. W. Gibbs and H. L. Colston, "Irony in Talk Among Friends in *Irony in Language and Thought: A Cognitive Science Reader* (London: Lawrence Erlbaum Associates, 2007), 339.

4. Francis M. Cornford, "The Eiron and the Alazon," in *The Origin of Attic Comedy* (London: E. Arnold, 1914), 136–38; Gloria Lotha and J. E. Luebering, "Irony," *Encyclopaedia Britannica Online*, http://www.britannica.com/EBchecked/topic/294609/irony [last accessed November 14, 2012].

5. John Wilkins, *An Essay Towards a Real Character, and a Philosophical Language* (London: Printed for S. Gellibrand [etc.], 1668).

6. R. Chambers and R. Carruthers, "Dr John Wilkins," in *Cyclopaedia of English Literature* (Boston: Gould, Kendall and Lincoln, 1847), 446.

7. "Forget Apollo and Sputnik: How a Briton launched the space race in the 1640s," *Daily Mail*, July 17, 2009; J. L. Borges and R. L. C. Simms, "The Analytical Language of John Wilkins," in *Other Inquisitions, 1937–1952*, Texas Pan American Series (Austin: University of Texas Press, 1975), 101; E. J. Bowen and Harold Hartley, "The Right Reverend John Wilkins, F.R.S. (1614–1672)," *Notes and Records of the Royal Society of London* 15 (1960): 47–56; John Wilkins, *The Discovery of a World in the Moone, Or, A Discourse Tending to Prove, That 'Tis Probable There May Be Another Habitable World in That Planet* (London: Printed by E.G. for Michael Sparke and Edward Forrest, 1638).

8. S. Auroux, "Theories of Grammar and Language Philosophy in the 17th and 18th Centuries," in *History of the Language Sciences: An International Handbook on the Evolution of the Study of Language from the Beginnings to the Present*, volume 2 of *Handbücher zur Sprach- und Kommunikationswissenschaft* (Berlin: Walter de Gruyter, 2000), 1038.

9. S. Clauss, "John Wilkins' Essay Toward a Real Character: Its Place in the Seventeenth-Century Episteme," *Journal of the History of Ideas* 43, no. 4 (1982): 531–53.

10. P. Janton and H. Tonkin, "Esperanto and Planned Languages," in *Esperanto: Language, Literature, and Community* (Albany: State University of New York Press, 1993), 1–22; C. K. Ogden, *Basic English: International Second Language* (San Francisco: Harcourt, Brace & World, 1968).

11. Janton and Tonkin, "Esperanto and Planned Languages," 1–22; M. M. Slaughter, "Introduction," in *Universal Languages and Scientific Taxonomy in the Seventeenth Century* (Cambridge, UK: Cambridge University Press, 2010), 1–11.

12. Slaughter, "Introduction," 1–11.

13. W. J. Clark, "The Earliest British Attempt," in *International Language: Past, Present & Future* (n.p.: Nabu Press, 2012), 87–92; V. Salmon and F. Lodwick, *The Works of Francis Lodwick: A Study of His Writings in the Intellectual Context of The Seventeenth Century*

(London: Longman, 1972); Thomas Willard, "Sir Thomas Urquhart of Cromarty: 'The Jewel,'" *The Modern Language Review* 82, no. 4 (1987): 917–18.

14. David Cram, "Dalgarno, George (c.1616–1687)," *Oxford Dictionary of National Biography*, May 2006, http://www.oxforddnb.com/view/article/7023.

15. Jorge L. Borges, "The Analytical Language of John Wilkins," in *Other Inquisitions, 1937–1952* (Austin: University of Texas Press, 1964).

16. D. Knox, "Ironia Unmasked," in *Ironia: Medieval and Renaissance Ideas on Irony* (New York: Brill, 1989), 72.

17. Ibid.

18. David Cram, "Universal Language Schemes in 17th-Century Britain," *Histoire Épistémologie Langage* 7, no. 2 (1985): 34–44.

19. Bowen and Hartley, "The Right Reverend John Wilkins, F.R.S. (1614–1672)," 47–56.

20. Marie-Christine Claes, "Marcellin Jobard, un visionnaire dévoré d'ambition humanitaire [Marcellin Jobard, a visionary humanitarian consumed by ambition]," *Scientific Connection* no. 20 (2008): 20–23.

21. Chelsey Parrott-Sheffer, "Lithography (printing)," *Encyclopaedia Britannica*, http://www.britannica.com/EBchecked/topic/343748/lithography [last accessed August 9, 2012].

22. Marie-Christine Claes, "Jobard invente le précurseur du smiley en 1841 [Jobard invented the precursor of the smiley in 1841]," jobard. eu, June 23, 2012, http://www.jobard.eu/spip.php?article34&lang=fr.

23. Ibid.

24. Claes, "Marcellin Jobard, un visionnaire dévoré d'ambition humanitaire," 20–23.

25. Jean-Jacques Rousseau, "Essai sur l'origine des langues," in *Collection complète des oeuvres de J. J. Rousseau, Citoyen de Geneve*, volume 8 (Geneva: n.p., 1782), 357–434.

26. Alcanter de Brahm, *Alcanter de Brahm, L'Ostensoir des ironies, essai de métacritique, 1re partie, L'homme, la femme et la famille* (Paris: Bibliothèque d'art de 'la Critique', 1899).

27. Timothy J. Attanucci, "No Irony?" *Meta Magazine*, http://www. meta-magazine.com/index.php?id=29 [last accessed August 27, 2011]; S. Zank, "Gentle Irony," in *Irony and Sound: The Music of Maurice Ravel,* Eastman Studies in Music (Rochester, NY: University of Rochester Press, 2009), 36.

28. W. C. Booth, "Is It Ironic?" in *A Rhetoric of Irony* (Chicago: University of Chicago Press, 1975), 55.

29. W. C. Booth, "Learning Where to Stop," in Ibid., 206.

30. M. B. Parkes, "Plates 34-35, The Percontativus used by two sixteenth-century London Printers: Henry Denham and Abell Jeffs," in *Pause and Effect: Punctuation in the West* (Berkeley: University of California Press, 1993), 218–19.

31. Zank, "Gentle Irony," 36.

32. James Kirkup, "Obituary: Hervé Bazin," *The Independent*, February 23, 1996.

33. H. Bazin, *Vipère Au Poing* (Paris: Éditions Garnier, 1948).

34. H. Bazin, "Les points d'intonation," in *Plumons l'oiseau* (Paris: B. Grasset, 1966), 141–43.

35. Bazin, "Les points d'intonation," 142.

36. Bas Jacobs, "Irony Mark, and the Need for New Punctuation Marks," Underware, http://underware.nl/logotypes/irony_mark/ [last accessed September 30, 2011].

37. Ibid.

38. "Nieuw: het ironieteken [New: the irony mark]," *Talk of the Town*, March 15, 2007, http://towntalk.wordpress.com/2007/03/15/nieuw-het-ironieteken/; Bas Jacobs, Personal correspondence, September 2011.

39. "A New Style," *The Baltimore Sun*, http://www.baltimoresun.com/about/bal-redesign-storytype,0,972889.htmlstory [last accessed August 28, 2011].

40. Jean F. Porchez, "Mencken Text," Typofonderie.com, http://www. typofonderie.com/alphabets/view/MenckenText [last accessed August 28, 2011].

41. Jacques Kelly, "H. L. Mencken, Pioneer Journalist," *The Baltimore Sun*, September 18, 2005.

42. H. L. Mencken and A. Cooke, "An Introduction to H. L. Mencken," in *The Vintage Mencken* (New York: Vintage Books, 1955), xi.

43. H. L. Mencken, "Notes on Journalism," *Chicago Daily Tribune*, September 19, 1926, G1.

44. Search for "ironics," *Baltimore Sun,* archives | baltimoresun.com, http://pqasb.pqarchiver.com/baltsun/results.html?st=advanced& QryTxt=ironics&type=historic [last accessed August 30, 2011].

45. Keith Waterhouse, "Terror Betting for Guys and Dolls," *Daily Mail*, November 20, 2003.

46. Keith Waterhouse, "Smoke Gets in Your Eyes and Up Their Noses," *Daily Mail*, March 30, 2006.

47. Keith Waterhouse, *English Our English: And How to Sing It* (Penguin Books, 1994); Keith Waterhouse, *Waterhouse on Newspaper Style* 2nd revised edition (New York: Viking, 1989).

48. Mike Molloy, "Keith Waterhouse," *The Guardian*, September 4, 2009.

49. Richard Morrison, "Ha Ha Hard," *The Times*, January 26, 2008.

50. "Bernard Levin," *The Times*, August 10, 2004.

51. Frances Stonor Saunders, "How the CIA Plotted Against Us," *New Statesman*, July 12 1999.

52. Bernard Levin, Op. Ed., *The Times*, February 23, 1982.

53. Brooke Crutchley, "Letter: Visual Rhetoric," *The Independent*, January 3, 1994.

54. F. Wheen, *Tom Driberg: His Life and Indiscretions* (London: Chatto & Windus, 1990).

55. "Lord Bradwell," *The Times*, August 13, 1976.

56. Christopher Hitchens, "Reader, He Married Her," *London Review of Books*, May 10, 1990, 6–8.

57. Nick Assinder, "Driberg Always Under Suspicion," BBC News, September 13, 1999, http://news.bbc.co.uk/1/hi/uk_politics/446305.stm.

58. Roger Hutchinson, "Aleister Crowley Has Been Dead 50 Years. But We're Still Under His Spell," *The Scotsman*, May 11, 1999.

59. D. E. Knuth, "Digital Typography," in *Digital Typography*, CSLI Lecture Notes (CSLI Publications, 1999), 1–18.

60.   "Sarcasm," *Oxford Dictionaries Online*, http://english.oxford
      dictionaries.com/definition/sarcasm [last accessed October 4,
      2011].

61.   Nathan Hoang, Personal correspondence, June 2012; Nathan
      Hoang, "Advertisements/Sartalics," nathanhoang.com, http://
      nathanhoang.com/advertisements/sartalics.html [last accessed
      August 12, 2012]; Victoria Kamen, "Sartalics: Company Devel-
      ops Sarcasm Font," *Huffington Post*, August 5, 2011, http://www.
      huffingtonpost.com/2011/08/05/sarcasm-font-_n_919845.html.

62.   Nathan Hoang, Personal correspondence, June 2012; Nathan
      Hoang, June Kim, and Blake Gilmore, "Sartalics," http://sartalics.
      com/ [last accessed August 12, 2012].

63.   Nathan Hoang, June Kim, and Blake Gilmore, "@Sartalics," Twit-
      ter, August 2012, https://twitter.com/sartalics; Nathan Hoang, June
      Kim, and Blake Gilmore, "Sartalics," YouTube, August 2012, http://
      www.youtube.com/user/sartalics [last accessed August 12, 2012];
      Hoang, Kim, and Gilmore, "Sartalics," http://sartalics.com/; Penny
      Speckter, Personal correspondence, March 2012.

64.   Hoang, Personal correspondence, June 2012.

65.   N. Hoang, J. Kim, and B. Gilmore (@Sartalics), "That last set of
      backslashes was to convey a Mean Girls–like satirical tone instead
      of sarcasm. Sartalics are versatile, \dawg\," Twitter, August 5, 2011,
      http://twitter.com/Sartalics/status/99712238373445633.

66.   Global Web Stats, *W3Counter*, http://www.w3counter.com/
      globalstats.php [last accessed July 12, 2012]; Hoang, Kim, and Gilm-
      ore, "Sartalics," http://sartalics.com/.

67.   Cristen Conger, "Can Twitterblitzing Start an Effective Twitter
      Trend?" *DiscoveryNews*, August 19, 2011, http://news.discovery.com/
      tech/can-twitterblitzing-start-twitter-trend-110819.html; Hoang,
      Kim, and Gilmore, "@Sartalics," Twitter; Kamen, "Sartalics: Com-
      pany Develops Sarcasm Font."

68.   Cvlrymedic (screen name), "TIL There Exists a Font to Repre-
      sent Sarcasm in Type. Reddit Should Add This to Their Type
      Formatting," Reddit.com, December 11, 2011, http://www.reddit.

com/r/todayilearned/comments/n8kp4/til_there_exists_a_font_to_represent_sarcasm_in/; Glenn McAnally, "Sarcastic Font," glennmcanally.com, 2004, http://glennmcanally.com/sarcastic/index.htm [last accessed August 12, 2012]; Lauren R. Orsini, "Sarcastic Font Movement Sees Revival on Reddit," *Daily Dot*, December 12, 2011, http://www.dailydot.com/society/sarcastic-font-movement-sartalics-revival/; Russell Smith, "Sarcasm in E-Mail Needs to Be Signalled. Yeah, Right," *The Globe and Mail*, September 10, 2012; Erene Stergiopoulos, "The Typography of Sarcasm," *Toronto Standard*, January 2, 2012, http://www.torontostandard.com/culture/the-typography-of-sarcasm.

69. "Program," in *Fifteenth International Unicode Conference*, The Unicode Consortium, August 1999.

70. "Code Charts—Scripts," The Unicode Consortium, http://unicode.org/charts/#scripts [last accessed September 22, 2011].

71. A. Tsigie, B. Beyene, D. Aberra, et al, "A Roadmap to the Extension of the Ethiopic Writing System Standard Under Unicode and ISO-10646," *Fifteenth International Unicode Conference*, The Unicode Consortium, September 1999.

72. Tara Liloia, "The Sarcasm Mark," *Liloia.com*, August 8, 2001, http://www.liloia.com/archives/000211.php.

73. "Tilde," *Urban Dictionary*, http://urbanup.com/5510913 [last accessed October 4, 2011].

74. B. Danet, "ASCII Art and Its Antecedents," in *Cyberpl@y: Communicating Online*, New Technologies / New Cultures (Oxford, UK; New York: Berg, 2001), 194.

75. Lea Goldman, "The Universal Sign for 'Annoying,'" *Forbes*, October 14, 2002, http://www.forbes.com/global/2002/1014/026a.html.

76. Tony Long, "Sept. 19, 1982: Can't You Take a Joke? :-) | This Day In Tech," *Wired.com*, September 19, 2011, http://www.wired.com/thisdayintech/2009/05/dayintech_0504/.

77. Goldman, "The Universal Sign for 'Annoying.'"

78. Long, "Sept. 19, 1982."

79. Jennifer 8. Lee, "Is That an Emoticon in 1862?" *New York Times,* January 19, 2009.

80. Mergenthaler Linotype Company, "General Maintenance," in *Linotype Machine Principles* (New York: Mergenthaler Linotype Co., 1940), 410–20.

81. Lee, "Is That an Emoticon in 1862?"

82. Michael R. Smith, "Cartoons, Comics and Caricature," in W. D. Sloan and L. M. Parcell, eds., *American Journalism: History, Principles, Practices* (McFarland & Company, 2002), 343–49.

83. "Typographical Art," *Puck,* March 1881, 65.

84. Ibid.

85. D. T. Blume, "The Collections: An Overview," in *Ambrose Bierce's Civilians and Soldiers in Context: A Critical Study* (Kent, OH: Kent State University Press, 2004), 329–35.

86. Ambrose Bierce, "For Brevity and Clarity," in *The Collected Works of Ambrose Bierce* (New York: Neale Pub. Co., 1909), 385–88.

87. "Cachinnation, Snigger," Google Ngram Viewer, http://books. google.com/ngrams/graph?content=cachinnation,+snigger& year_start=1700&year_end=2000&corpus=0&smoothing=3 [last accessed August 13, 2012]; Oxford English Dictionary, "Cachinnation, n.," *Oxford English Dictionary,* http://www.oed.com/view/ Entry/25817 [last accessed August 14, 2012].

88. Ralph Reppert, "Punctuation Larks," *Reader's Digest,* May 1967, 160.

89. Zoran Kuzmanovich, "Strong Opinions and Nerve Points: Nabokov's Life and Art," in J. W. Connolly, ed., *The Cambridge Companion to Nabokov,* Cambridge Companions to Literature (Cambridge, UK: Cambridge University Press, 2005), 11–30.

90. Vladimir Nabokov, *Strong Opinions* (New York: Penguin Books, 2012), 112–14.

91. Benjamin Zimmer, "The Prehistory of Emoticons," *Language Log,* September 21, 2007, http://itre.cis.upenn.edu/-myl/languagelog/ archives/004935.html.

92. Josh Greenman, "A Giant Step Forward for Punctuation¡," *Slate,* December 21, 2004, http://www.slate.com/articles/

news_and_politics/low_concept/2004/12/a_giant_step_forward_
for_punctuation.html.

93. Martin K. Speckter, "Interrobang," *Type Talks*, November–
December 1968, 17.

94. Josh Greenman, Telephone interview, December 2009.

95. Choz Cunningham, "The Snark>>History," thesnark.org, June 13,
2007, http://thesnark.org/history.

96. Choz Cunningham, "The Snark >>Design," thesnark.org, June 14,
2007, http://thesnark.org/design.

97. Ibid.

98. Andrea Gordon, "Hitting the Mark with Sarcasm," *Toronto Star*,
January 15, 2010.

99. "SarcMark," Trademark Electronic Search System, March 29,
2011, http://tess2.uspto.gov/bin/showfield?f=doc&state=4008:57
pomo.2.1; "SarcMark.net," Whois search results, http://reports.
internic.net/cgi/whois?whois_nic=sarcmark.net&type=domain
[last accessed August 15, 2012]; Douglas J. Sak, "Font for a Punctuation Mark, U.S. Patent D608,820," January 26, 2010, http://www.
google.com/patents/USD608820.

100. Douglas J. Sak and Paul Sak, "SarcMark Info," SarcMark.
com, http://02d9656.netsoljsp.com/SarcMark/modules/user/
commonfiles/newmarkinfo.jsp [last accessed July 30, 2011].

101. Ki M. Heussner, "Sarcasm Punctuation? Like We Really Need
That," ABC News, January 18, 2010, http://abcnews.go.com/
Technology/sarcasm-punctuation/story?id=9585453.

102. Gordon, "Hitting the Mark with Sarcasm"; Matthew Moore, "Sarcasm Mark Aims to Put an End to Email Confusion," *The Daily
Telegraph*, January 15, 2010.

103. Nick Broughall, "SarcMark: For When You're Not Smart Enough
to Express Sarcasm Online," *Gizmodo Australia*, January 13, 2010,
http://www.gizmodo.com.au/2010/01/sarcmark-for-when-youre-
not-smart-enough-to-express-sarcasm-online/.

104. Tom Meltzer, "The Rise of the SarcMark—Oh, How Brilliant," *The
Guardian*, January 20, 2010.

105. "Open Sarcasm Manifesto," Open Sarcasm, February 16, 2010, http://www.opensarcasm.org.
106. Heussner, "Sarcasm Punctuation?"
107. Bobbie Johnson, "Smile...That Will Be £10,000, Thanks," *The Guardian*, December 12, 2008.

Illustration Credits

Figures 4.2, 4.4. and 4.7   The Tschichold family.

Figure 4.3   Courtesy of Hoefler & Frere-Jones.

Figure 4.5   Author's collection.

Figure 4.6   Public domain image taken by Adrian Pingstone and courtesy of Wikimedia Commons.

Figure 4.8   Courtesy of Stan Carey (http://www.stancarey.com).

Figure 4.9   Courtesy of Felix O.

Figure 4.10   Courtesy of the Michigan State University Libraries.

Figures 5.1 and 5.2   Courtesy of David Gesswein at pdp8online.com. Reprinted with permission of Alcatel-Lucent USA Inc.

Figure 5.3   Florence State Archives, V Serie Strozziane, n. 1207. By permission of the Ministry of Heritage and Culture. Further reproduction prohibited.

Figure 5.4   Courtesy of Guy Pérard of typewriters.be.

Figure 5.5   Public domain.

Figure 6.1   Leiden University Library, ms. VGQ 8, ff. 44v-45r.

Figure 6.2   Courtesy of the Thomas Fisher Rare Book Library, University of Toronto.

Figure 6.3   Author's collection.

Figure 6.4   Corpus Christi College MS 139, f85r. Image courtesy of the Master and Fellows of Corpus Christi College, Cambridge.

Figure 6.5   © The British Library Board. L.9.e.7, f.27.

Figure 6.6   © Allen Fredrickson/Icon SMI/Corbis.

Figure 6.7   Doonesbury © 2003 G. B. Trudeau. Reprinted with permission of Universal UClick. All rights reserved.

Figure 7.1   Bodleian MS. Gr. Class. a. I(P) ii. Courtesy of Bodleian Library, University of Oxford.

Figure 7.2   Oxford, Christ Church, MS lat. 88, fol 34. Courtesy of the Governing Body of Christ Church, University of Oxford.

Figure 7.3   Gutenberg Bible, volume 2, Old Testament, Lamentations, page 99 verso. Harry Ransom Humanities Research Center, the University of Texas at Austin.

Figure 7.4   *Gutenberg-Forschungen*, Gottfried Zedler. Leipzig: O. Harrassowitz, 1901.

Figure 7.5   Public domain.

Figure 7.6   Florian Hardwig.

Figure 7.7   Author's collection.

Figure 8.1   SAL MS 223, f30v. Courtesy of the Society of Antiquaries of London.

Figure 8.2   New York, Columbia University, Rare Book and Manuscript Library, Plimpton MS 021, fol. 103 verso.

Figure 8.3   *Gentleman's Magazine*, December 1741. SC 1490. Courtesy of Edinburgh University Library, Special Collections Department.

Figure 8.4   Public domain.

Figure 8.5   Scanned by Jim Vadeboncoeur, Jr., public domain image.

Figure 9.1   © The British Library Board. Royal MS 5 D.x, fol. 9 recto.

Figure 9.2   Ryland Medieval Collection, Latin MS 155, fol. 70 recto. Reproduced courtesy of the University Librarian and Director, The John Rylands Library, The University of Manchester.

Figure 9.3   New York, Columbia University, Rare Book and Manuscript Library, Plimpton MS 025, fol. 56 verso.

Figure 9.4   BANC MS UCB 045. Part 1, text 1, fol. 1 verso. Courtesy of the Bancroft Library, University of California, Berkeley.

Figure 9.5   Courtesy of University of St Andrews Library, classmark Typ NL.A85JT (photograph by Daryl Green).

Figure 9.6   Inc-ii-856, image 149. Universitäts- und Landesbibliothek, Technische Universität Darmstadt.

Figure 9.7   Public domain.

Figure 9.8   Courtesy of Laura K. Balke.

Figure 9.9   Courtesy of Todd Chatman.

Figure 10.1   P. Oxy. xxiv, 2399; Pack2, 2194. Courtesy of the Egypt Exploration Society and Imaging Papyri Project, Oxford.

Figure 10.2   © The British Library Board. Codex Sinaiticus, fol. 200b. Matthew 2:6.

Figure 10.3   MS. Bodley 819, fol. 16. Courtesy of Bodleian Library, University of Oxford.

Figure 10.4   Courtesy of the Thomas Fisher Rare Book Library, University of Toronto.

Figure 10.5   Bayerische Staatsbibliothek, 4 Polem. 2534, fol. 4v.

Figure 11.1   Public domain.

Figure 11.2   Image taken from Plumons l'oiseau: divertissement by Hervé Bazin © Grasset & Fasquelle, 1967, Paris.

Figure 12.1   Author's collection.

Figure 12.2   Author's collection.

Figure 13.1   Public domain.

Figure 13.2   Cardo, Share, Century, and Dolly typefaces courtesy of Underware.

Figure 13.3   Douglas J. Sak, President, Sarcasm, Inc.

Index

KEY TO SYMBOLS

Page numbers in *italics* refer to figures.